I0805898

THE GLOBAL INNOVATOR

HOW NATIONS HAVE HELD AND LOST THE INNOVATIVE EDGE

THE GLOBAL INNOVATOR

HOW NATIONS HAVE HELD AND LOST THE INNOVATIVE EDGE

HESHAM HAFEZ, PH.D.

CO–AUTHORS

KENNETH LIPARTITO, PH.D.

PATRICIA WATSON, PH.D.

THINK TWICE BOOKS

WASHINGTON, D.C.

THINK TWICE BOOKS

Copyright © 2022 by Hesham Hafez, PhD

All rights reserved. No part of this book may be used or reproduced in any manner without written permission from the publisher, except in the context of reviews.

Published in the United States by Think Twice Books, an imprint of Ideapress Publishing.

Ideapress Publishing | www.ideapresspublishing.com

Cataloging-in-Publication Data is on file with the Library of Congress.

ISBN: 978-1-64687-074-5

Special Sales

Think Twice Books are available at a special discount for bulk purchases for sales promotions and premiums, or for use in corporate training programs. Special editions, including personalized covers, a custom foreword, corporate imprints, and bonus content, are also available.

"Dedicated to my family and in loving memory of my late parents; my mother, who taught me to be a critical thinker, and my father, who continually pushed me to impart my experience and knowledge, which was the groundwork of the innovation model: observation, critical thinking, execution, and ultimately value creation."

CONTENTS

PREFACE

I am a paper trader, and my neighborhood is the world. This makes me part of a long tradition, for humans have travelled, moved, traded, and exchanged goods, practices, and ideas for millennia. This history of movement and connection has been the most important stimulus to a process that I have been studying and trying to implement in my own business for some time: innovation. Innovation, which is how people make, or fail to make, creative, valuable, beneficial changes to their environments, is something that feeds off of creativity, diversity, and connection. I can tell you from experience that it benefits enormously from a free and open society where people can try out, test, and challenge their beliefs. I know what it is like to be missing those opportunities. I was born and raised in Egypt under the Nasser regime. He had vowed to create a modern egalitarian society, but after his death my country experienced a revival of Islamic fundamentalism. I saw Egypt come under the sway of conservative Muslim clerics and witnessed the growth of extremists who assassinated Anwar Sadat. Now, don't get me wrong. I am a citizen of the world and regardless of race and religion these are my beliefs about how to be an innovator. But I am also a Muslim and I do not believe that religion is always the enemy of innovation. To be an innovator I believe that one must have clear values, the sort of values that are learned in childhood. Faith and religion are the great source of many of our values in the world. And some of the most important innovators have been inspired by a desire to share their values, to make the world a better place. Because that's what innovation is — adding value. You cannot add or offer new values to your partner or customer or co-worker if you don't have values to start with.

But those values need a chance to flourish, and to be communicated to people, often those from very dissimilar cultures who view the world quite differently. Travel, trade, and exchange are closely linked to innovation and creativity in my mind, because that is where one gets the chance to test new ideas and draw from and learn from others. Even as a boy I longed to travel the world. And as I'll tell you, I got my wish! I was also something of a handful when I was a child, sometimes too curious and independent for my parents' patience. I grew up in a house of learning with parents who were both teachers. They taught me how to be observant, to think critically, and be true to my values. But that also made me question my teachers, even my religious teachers. This attitude, combined with my strong values rooted in education and a desire to see the world, set me on my journey. By the time I was thirteen, I realized I could never speak or think freely in Egypt. It was my home, and it is part of the long history of the Islamic World. At times Islam, like Christianity and Judaism, like Confucianism and Hinduism, has been a great teacher of values, and a great incubator of ideas and inventions. But cultures and societies have risen and fallen when it comes to innovation. And when I was growing up, one of the world's great seats of learning, science, technology, business, and innovation was Europe. So, I set my sights on studying there, moving to Austria for education. My ability to learn languages was an enormous asset in Europe. I already spoke English and quickly picked up German, as well as Spanish and French.

These experiences shaped my view of the world and of business. Here I was, an Egyptian, who grew up in the Islamic world, but who had become educated in Austria, in a new language, in a culture vastly different from what I had experienced as a boy. These experiences convinced me that to be creative and innovative, one must be able to deal with a variety of people and values. It is an important way to widen one's creative scope. If your experiences are too limited or narrow, if you are not open to seeing the world through the eyes of others, you will find it very hard to be innovative. And by that I mean not simply doing what others are already doing, even if better. I mean doing something new, something that no one had thought to do before. That's hard work, and you will need as wide a scope and imagination as you can get.

Over my life I have travelled, worked, studied, and lived in many places in Europe, in the Middle East, Asia, and the United States. These experiences not only shaped my view of the world and of business, they also taught me something else. It is vital to learn about other people and their ways if one wants to remain sharp, creative, and innovative in business. Sometimes even the humblest of interactions with others has something to teach you. For all my globetrotting the way I learned to read people and interact with them came from the work I did as a student studying in Austria. To earn money and learn the language, I worked as a waiter in a restaurant and disco club during my student years. My advice is never to be too full of yourself to take such work. The hospitality business is the best training ground for learning about people, which is a critical part of doing good business.

Later, I moved for a time to still another new world, the United States, where I studied at the Harvard Business School. Here I was first introduced to this idea of innovation by my professors. At first, I couldn't understand why they were teaching us about innovation; I didn't have any idea what it was at that point in my life. But soon I started to learn about the differences between revolutionary and evolutionary innovation, the ways that innovators came up with their ideas, and the work they did to execute them. I got *really* hooked. I began to think about the circumstances that engendered innovation throughout different cultures, throughout time. I read histories about the regions where I was doing business, and learned about the extraordinary advances made in ancient China and in the Islamic empire during the Middle Ages, the Renaissance in Europe, and the great Industrial Revolution that emerged in Great Britain and then in the United States. What factors coalesced to trigger such an intense flourishing of culture and innovation in these societies? It seemed that they shared many similar policies and practices such as the promotion of immigration, an openness to other cultures, stable governments that supported business and contributed to new technology, a widespread educational system, strong and creative financial institutions open to funding entrepreneurial endeavors, and varying degrees of freedom of religion and thought. It seemed that my own experiences with different parts of the world fit the patterns and models of how innovation can work, and where it could break down.

Between my own personal journey, my work in diverse cultures and places, and my academic experiences at Harvard and in Austria, I began to think about models of innovation. How does it work, what causes some people and some societies to be highly creative and leaders of innovation and masters of change, while others fail to achieve such things, or even fall from the heights of innovation to become second rate economies? A lot of my ideas about innovation, in fact, are like those of Joseph Schumpeter. Maybe it was fate, since I studied in Austria at Graz, in fact, the very same university he once taught at. Schumpeter emphasized the revolutionary potential of innovation, to sweep away early or inferior products, firms, or ways of doing, "creative destruction" he called it. Likewise, I agree that as a whole, innovation is about making something new or changing what came before or adding new value that did not previously exist. These issues are really historical in nature and raise questions about change over time, about process, about the rise and fall of societies and civilizations. So, I realized the only way to really develop and test my models and ideas about innovation was to engage in history.

I was especially taken with the histories of the places where I had lived and worked: The Middle East, Europe, East Asia, the United States, and China. I thought it was important that other people hear about this history and draw from the experiences that I had myself so they could have a model of innovation, so that policy makers and business leaders could understand and distill the lessons of the history into ideas they could put into practice now, today, for nurturing and encouraging innovation. I wanted to write a powerful and compelling brief for innovation that would show, historically, what could be done with the right practices and policies, and I wanted it to be available to students and young people to inspire them to think and act creatively and also to push their governments to give them the chance to be innovators.

These are hardly modest goals, I know! But one lesson I did learn from my own attempts to innovate was that successful innovators draw together the people and talents they need to carry out their vision. And that led me to my co-authors, historians of business, science, technology, and innovation. We worked together for more than a year to look throughout history, refine a model of innovation, identify they key features innovative societies share, and bring the story right up to the present day by looking at the world's leading innovative societies, from the United States, Europe, and now especially China.

The result of our efforts is the book that you are reading. We have come to some conclusions that we think history bears out clearly, in terms of what innovative societies do when they work best. We also have outlined a process, not just a set of rigid policies and prescriptions, for seeing how societies make the transition to innovative leadership. And we have examined the current state of the world economy, in particular the contested relationship between China and the United States, in light of the long history of innovation as leadership has moved from one part of the world to another.

INTRODUCTION:

A Model of Innovation

Innovation, economists have long noted, drives economic growth. It makes societies wealthy, and wealth leads to power and influence in the world: militarily, diplomatically, culturally. Throughout history wealthy and powerful societies have been innovative ones, and innovative societies have been wealthy and powerful ones. Innovation does more than this. It makes societies creative in many ways, not just the narrowly economic. The quality of life reflects innovation in many areas, in the arts, in knowledge, in values and religion; all are shaped and changed by innovations.[1]

We would be doing the same things people did tens of thousands, indeed hundreds of thousands of years ago, if we did not have a way to change what we did, how we live, how we produce things, what we believe, how we understand and grasp nature. Innovation is the means, the process of that change. It is the doing of something new, the having of new ideas, the acquisition of new knowledge. New can be wholly new, as in no one ever did it before. Or it can be new for a society, people, or civilization. History is replete with both types of innovations. There have been occasional big breakthroughs—replacing hunting and gathering with settled agriculture, smelting metals to replace stone tools, mechanization and industrialization.

These are powerful innovations precisely because they spread from their place of origins across the globe. But anything truly new does not stay in place or keep its original form. Much of what we call innovation is a process of continual small changes, adaptations, improvements, that go on in time, and that occur as new things move from people to people, society to society.

I have seen this in my own life and experiences. In the world of business, if you do not reinvent yourself on a regular basis you quickly fall behind. I completed my education in business and economics in Austria, and then joined a commodities trading firm in that country, selling everything from tuna fish to gas masks during the Gulf War. Before long, I landed a better position in a paper trading firm in Vienna. I hit the road, travelling from place to place, crisscrossing Western and Eastern Europe, and then the Middle East and Asia, and learned how to read other cultures, observe and understand their values, blend in, and build networks of contacts.

My travels also convinced me of something else. I was a stranger, an outsider, moving to new cultures as vastly different as Western Europe, the Middle East, and East Asia. When I left Egypt to study abroad, I became an immigrant. When we look back at history, one of the striking things we are going to see is that creative and innovative societies are the ones that have been open to talented strangers. The ones that have allowed themselves to feel the currents of different cultures washing across their lands are the ones that have had the best opportunities to do something new.

With what I thought was a wealth of experience under my belt, I decided to open my own paper trading business and serve the markets of the Middle East. I settled in Dubai in 1994, which I found to be an extraordinarily cosmopolitan city, one that is receptive to new business ideas, tolerant, and welcoming to people from different cultures. I will tell you later about Dubai. It has the potential to become a seat of innovation, and its government is working very hard to make that come true. I started on a commission basis, trying to bridge customers with suppliers. But I quickly found that suppliers' doors were closed to me in Europe as well as in the United States. It was a clear lesson that adds another chapter to my story of innovation. You can come up with great ideas, but executing them requires an opportunity. Not every society is good at giving people that opportunity, particularly new people with new ideas. Innovative societies have to find ways to get capital and other resources into the hands of creative newcomers if they want to stay ahead of the innovation curve.

I had to come up with a pioneering way of doing business, one that would allow me to open new trading networks. My only chance was to go to Asia. Nobody believed in Asia at that time, but I had a vision that it was the place where I could buy quality paper at competitive prices and sell to my customers in the Middle East. I travelled to Indonesia, Taiwan, and South Korea. I learned the Indonesian language so I could blend into society and talk to people in the mills in their native tongue. These countries didn't have the know-how to export their own paper because their mills were not well known in the world. I opened offices in South Korea, Hong Kong, and Shanghai in 1996, and Malaysia in 1997. I have dedicated myself to understanding the mentality of the people with whom I was working in Asia. It was like I was traveling a modern-day Silk Road, that ancient overland route that brought together the East and West. We will hear more about the Silk Road shortly. But here I was, once again bridging the East, the Middle East, and the West.

Changes in technology are also a major part of what we think of as innovation, though as we will see, technology in the narrow sense is not all there is to innovation. Still, I had to face up to what were some of the most radical technological changes affecting the economy in my own world. The Internet was leveling the playing field between customer and supplier, adding a new transparency to my industry that called for a decidedly different model of business. I shifted from a commission-based model to one that was finance-based. Today we are providing financing to paper mills in Asia and our customers in the Middle East through a network of banking partners all over the world. But sustaining advantages in the paper commodity business continued to grow increasingly challenging in the face of regulatory changes, shifting market conditions, geopolitical risks, international tax reforms, and volatility in prices.

Forms of Innovation

These are the sort of issues that innovation embodies. And because innovation is so fundamental to human history, many authors have grappled with the word, to give it clarity and to understand how it occurs.[2] We can certainly recall the work of Austrian economist Joseph Schumpeter, who has inspired my own work, as well as the work of many other students of innovation. Schumpeter's key idea of creative destruction explained how path-breaking innovations, particularly in technology, operations, manufacturing processes, and economic organization, led to great improvements in productivity and created new, exciting, and valuable products (or even services) for people, while sending outmoded products or inferior processes to the dustbin of history. More broadly, innovation involves deliberate applications of information, imagination, and initiative to produce new or different values, products, processes, or resources. According to Peter F. Drucker, "An innovation is a change in market or society. It produces a greater yield for the user, greater wealth-producing capacity for society, higher value or greater satisfaction."[3] New technology, plus the reorganization of resources and inputs so that productivity increases are crucial ways that out material and economic lives improve, there is no doubt.

This is an important insight, but the strictly economic, productivity enhancing innovation is only part of our story. Human beings can alter their natural, social, and cultural environments in all sorts of ways that create new values—in knowledge, in beliefs and religions, in art and aesthetics, and all of these have been part of the global innovation process. Public innovations that improve cities by providing clean drinking water and easy disposal of waste make life more pleasant and healthier. Artistic innovation provides pleasure and satisfaction on its own terms. Throughout most of history, before economic growth became common and expected with the Industrial Revolution, the world economy hardly grew at all. Many innovations had little to do with improving labor productivity.[4] But that does not mean societies did not innovate, create, and come up with new goods, new entertainments, new pleasures and means of satisfaction. And even today, some of the most innovative sectors are concerned with media and communications. Much of social media has little to do with improving our productivity (and indeed may be distracting us from being more productive). But media provides other things we value, such as information, connection, and entertainment. So innovations can be detrimental as well as beneficial, as with nuclear energy, fossil fuels, and social media once again.

On balance I think innovation has helped more than harmed human life. But we need to account for the full range of ways people have innovated, the ways that innovations have added to or changed values. This is because the long term process of innovation is always uncertain and not predictable. What seem to be small changes in the one realm may lead to larger, more productive consequences later. Humans toy and tinker all the time. What at one time were dismissed as follies, such as putting people into flight or into cars that drive themselves, may lead to striking breakthroughs down the road. Today, the cutting edge of information, artificial intelligence, and data science involve multiple areas of human endeavor and skill: art, literature, design, ethics, biology, brain science. Since innovations are changes of value, they even can reshape how people think of themselves and what matters to them, as when a people adopt a new religion or when they embrace a new intellectual orientation and come to see the world through new eyes. Think about how the spread of Christianity or Islam, the rise of modern science, or the view of the pale blue dot of earth from the moon has remade our sense of ourselves.[5]

Since innovations come from many sources and have appeared historically in many different places, they do not necessarily occur all at once or spread evenly across the globe. This is why only some people or some societies are the creators, or early adapters of innovations. So, innovation is closely connected with the rise and fall of civilizations. The same is true at the level of individual firms and organizations. Innovation is necessary for firms to endure and grow. Some firms may survive for a while by exploiting existing intellectual capital or drawing down internal savings. Others may be able, for a time, to block competition. But innovation is both continual and cumulative. Non-innovative firms will not be able to stave off the decay of entropy forever. The tech industry is strewn with such victims of creative destruction as AOL, Blackberry, Palm Pilot, Microsoft's Zune (a failed competitor of the iPod),

Sony's Betamax, the Segway, and LaserDisc demonstrate.[6] In fact, nearly nine out of every ten *Fortune 500* companies first listed in 1955 are, according to one economics professor, "gone, merged, or contracted" which "demonstrates that there's been a lot of market disruption, churning, and Schumpeterian creative destruction over the last six decades.[7]

These sorts of creative-destructive or revolutionary innovations often require a certain type of thinking. It is best summed up by the famous saying of the playwright George Bernard Shaw: "You see things; and you say 'Why?' But I dream things that never were; and I say 'Why not?'" But many innovations are much more evolutionary—they improve, modify, or change that which already exists. It is the difference between the first car or the first PC and the many improvements and redesigns of cars and computers in the years since their first appearance. As historian Mark Kurlansky has argued, "Gutenberg did not invent the printing press, Robert Fulton did not invent the steamboat, and Thomas Edison did not invent the light bulb. Rather, these were people who took existing ideas or machines that were not suiting society's needs and reworked them into technologies that did. It says something about our world that we seldom remember the person who came up with an idea, but canonize the pragmatist who made it commercially viable."[8] Mark Zuckerberg "borrowed" the idea for Facebook from his classmates, the Winkelvoss brothers, who had developed a similar social networking site at Harvard. He then turned it into an enormously successful, yet controversial, global financial empire with a market capitalization of over $575 billion.[9]

It is not always easy to distinguish between an evolution and a revolution. Sometimes small, incremental improvements suddenly add up to something radically new. The Internet can trace its origins back to the early Department of Defense-funded mainframe computer networks of the 1950s. For decades these networks were small and closed, used mainly to share information and computer time (timesharing) between big expensive machines. No one ever imagined that gradually, with minor but important improvements (some quite subtle in the form of standards and protocols, as well as software products such as the first browser), out of these humble beginnings the World Wide Web would emerge nearly half a century later. But once it did emerge, once the tools were all in place, the Internet became a revolutionary technology.

What this tells us is that both revolutionary and evolutionary innovations play vital roles in the development of ecosystems of technology, industry, and even business. In the long run, evolutionary innovation needs revolutionary innovation to push the boundaries and tap new potentials. Evolutionary change provides the long- run stability and durability of important breakthroughs, modifying them to changing circumstances and improving them by exploring their untapped potential. In a well-functioning innovative society, the two sides of this process are constantly at work—revolutionary breakthroughs triggering evolutionary improvements, which can then accumulate into a new revolutionary change.[10]

Making Society Innovative

Now that we have a better handle on what innovation is, and what it looks like, the next question to ask is--- what causes innovation? What conditions make it possible? And most importantly, why are some parts of the world highly innovative, and others much less so? We know that wealth and technology are not evenly distributed across the earth. Given the close connection between innovation, economic improvement and growth, and wealth it seems that innovation is not evenly distributed either. A glance at history confirms this impression as well. There have been great flourishing of new ideas, practices, and knowledge in some places—ancient Greece, medieval China, industrial Britain—while other places either remained outside the orbit of these creative and innovative places, or only slowly came to gain access to their innovations. And these patterns are not just in the past. They persist to the present day, despite far higher levels of trade, faster means of communications and transportation, and much greater spread of knowledge and literacy than ever before. Even the most universal of resources, scientific knowledge, is not evenly distributed across the globe. Physics and chemistry are the same whether practiced in Chicago, Paris, Delhi, or Shanghai. Given the flow of knowledge, capital, and people, and the vast and almost instantaneous availability of information, there is no reason for innovation to concentrate among some nations and not others. Yet by almost any measure it is clear that nations differ significantly in their rate of innovation, their creativity and contributions to science and technology, and their level of productivity.[11] So why have some parts of the world at some times been great engines of innovation and seas of creativity, while other places have not been? And why did places that were once at the forefront of innovation stagnate and fall behind? Given the crucial role of innovation in matters of wealth, power, and economy, we also want to know, which places will be leading innovation in the coming years, and which places might be in danger of losing the competitive, innovative edge.

These questions are at the heart of this book. As we will see, not only have some places emerged as the great hubs of innovation in some periods, but the seat of leadership has moved continuously. Once great empires of innovation, from ancient Rome to the Islamic caliphates to imperial China, have fallen, while formerly marginal parts of the world, such as Northern Europe or North America, have risen to prominence. Even today, moreover, while there are many places that are innovative to some degree, a few places stand out among the pack, the high-level innovators such as the United States, Japan, Germany, Sweden, and increasingly South Korea, Israel, India, Singapore, and Hong Kong. Many other places, such as Australia, Spain, Austria, and Italy are just solidly mid-level. And still other parts of the world in Africa, the Middle East, and Latin America, remain far behind.[12] Though of course as history shows, there is no reason this list might not look radically different in twenty or thirty years! But our concern is especially with the great innovation leaders of history, the places that for a time stood out from the rest, who became the creative engines of innovation often spreading and seeding their ideas, practices, products, and technology to other corners of the globe.

Why Societies Are Innovative: Some Old Models

Many great thinkers have pondered this question, why are some places innovative while others are not? Why do some places catch up fast, and others stay behind? What is the key here, the secret to making a society innovative? Our friend Joseph Schumpeter, for example, argued that the individual entrepreneur was the key. These innovators did not just make profits for him or herself, or even just build a successful company. They acted radically and changed the entire economy, contributing to overall economic growth by enhancing productivity. To Schumpeter, innovative societies were societies that gave maximum freedom to individual entrepreneurs.

After World War II, and particularly among Western nations, focus on the individual gave way to focus on the organization, especially the large multinational corporation. It was believed that strong, vertically integrated corporations were the progenitors of most innovations. Strong private firms would provide the leading edge of research and development and especially the commercialization of innovations. Nations that lacked big, vertically integrated corporations would tend to be less innovative, unable to compete in the race to develop and diversify new products, processes, and techniques, which were expensive to create and needed to be produced at low cost through economies of scale. This made a lot of sense when big American corporations were dominant in so many industries and sectors of manufacturing that in Europe and Asia there was talk of an unstoppable "American Challenge" to economic supremacy. The problem child among the advanced industrial world in this regard was England, which was said to lack both the strong, integrated corporate sector and had failed to invest sufficiently in scientific and engineering education, preferring instead a higher education system that produced liberal arts scholars and generalist gentlemen and women.[13]

But in the 1970s and 80s the era of American corporate dominance seemed to be waning. Nations ranging from Japan to Germany to eventually even France and England bounced backed or caught up while others such as South Korea, Taiwan, and Singapore were on the rise. New models were afoot. These models stressed a new, more central role for government. Bold programs that focused on new research efforts, in the manner of the successful Manhattan Project that built the atom bomb or the race to the moon that required innovations in materials, fuels, and propulsion and computers seemed to offer positive examples of government led innovation. For a time it seemed that the most successful nations were those that had hit on the formula of government led research or government-business collaborations and publicly-directed strategies for innovation. Japan and its storied Ministry of International Trade and Industry (MITI) seemed able to command and direct the nation's firms and researchers to learn how to enter and eventually dominate whole industries or sectors—steel, automobiles, consumer electronics, silicon chips. Such overt industrial policies were followed by a number of Asian economies, a tradition carried on in China and South Korea today.[14]

Then things changed again and the seemingly unstoppable rise of Japan stalled. The government led model was challenged by a new political economy rooted much more in the private sector. Ronald Reagan in the United States and Margaret Thatcher in the United Kingdom had ushered in a new respect for the "supply side" of the economy that placed much more emphasis on new firms, startups, and nimble entrepreneurs than on large incumbents. It was crucial, the new supply side theorists argued, to encourage firms and individual entrepreneurs to innovate. Popularizers of these ideas such as economics writer George Gilder predicated that if governments would step back from trying to regulate and manage their economies and let private initiative take over, there would be radical improvements in technology and a flourishing of new innovations that would usher in a golden age of economic growth.[15]

By the 1990s, it became clear that large firms could be overwhelmed and even defeated in the race to innovate by small startups that were hungrier for profits, more knowledgeable in emerging areas of technology, and more nimble in moving into and dominating those new sectors. The virtues of the startup seemed confirmed by the success of the computer and software firms that burst onto the scene in Silicon Valley and elsewhere in these decades, challenging and in some cases toppling long established big players like RCA, Control Data, Honeywell, and others. The problems faced by the once highly touted giants were summarized and analyzed by Clayton Christensen in his best seller, *The Innovator's Dilemma*. He argued that incumbent firms were handicapped when it came to innovation because they had no choice but to focus on existing markets and serve existing customers, and thus were badly positioned to recognize new opportunities or to serve small, but growing emerging markets.[16]

To unleash the power of startup innovators and supply side forces, the new thinking, sometimes called "The Washington Consensus" or "neoliberalism," was that government should be much smaller, that markets should be much freer, that private capital should flow into the hands of creative entrepreneurs with as few restrictions as possible. Tearing down barriers such as tariffs would also unleash these forces on a global level, with trade, capital flows, and exchange of knowledge eventually spreading the benefits of innovation to all nations and equalizing the incomes of rich and poor regions of the world.[17] Especially in the West, old style government policies and big government-funded research projects lost favor. Government still had a role to play in innovation. Innovators needed educated workforces, so investments in education to enhance "human capital" were if anything more important. And the state could incentivize would-be innovators, but less by giving them money or material resources and more by stabilizing the legal and political environments. Particularly important were intellectual property laws—patents and copyrights. Strong intellectual property laws would allow innovators to exploit and profit from the fruits of their labors, thus encouraging more people to innovate. Stability included price stability, which required an independent central bank that would not debase the currency. Crucial to building the necessary system, it was argued, were open, democratic, and transparent political systems accountable to the people. Dictatorships and other forms of authoritarian governments tended to suppress free thinking and bold private action, or else keep all resources and opportunities locked up for insiders and supporters of the regime in a form of "crony capitalism."[18]

Law, property, and institutions now became the magic elixir that explained economic success. The record of the past, it was argued, revealed a consistent pattern of open and free societies with good laws and strong property rights emerging as the most creative, successful, and wealthiest. Conversely those societies that did not embrace such policies tended to either second rate status or to lose ground once they backed away from openness and competition. In perhaps the most ambitious survey of this kind, economists Daron Acemoglu and James Robinson examined and catalogued the record of diverse societies and nations over centuries of history to discover *Why Nations Fail.*[19] Their survey fit the open society model, with the failures being places that either declined to embrace or gave up on openness, inclusiveness, and competitiveness. Closed societies without democratic and responsible governments created institutions that extracted and expropriated wealth for the few. In the end, these societies could not keep up with change and innovation and new opportunities, losing ground to more open and competitive societies.

By the early 2000s theories of innovation seemed to have settled on a consensus of this sort. The world would move toward the open, democratic model of the West. At the same time, the movement of people, goods, capital, and ideas across borders would allow innovations to spread, so that things invented in once place would become available for other people to use, adapt, and improve upon in all parts of the world. Over time, the force of innovation would spread the benefits of technology, and hence economic growth, worldwide, leading to a convergence among nations. There seemed little reason to believe that any people could not adapt the benefits of innovations or indeed become successful innovative participants themselves.

As it has turned out, however, the world has not converged as expected. Differences in income and wealth remain, and in some cases have grown more pronounced, especially between the advanced first world and the poor third world.[20] The assumption that innovation, growth, and economic success necessarily meant adoption of the Western democratic model of government also no longer holds. Few now argue that China's prosperity will lead to democracy. And a long look over history makes it clear that the range of governments in innovative societies is much more diverse than simply those of Western-style democracies. Where there has been progress among nations, as with China most notably, it has **not** come by adapting Western-oriented notions of openness and democracy or reducing the role of the public sector in favor of the private. If we look across the globe, we see that democracy is hardly a universal attribute of successful innovative places: Besides China, South Korea, Singapore, Malaysia, Dubai, even Japan and Taiwan are either not democratic or are run by long standing parties that hardly ever lose elections. Sometimes power stays within the same family, as with Singapore; in other cases it is monopolized by a relatively small group of elites from the same universities and with similar backgrounds.

China has come further and industrialized faster than any other economy in history by building the world's most extensive manufacturing ecosystem manned by 150 million low-cost workers.[21] The nation has been widely criticized as a haven for copycats and intellectual property pirates. But copying and pirating have been used throughout history by nations that want to catch up to the economic leaders, as we will soon see. In fact, one might say that stealing is both the highest form of flattery and also the way that formerly closed and benighted nations come into the global competition for innovation. In 2006, Chinese party leaders began to heavily promote "indigenous innovation" through an economic and political campaign that is now pressing the nation's entrepreneurs to evolve rapidly beyond their reliance on foreign technology. Under the strong leadership of President Xi Jinping, Beijing is intensifying its efforts to accelerate homegrown innovation. In 2017 the government announced a comprehensive plan to make it the world's primary Artificial Intelligence (AI) innovation center by 2030, and Beijing is bankrolling that enormous effort. It is already employing AI through its advanced facial recognition technology throughout the nation to keep a close eye on its citizens, and Chinese companies use it to track the whereabouts of workers.[22] China is now crashing "headlong into the foundational principles of the Internet in market-based democracies: online freedom, privacy, free international markets and broad international cooperation."[23] "Can a country like China with lots of money combine repression, creativity, and economic success based on that creativity? If the answer is yes, then we will have to rethink everything."[24] We need a new way to explain why nations innovate.

In the recent and comprehensive survey across nations, Mark Zachary Taylor concludes that none of the existing explanations for innovation is adequate to account for these persistent differences and variations.[25] The verdict of history and the evidence of the great variations across many different societies today make clear that there is not a "one best way," as predictors of the Washington Consensus hoped just a decade or so earlier.

There are many ways to accomplish the same thing, and what might make one place highly innovative does not simply translate directly to another. Becoming innovative, in other words, often requires innovative thinking and innovative policies that might not be found in existing societies. But that does not mean we cannot find solution to the innovative equation either. We may not find "the" answer; many different resources and factors can contribute to innovation and it is unlikely that we will find any society that combines all of them in just the right amounts. But we can identify what makes places likely to be innovation leaders, and what is likely to keep them back.

How to Make an Innovative Society: A New Model

Let me offer you my answer, based on my own deep experiences across the globe. We can start very simply with a model that will help explain how innovation occurs.

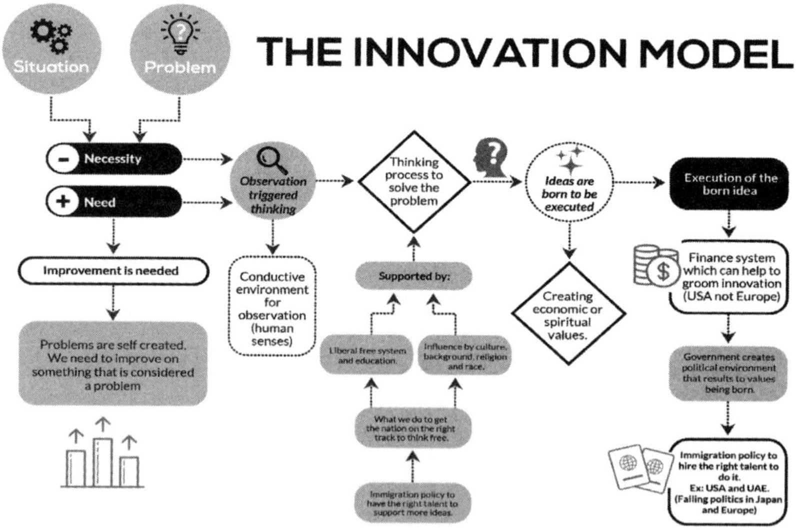

My model begins with the universal ability of all people to see and observe the world around them. This is a crucial feature and no people lack the potential for this sort of creativity. That is also the reason we need to give everyone a chance to express themselves. You don't know where the next great idea or observation is going to come from, and the more eyes that are looking out for it, the better for all of us.[26] The more diverse those eyes, and brains and hands, the better yet still.

This brings us to our first principle of innovation:

1. Innovation starts with observation and critical thinking. The more people observing, the more chances of producing something new and improved. So innovative societies will activate all their potential talent. Throughout history the opportunity to innovate has been limited and confined, often taking women, the enslaved, the marginalized and minority out of the equation. But the society that does the best at engaging and diversifying its talent pool will be best positioned to win the race.

Observing and critical thinking by open minded observers starts the process. So innovative societies cannot be too strongly attached to conventional wisdom, to doing things "how they have always been done," or hemmed in by religious orthodoxies or political ideologies that could frustrate would-be innovators, snuffing out creative thinking before it even begins. Openness to new ideas and opportunity for would-be creators, I believe, are characteristics found in the most innovative societies.

Critical thinkers also need the tools to analyze and this starts with investments in education. And not just any educational system either. The most successful places will tune education to be deeply thoughtful, fostering creativity. The education systems of Asia, for example, put much less emphasis on independent exploration and trial by the child than do those in the West. As I have seen from my travels (and my own family as my wife is from Malaysia), in China, South Korea, and Malaysia children at home live in a more structured environment, with everything done for them, whereas in America and Europe they are given much more freedom to explore. Some of the most innovative societies today, such as Finland and Sweden, also have some of the most open approaches to education, with much emphasis on exploration by the child. The same differences can be found at higher levels, where in Asia there is so much stress on cramming for high-stakes exams and rigidly adhering to a standard curriculum. Recognizing that educational principles may be too stifling to keep up the innovative edge, governments in much of Asia are now trying to reform education to be more creative and open.[27]

Finally, innovators need to be able to execute their ideas. They need access to capital and resources. They need the support of governments, in things ranging from patents and property rights, to courts and laws to enforce those rights, to the basic infrastructures of transportation, communications, education, and high-level research that they cannot perform by themselves. Innovative societies build these institutions. If a nation's financial system is too closed, too risk averse, then people with new ideas will move elsewhere to get the funding they seek. Strong financial institutions get innovators resources to execute their designs. Though as we will see, too much emphasis on finance and making money purely by financial manipulation can also lead societies off the path of innovation. Likewise, the government being too controlling, focused too much on protecting vested interests or incumbent firms will have the same effect. It is clear, as with the example of deeply flawed states ranging from the former Soviet Union to Sudan and North Korea today, governments can severely inhibit innovation, as they are far too averse to challengers and independent thinkers. But outside of the extremes, it appears that a wide variety of political systems can successfully foster innovation, so long as those states are stable. Here a culture tolerant of failure can be helpful. Failure is a great teacher and few innovators have ever got things exactly right the first time. Only by trying, failing, trying again, did they finally succeed. The playwright and poet Samuel Beckett said it best: "Ever tried. Ever failed. No matter. Try again. Fail again. Fail better."[28]

The record of the past offers powerful lessons because it provides many different examples of many different societies doing things in many different ways. And just as importantly, history allows us to see how ideas, technologies, practices, and values get passed on from place to place over time. What one society has achieved can be learned and adapted by another society. But an important caution here. Economists often write as though places merely need to move out to the technological frontier by learning and adapting best practices. As they do they will grow and catch up. Except of course as we have seen catching up is hard to do, and it does not seem to happen historically nor is it happening today. A small number of places may catch up and indeed may move ahead, but many places do not. Even scientific knowledge we see cannot be simply "spread" across the earth so that everyone is quickly at the same level. So my model is historical, in the sense that the past does not offer a simple roadmap to the future. Innovation is cumulative and always occurring, so that catching up is less a matter of adapting what's already there then coming to innovation in a new way.

This brings us to our second principle of innovation:

2. To learn, catch up, and adopt is itself a form of innovation. Societies must be able to adapt and absorb what is out there, and that is itself a matter of being creative, being able to learn and execute, no different than inventing from scratch. There is no easy road of simply adopting.

To put it another way, learning is crucial, but it is active, creative, and innovative, not passive. If we go back to the basic model, we see that becoming innovative by learning involves all the same steps and benefits from all the same resources: education that is open and creative; opportunity deep and broad across society to activate as many potential innovators as possible; the favorable conditions for executing what one has come up with.

This brings us to our third and most important principle of innovation:

3. Innovation requires connection. Historically, places that were at the center, the confluence of many ideas, many practices, technologies, that received multiple cultural influences from many different parts of the world, have a much better chance of learning, catching up, and becoming innovation leaders themselves. Put another way, an open mind needs lots of nourishment from many different sources.

Openness to others, I will argue, has been the key to innovation leadership in history, as it is now. In contrast to most studies, which seek the solution to the innovation equation strictly from within a society's traits and characteristics, I want to place a lot more emphasis on the extrinsic force of connection, communication, and exchange. These are the powerful "opening" forces that stimulate thought and creativity, provide challenges to existing ways, and bring in new products, ideas, knowledge, and technology, the resources that innovation can operate on.[29]

A place that wants to be innovative should ask these questions: Is it open to people from many backgrounds, ethnicities, and religions, or does it expect narrow conformity to just one way of life? Is it connected to other societies, or is it closed off? We know what a closed society looks like—North Korea! It's at the opposite end of the innovation scale. Accepting people with different backgrounds also opens a culture up to other value systems, other religions. In fact, religions are the great source of many of our values in the world. Some of the most important innovators have drawn upon their values and used their breakthroughs to make the world a better place without benefitting financially. Both Jonas Salk (the "Father of Biophilosophy") and Albert Sabin invented polio vaccines and refused to patent them. Instead, they donated their discoveries for the benefit of mankind.[30]

An open society does not take just the form common in Western democracies. This is why all the efforts to identify the key political structures for innovation have failed. They took too narrow a view, assuming that Western style political systems and values were the only form of openness. In fact, openness can occur in many ways, without necessarily requiring a place to look exactly like the United States. It may be through trade and exchange, as was true throughout the Middle East and the Mediterranean in the Middle Ages and Europe in the Age of Exploration. Think about how the movement of goods from the Americas changed diets around the world. Italian food may be unthinkable without tomatoes, but tomatoes only arrived after Columbus because they are indigenous to Peru. And Peru also gave Ireland its potatoes that are the stable of the diet there. Though Peruvian food, with its varied and creative use of potatoes, also takes some of its signature dishes from recipes derived from its many Asian immigrants.

Connections may also come from the spread of a powerful, fundamental value that unites people under the banner of a religious community, as was true across the Middle East, India, Southeast Asia, and North Africa during the Golden Age of Islam or Europe under the Church of Rome. Connections might be part of a concerned and deliberate policy of learning and borrowing and taking back home, as Japan did when it sought to catch up to the West in the Meiji Period. It might come from competitive borrowing, indeed stealing as Western nations did from each other during the Industrial Revolution. It might come from an open door to ambitious immigrants from around the globe as the United States did in the nineteenth century. But there has to be some portal of connection that brings places into contact with each other. Without that contact, learning cannot take place, the mind and imagination will not be stimulated, new and better practices from abroad cannot be brought into the innovation system.

The Innovation Connection

As we now know, the world did not just suddenly become connected. The movement of people, goods, knowledge, and ideas has a very long history. It began 200,000 years ago with a great and continuous migration of humans out of Africa to cover nearly every niche and environment of the earth. Over the millennia people moved, contacted, mixed, exchanged, and sometimes fought and conquered. But all of human history is one long process of entering new habitats, adapting to new environments, and making connections and exchanges among other groups doing likewise. As we will see in the next chapter, for example, the trading civilizations of the Middle East and surrounding areas were one of the major centers of innovation in the ancient era. They were a key linkage between the great civilizations of India and Asia and the cities in present day Iran and Iraq, Turkey and Greece. Such connections in fact became a major stimulus to innovation through the Eurasian landmass. The importance of such cross-cultural connection is certainly something I appreciate as a man who came from the Middle East and then moved East and West.

There are always some people who are willing to take risks and look for adventure. I know because I am a trader in my blood and taking risks is in my DNA. Our ancestors took to the high seas in tiny boats and canoes to populate the massive Indonesian archipelago, and went on to Australia, New Zealand,

and the tiny islands of the vast Pacific Ocean. They were the first entrepreneurs in a sense, making connections, bringing people to new lands, new environments, where they would adapt what they had learned at home and engage in a process of innovation to make a new life in a strange and foreign place. That's something I can certainly understand, how risky, difficult but also potentially rewarding such moves can be.

Consider just one famous example of how this process worked. Along the famed Silk Road built by the Chinese during the Han dynasty (206 BCE – 220 CE), caravans of a thousand camels transported precious goods like silk, spices, gold, and gemstones between the central Chinese city of Xian (then the capital) and Constantinople (now Istanbul). By land and by sea, this tidal wave of trade dominated global commerce for centuries. It was carried over an enormous network that not only moved merchandise, but also linked cultures in unprecedented ways, transmitting new ideas and revolutionary technologies along the way.[31] One example of what these connections led us to was paper and printing. Their movement, starting in China and then spreading across the world, made them arguably the most revolutionary innovations and facilitators of change in history, much like the Internet today. Muslim merchants travelling the Silk Road in the eighth century carried Chinese paper west to the Islamic world.[32] By that time, Muslims had also learned the secrets of Chinese papermaking and the technology spread rapidly throughout their far-flung empire that mediated between the cultures of the Far East and Far West. Papermaking technology spread from the Muslim world in northern Africa to Andalusian Spain where it developed into a formidable industry. During the Renaissance, another Chinese innovation, printing traveled a similar route, ending up in northern Europe, where it underwent a creative transformation. Gutenberg's development of the printing press with movable type formed a pivotal innovation that helped launch an era that surged with creativity, new ideas in arts and science, social justice, and religion. Victor Hugo once said that, "The invention of printing is the greatest event in history. It is the mother of all revolution .... Printed thoughts are everlasting, provided with wings, intangible and indestructible. They soar like a crowd of birds, spread in all four directions and are everywhere at the same time."[33] With paper and printing, people were freed from their dependence on scribes. They now had a light, portable media to record and store ideas, and to transmit them to other people, giving birth to a profoundly interconnected world.

Interconnectivity of this sort has been one of the driving forces of civilization, continuing right up to the present day, aided by telegraphs, telephones, televisions, radios, and now the Internet. We are poised to make another leap in interconnectivity with 5G technology that allows the transfer of data and voice at hyper speed. This will set new standards for digital commerce, communication, health care, education, military operations, and transportation. China's state-supported Huawei is leading that innovation race, with Ericsson and Nokia a distant second and third, and the United States, says Thomas Friedman, is "woefully—even disgracefully—behind."[34]

China led the world in the development of new technologies during the Silk Road era, and is now very consciously positioning itself to become the global innovation leader once again, even adopting as its key trade policy the "Belt and Road Initiative," deliberately reminiscent of the glory days of the Silk Road of long ago. During its forty-year rise to become the world's second largest economy, China has become a formidable, innovative player in the global tech arena.[35] There is much at stake in the innovation race, since the nations that innovate consistently are the ones that will be the most powerful over time. They will generate greater wealth, provide people with more and better jobs, and exert more influence over world politics.

I've placed great emphasis on what nations can do to become innovative. But here we might stop a minute and ask, "where is innovation located, actually?" Within any nation, within any society, after all, there are bound to be highly innovative and progressive areas and more stagnant and backward places. No one would deny that Silicon Valley is a unique cluster of highly innovative people and firms, while in the poorest, least educated parts of Mississippi or the deindustrialized rust belt of America things are either stagnant or moving backward. China's Pearl River Delta is a vibrant and innovative manufacturing center, but in parts of China's rural interior life is little different than a century ago.

The great urbanist Richard Florida argues that cities are the engines of innovation. They are the connection zones that bring people, capital, ideas, firms, knowledge, and other crucial resources together in ways that bring forth innovation. Look at the United States or any advanced nation today and you will see that the vast amount of economic activity is occurring in key global cities, as are the vast amount of innovation.[36] And throughout history cities and regions, valleys and trade entrepôts, have been crucial sites of learning, creativity, and innovation. In almost any era the innovative leader has also had the leading cities where the cutting edge of innovation was taking place—Athens, Rome, Alexandria, Venice, Florence, Antwerp, London, Manchester, New York, Detroit, Los Angeles, Tokyo, Beijing. The great Roman Empire was an empire of cities. The Islamic Empire at its height has been called a series of cities connected by trade routes.[37] This is true today as well. Cities like my home, Dubai, as well as Singapore and Hong Kong, are trying to follow a pattern we will see throughout history—connecting themselves by lines of commerce to people and places, providing access to capital to anyone who has a good idea to try, welcoming talented and ambitious outsiders.

So I agree that this clustering and bringing together is absolutely crucial, my Third Principle of Innovation. And we will travel to the great cities, regions, and valleys of innovation in history. But until two hundred years ago only 7 percent of the world's population was urban, so much activity took place outside of cities in history as well.[38] We need to cross into and over the lands of empires, and look at the rise of the nation state, political and geographical forms that have also been crucial to innovation. These larger political entities matter in part because cities and districts also depend on the public goods and political stability that states provide. Even when cities have gone it alone, they have been more city-states than just urban places—as with Italian Renaissance cities that raised armies and controlled agricultural lands. Much innovation, moreover, takes place because goods, people, and economic activities are traded across the urban-rural landscape. Cities need hinterlands and hinterlands feed cities, literally with food but also supply the raw materials that cities process. So to understand innovation we cannot rest with just one level of society, we have to look at many, some bigger than just cities, and others, such as religious communes, ethnic networks, guilds, merchant trade organizations, multinational enterprises, some smaller.

Connections are not the only thing that matter of course, but as we will see throughout history they have been a key part of what makes a society innovative. And they have been crucial especially to the places that emerged as the great centers of learning, knowledge, and technology. Today, in a global age, innovation is truly global, and connections matter more than ever before. My prediction is that the places that have mastered the art of learning from and connecting to other places will be the innovative leaders. Places that are building walls and closing themselves off are setting themselves up for failure.

There is one final point, a possible Fourth Principle, that we have to remember before we can embark upon the journey of history to see how innovation has unfolded. Too many studies of innovation have been static. They look for the enduring features that explain innovation everywhere and for all time, like a simple recipe. But our explanation is not static, it is historical. True, Principle Three, connections, can be found in all innovation societies, but it is not a static. It is flowing, changing, adaptable, taking many different forms in many different periods. Indeed it has to be flexible and fluid because of the cumulative nature of innovation. Although it happens occasionally that knowledge is lost and must be rediscovered, for the most part in world history ideas, practices, and technologies do not disappear but are passed on and claimed (innovatively!) by other peoples. By claimed we mean that they are improved, adapted, embedded, and learned in the new context of a different society. They change. And these changes mean that what might be effective or successful in one period is not necessarily so in another.[39]

To take one example. Britain was the first industrial nation. But it created the complex of machines, factories, methods of production and knowledge of materials, energy and chemicals that were needed for industrial processes without much investment in higher education and formal science. Those places that followed, adapted, and in some cases stole the secrets that Britain had pioneered and did so with much greater use of formal education and investments in science. The nature of industrialization had changed and the artisanal innovators that had served Britain so well were no longer sufficient as Germany and the United States became leading industrial nations.

We will see this again and again in history. To do innovation requires connections; connections stimulate learning and thinking; adapting what is already out there requires innovation too; innovation changes what was adapted or acquired into something new—we might say an innovation of an innovation. The hand of history moves and the next step will require doing something different from the previous one. This cumulativeness makes any predictions about what will work, what will assure a society can be at the cutting edge of innovation, futile. The hand of history is always changing the rules of the game. That is why the best move is to be as connected as possible.

These are the patterns of history. A story of radical innovations transforming human life, a narrative of innovation centers and leaders emerging for great moments of flourishing, but then also dying away and passing along what they learned and achieved via trade and interconnection to other societies, which pick up the mantel of innovation. It is a story with important lessons for today, especially as we watch the growing competition between China and the United States become a source of friction and perhaps antagonism, about who will dominate important innovations that are on the horizon.

Linking past, present, and future innovation, the chapters that follow will explore how innovation occurred in pivotal civilizations in the past, and examine contemporary trends in places like Silicon Valley where many Chinese engineers have hit the "bamboo ceiling," grown tired of the lack of real opportunities to advance, and are returning back to their homeland in record numbers to start well-funded new ventures.[40] We will consider which lessons from the past are most useful today. We will follow the process by which innovation leadership passes from one part of the world to another. And we will examine the changing patterns of innovation over time to see if we are entering a wholly new era, or if the recent changes occurring in the United States and China are merely one moment in a larger story that portends a new, even more radical era of global innovation that is unfolding before us.

CHAPTER 1:

Innovation and Human History

The story of innovation is deeply forged into our existence on earth. It is more ancient than even the Silk Road of two thousand years ago. One definition of being human, in fact, is *homo faber*, or the tool maker. Now, some animals do use tools. But it was our big-brained hominid ancestors who turned this skill into a means to survive, thrive, multiply, and evolve. Some 40,000 years ago early Homo sapiens had developed an impressive array of stone tools, specialized devices for carrying out work and manipulating the environment. These tools were not just one- off creations, immediate responses to some need, but standardized forms. Humans had begun to actively think about creating and making things. It was about the same time that the first cave paintings appear. In a burst of creativity, early Homo sapiens and their Neanderthal cousins were finding ways to express themselves in material artifacts and art.

We often forget that tool-making or what we now call technology is closely connected to art and expression. Indeed, some of the earliest manipulations of stone and metal were done not to serve practical ends but to adorn the body, worship the gods, or to provide pleasure and beauty in an otherwise drab environment. When we look at the artifacts of pre-history we find bracelets, combs, rings, and decorated bowls, as much as we do needles, knives, hammers, and axes. This is not just some quirk of pre-history either. When aluminum was first refined into a metal, its original use was for jewelry and only later pots and pans. As we shall see, art, religion, and cultural values have often provided a powerful stimulus to innovation and creativity, as with the construction of the great cathedrals of the High Middle Ages, or the pyramids of ancient Egypt.[1]

About ten thousand years ago, the human race had its first macro, or maybe more accurately, supra technological breakthrough: agriculture. Through a long, slow process of learning, in the Middle East, in Asia, and a bit later in Central America and the Andes of South America, humans domesticated plants as a main food source. By selecting and breeding those with characteristics that fit and served human needs, they created wheat, rice, potatoes, millet, sorghum, and a host of other grains, cereals, and tubers they could cultivate and harvest in a dependable annual cycle. This pivotal breakthrough was most likely achieved by women.[2]

The First Macro Innovation

Agriculture changed everything. It allowed permanent settlements. No longer did hunters and gatherers have to live a semi-nomadic existence fanning out in search of sustenance. It facilitated the growth of cities, or places that did not provide their own food but specialized in other activities such as manufacturing, services (including temples and religion) and, for better or worse, politics, all fed by the food growers. Agriculture permitted human populations to increase, since cultivated crops supported a far higher density of people than did hunting and gathering. These larger populations with specialization and a division of labor also included some who devoted their time to trying to make new and better things: The first entrepreneurs.[3]

Human societies could now support a wide range of specialists who pushed innovation. Since most of time, labor, and capital still went into procuring food, the largest group in society was those who grew the food itself. These simple farmers were also a major source of innovation in agriculture, though we know very few of them. Other specialists included artisans who produced all sorts of nonagricultural products—cloth, jewelry, glass, and somewhat later, capital goods in the form of metals and metal implements made of lead, copper, bronze, and eventually iron and hard alloys of iron such as steel. Still other specialists handled religion—priests--and politics, an emperor or king or queen, his or her retainers and retinue, and smaller royalty and nobility. These "eaters" were also innovators in their own right, whether curating ideas about the sacred, developing new forms of political organization, managing public works, recording information, or producing written documents and texts.

Agriculture spread throughout the world, changing and adapting to climate and soil conditions. The imitators too abandoned their nomadic past for a settled, agrarian life. This was the long, slow period of evolutionary improvement following the revolutionary innovation. An important part of that process was contact among different peoples, which allowed for modification of the original prototype. Agriculture adapted to the dry wheat fields of the Middle East, the humid valleys of Central America, the arid altitudes of the Andes, and the aquatic deltas of the Far East. Likewise, incremental improvements in animal husbandry adapted domestic beasts to different conditions and tasks, or improved the work that could be extracted from them, just as we look to engine designers and car manufacturers to squeeze more horsepower or greater fuel economy out of our car engines. Early Stone Age horse collars were replaced with chest harnesses, which went around the sturdiest parts of the animal and did not constrict breathing. This literally increased horsepower.

A thousand years after agriculture appeared, humans began smelting metals. The move from stone to metal was a big innovation, and it was followed by a series of smaller ones. Humans first melted and cast copper, then mixed it with tin to make the much harder alloy, bronze. Bronze allowed people to make much sharper-edged and more durable tools. The Bronze Age and following Iron Age yielded another flourishing of innovations, many designed to improve and enhance agricultural productivity, such as hoes, scythes, sickles, the wheel, and wheeled means of transport. With agriculture, harvesting speed is always critical. When crops ripen, they do not wait leisurely in the field to be gathered. They peak and start to decline and rot quickly, and all at once. So, tools of the harvest were crucially important. Other innovations in this period included potter's wheels to throw clay and mass produce vessels for holding and storing the harvest and carrying water. And it was in this period humans started writing, a technology that evolved out of the need to measure and track goods.

Early agriculturalists improved the other end of the process as well—planting. They replaced wooden hoes and simple scratch ploughs for turning the soil with metal implements. Hoes and wooden sticks had served adequately in the cradle of agriculture in Africa and the Middle East, but heavy ploughs with iron plough shares were needed to turn the deeper, thicker soils to the north in Europe. By the time the ancient Greeks were enjoying their classical period, humans had at their disposal the basic array of simple tools for moving heavy objects and building: The lever, the incline plane, the screw (really another form of the incline plane), and the pulley. Other expenditures of agriculture's caloric abundance were thrown into making perhaps the most advanced and sophisticated system of technology in the premodern world—ships, both sailing and oar-driven. Ships were the main form of transportation before railroads and internal combustion engines.

Ancient ships could be large or small, but they were complicated because they needed a system of sails to master the winds, or if galleys, a hold full of oarsmen. They required a method of control that allowed them to move where desired and navigate currents. They had to be robust enough to deal with the open seas and unpredictable storms, yet light and small enough to get to shore or dock. Sailors needed detailed knowledge of land, sea, currents, and dangerous tides and obstructions, something that could only be won from hard-earned experience. And they needed some advanced science and mathematics to make and use maps (a slowly developed innovation) and tools of navigation, which also evolved slowly in different civilizations over centuries, indeed millennia. There was, in short, a significant amount of technology in shipping and sailing, particularly when covering long distances. Like agriculture, many of these improvements and innovations were made by anonymous artisans and sailors.

Ships were important for another reason. They allowed a society to trade and have contact with many other societies quite distinct and distant from their own. They still do, with container ships probably the most important factor in the growth of global trade today. Sailing was not the only way to get around in the past; we will talk about the overland trade and routes, such as the famous Silk Road. But when agricultural societies produced surplus products, one thing they could do with them was trade with other people. Trade, particularly in the premodern, preindustrial era, was one of the main drivers of economic growth. By specializing in some goods, they could make, or make more efficiently, and trading for others they could not, people followed the classic "Smithian" model (named for Adam Smith, of course) of growth.[4]

Trading Civilizations

Trading in the civilizations of the Middle East and surrounding areas developed a high degree of sophistication in ancient times. That is not surprising when you look at a map, given that the region was positioned in the middle of a number of important other civilizations and societies. The ancient Middle East connected the Mediterranean to India and China to the East and from the Mediterranean to the North and West of Europe. It had access to the vast Indian Ocean, which would emerge over millennia as the great trading sea of the world, well before Columbus and his European followers mastered the Atlantic. Trading in turn stimulated a variety of business innovations.

Consider one of the great civilizations of the region, Babylonia, which arose in Mesopotamia about 3,800 years ago. Succeeding earlier dynasties such as the Sumerians and the Assyrians, Babylonians developed surprisingly modern-sounding trade and exchange mechanisms. They had a monetized economy based on silver, used debt and credit, had negotiable instruments that could be assigned to third parties, and housed a class of specialized merchants who benefitted from a stable government that provided standardized weights and measures, infrastructures of transportation such as canals, and a code of laws under their most famous ruler, Hammurabi. Prices fluctuated with supply and demand and producers responded, with farmers putting more land under cultivation when prices were steep and bringing more produce to the market to sell. We know all this for one simple reason. The Babylonians, like their predecessors and like the Chinese and the Incas independently, had developed and made use of written language. When scholars deciphered their cuneiform script, they discovered that much of the writing concerned business transactions, prices, and quantities of goods.[5]

Now we don't want to make ancient Babylonia into a modern capitalist economy. Most people still lived and worked on the land, and were illiterate. Trade, particularly long-distance trade, was rare. Slavery and serfdom were common and extensive. But where trade was possible, it not only occurred but people could also be quite innovative in developing the tools, in this case the financial and business tools, for carrying it out. As we will see, different societies invented or reinvented these tools again and again when they had the opportunity to engage in trade.

One reason that these ancient societies differed from what we would think of as a modern capitalist economy was, they still lived a very precarious existence. They lived in a "Malthusian" world where bad weather, sudden disaster, or even a disappointing harvest year could spell famine, starvation, and death from opportunistic diseases. Good harvests encouraged the population to grow but that just meant more mouths to feed. Though farmers responded to the new demand, they did so by stretching resources to the maximum, putting into cultivation more and more marginal, low productivity lands—the famous "law of diminishing returns." All it took was one or two bad years, maybe caused by some random fluctuations in weather, and the population exceeded the available calories. Plagues lurked just outside the gates of these societies, ready to swoop in as soon as hunger made the population vulnerable. Diseases also followed the routes of trade, most famously the deadly bubonic plague. If trading goods between people who had different skills and made different products was a net gain for humans; trading germs between populations that had different levels and types of immunity was a net gain for the disease microbes.

In a world where even basic caloric security was almost non-existent, it could be risky to stray too far from accepted practices. Innovation, particularly in the great agricultural sector, tended to be highly incremental, even if agriculture itself had been a radical breakthrough. In fact, until quite recently "innovation" was not a positive word. People might have sought out new things and changed when it benefitted them, but they were still quite wary of the new and untested. Innovation was, in ancient Greek and Latin as well as many other languages, a word to be suspicious of, signaling a troubling or unwelcome novelty, even a sacrilegious deviance, a vice forbidden by law and tradition, an upsetting of the established order.[6]

We should remember, even in our world, at any given time most technology is old technology. Much of the work of engineers and others responsible for it involves maintaining more than changing. Some things, from doorknobs and bookshelves to paperclips to electric fans have hardly changed over decades, even centuries.[7] If we look, we can see many of the artifacts of earlier innovations still on the earth. Take the pyramids of Egypt. The ancient Egyptians were probably the first civilization to develop special tools to make rope, perhaps as long ago as 4,000 to 3,500 BCE. Ropes of water-reed fibers, pulled by thousands of workers, allowed the Egyptians to move the heavy stones required to build their monuments. But the pyramids were not just a technological innovation. At one time historians thought that the pyramids could only have been built by slave labor. It turns out that this was actually not the case. We now know that these ancient builders were organized into private contractor teams, skilled artisans who combined human muscle and energy and what by our standards today seem incredibly simple machinery—ropes, incline planes, simple pulleys—into an effective building force. They were innovators who brought together tools, technology, and organization to build something that has stood for more than 4,500 years. In fact, the tools and the devices the pyramid builders used would not be radically changed or improved upon for thousands of years. Masons in Europe who put up the great cathedrals of the Middle Ages used mostly the same simple machines that the ancient Egyptians used. The radical breakthroughs in construction had to wait a bit longer.[8]

The cutting edge of innovation is where the rare and unusual lies. So, in this premodern world, the number of people engaged in risky, cutting-edge behavior was necessarily tiny. That was what made ancient trade so important;

it was highly risky, even dangerous, yet had the potential to greatly increase wealth and well-being. So those who engaged in high-risk trade inevitably represented a small portion of society, since very few societies could afford to put a majority of their resources into innovative but risky ventures. Societies that did engage in extensive trade had to maintain a precarious balance, one that was often not sustainable over the long run. But when they could maintain it, they often became the flourishing centers of innovation and creativity precisely because they had access to so many diverse products and goods, to so much diverse knowledge and ideas.

Innovation in the Ancient World

One society that, for a time, walked this balance beautifully was ancient Greece. Unlike ancient Egypt or Babylonia, Han China, or even their Roman successors, Hellenistic Greeks did not live in a vast agrarian empire with a central state and emperor ruler. Greece was comprised, rather, of a series of city-states--a model that would appear later in other parts of the world that also took advantage of trade and contacts to build innovative, creative societies. These city-states were hardly democratic by modern standards—they depended heavily on slave or semi-free labor for agriculture, mining, and artisan production, a labor force replenished by constant imports of new captives from war and piracy. Still, the lack of a central imperial state with draining high taxes plus the need for a citizen army to defend the city meant that a much broader group of the population benefitted from and could engage in profitable economic activity than in societies that were almost exclusively agrarian.

Starting roughly 500 BCE the Greek city-states became aggressive and dynamic traders. They invested in building bigger, faster, cheaper ships for trade. In the Greek *agora*, or urban marketplace, local products from surrounding peasant farmers were exchanged. In the more exotic *emporion*, the fruits of long-distance trade went on sale. In fact, taking advantage of specialization, ancient Greeks imported food from more productive locales—Sicily, Egypt, the Black Sea region—rather than striving for self-sufficiency. Under Alexander the Great, Greece extended its influence and power, conquering the Persian Empire to the East and Egypt, one of the major sources of grain production along the fertile Nile. The result was not just conquest, but an intermingling of Hellenistic knowledge, culture, and economy with the older Persian and Egyptian cultures, as well as access to the Red Sea through Egypt and contact with India and its Mauryan Empire. In Egypt the Ptolemaic Dynasty (Ptolemy had been one of Alexander's generals in his conquests), engaged in a substantial transfer of knowledge with the older Persian culture, leading to the founding of the great library and center of learning in Alexandria, one of the largest and most important centers of knowledge in the ancient world. Greece and Egypt maintained strong social and economic connections. Greeks migrated to Egypt and brought with them new crops such as durum wheat. They also increased production of their favorite beverage, wine. Iron farm implements from Greece went to Egypt as well, which in turn made use of its own technology such as waterwheels and water screws along with new canals and reclaimed land to improve agricultural productivity.[9]

Like the Babylonians and the Egyptians, Greeks also developed tools of business--debt and credit instruments, family-based merchant networks, and joint-stock companies and partnerships that outsiders could invest in as a means to mobilize capital. Private trade groups, money lenders, banks, and credit networks facilitated trade across the region. None of this was entirely new, as in fact Greece built on the earlier networks of trade set up by the Phoenicians and other early trade empires. These early traders had moved goods such as iron, copper, and silver from Spain to Tunisia, Italy, Crete and into the Aegean. Greece added to this trade network with one of the world's great business innovations--money, specifically a public money in the form of coin that could be used for trade between city-states in Greece, with foreign empires, as legal tender for taxes, and payment of debts. Public money backed by a political authority in this way can be a powerful stimulus to trade. It makes it possible for people in different societies to have a secure and well accepted means of payment, especially if the coining society is careful not to debase (remove precious metal) or over inflate the production of such medium. Greek coins would eventually be found all across the Mediterranean and Middle East, in Rome, among the Etruscans of northern

Italy and as far away as Marseille. It was one of the signs that they had mastered the art of long-distance trade.[10]

As with the Babylonians and their written language, we know how extensive these trade networks grew because of a surprisingly revealing historical source. In the case of the Greeks, it was shipwrecks. A trading society is a society that will inevitably suffer the perils of the sea. Greek wrecks reveal the vast extent of the trade in the number of amphorae, the ceramic vessels that carried olive oil and other valuable goods, which they left at the bottom of the ocean. During the height of Hellenistic Greece around 300 BCE the number of amphorae in shipwrecks jumped, an indication of the success of the trade networks and the utility of having a good means of monetary exchange. It's unfortunate, in fact, that innovation eventually replaced the rather expensive amphora with cheap but serviceable wooden barrels, around 50 CE. Wood deteriorates and disappears from the shipwrecks, and so our means of recording economic activity in trade in the ancient world disappeared as well.[11]

Greece was part of a broad Mediterranean world of trade and exchange and competing empires who borrowed from each other, learned from each other, and exchanged goods, technologies, and religions.[12] With strong economic competition and extensive networks of contracts, the Greek city-states became centers of all sorts of other innovations. They learned about new crops such as alfalfa from the Persians and grew it to feed livestock, which improved their agricultural productivity and expanded their economic base. Fed by improvements such as this as well as their vast trading relationships, Greek cities expanded, and became centers of learning and innovation. By 430 BC Athens had 40 thousand inhabitants. By comparison the cities of the earlier Bronze Age societies grew to only about 10 thousand in terms of population.

Greeks inherited the mathematical and astronomical knowledge as well as much of their technology from the ancient Egyptians and Babylonians and borrowed their alphabet and much nautical technology from the Phoenicians.[13] They also spread innovations such as their mastery of iron making and knowledge of astronomy (itself benefiting from contact with Persia and the Middle East) and medicine. They then developed one of history's most influential systems of thought and philosophy in the works of Socrates and his student Plato. New knowledge was developed in Plato's Academy and Aristotle's Lyceum and in the Great Library in Alexandria. At its peak, this institution was a combination of library and museum for mathematics, physics, geography, astronomy, and mechanics. Particularly under the leadership of Archimedes, the Greeks contributed to key developments in mechanics and technology, with gears, screws, and connecting rods to harness rotary power from water mills. In the writings of Archimedes, they also developed an abstract appreciation for how these tools and devices operated, bringing science and learning together with hands-on technology.[14]

One example of this productive mixture of mechanics and technology, science and abstract learning is the mysterious Antikythera Mechanism, a metal device found in 1900 by sponge divers in an ancient shipwreck. Fashioned around 200 BCE, the mechanism is a marvelously complex calendar of astronomical cycles, moon phases, planetary movements, and the zodiac. It is a Greek invention that clearly drew on Babylonian astronomy in a ship headed for Rome, then the dominant power in the Mediterranean.[15] A device this complicated would not be found in Europe for more than a thousand years.

In other cases, innovations were the result of artisanal labor, small changes and improvements in existing products or processes that added up to something strikingly new. Greek art is famous for its pottery, which was produced in large quantity for both practical needs, like the amphorae found in the shipwrecks, and also as decorative items for consumers. During the archaic and classical periods, a series of small innovations, ranging from a faster potter's wheel to continual experiments in firing the clay resulted in the magnificent and highly desired red figure and black figure ceramics. Even today we do not know exactly how to duplicate the results obtained by these largely anonymous artisans. Their experiments drew on neither science nor formal research but were typical of the way that innovations can come from all levels of society when people are able to put their ideas into practice.[16]

Even for the highly successful Greeks, though, there were limits to how far innovation could take them. As a society still dependent on the labors of numerous farmers working the land just to feed itself, the basics of agriculture and calorie production put the brakes on what could be achieved. Lack of agricultural machinery, an absence of nonhuman power sources, and no knowledge of fertilizer meant that agricultural productivity to sustain a growing population was always limited; something that imported foodstuffs could not fully overcome. And for all the advantages of the city-state model as a source of innovation, it faced threats from unified, imperial agrarian societies, most notably the rival Persians. In the end, it was another powerful territorial empire, Rome, that conquered Greece around 146 BC.

Of course, the fruits of Greek knowledge did not disappear. Much of it passed to the Romans. Rome as an extensive empire added one important feature to the ancient economy: great political stability. Under Roman rule and Roman administration, goods could move more freely and safely, along high-quality Roman roads, protected by the Roman military, administered by a fiscal and tax system to pay for all these services. Romans built harbors and warehouses where goods flowed into and flowed out of. Roman coins became the new widely accepted medium of exchange, an integrated monetary union across the entire territory, facilitating trade and movement. Under Roman rule a strong financial market grew up, with banks making mortgage loans for house and land purchases and commercial loans for shipping and trade. This financing was not based just on individual personal contacts but constituted a true market with a set interest rate. [17] The famous Pax Romana provided a framework of commercial law and dispute resolution and protection from piracy.[18] Good markets, good roads, good public work and strong trade relations allowed Rome at the height of its power to enjoy a standard of living comparable to that of eighteenth-century Europe.[19]

A significant part of Roman innovation focused on the public sector, as one might expect in a vast territorial empire. The Roman discovery of high-quality, waterproof concrete using volcanic ash spurred the construction of bridges, viaducts, and public buildings with impressive arch spans.[20] Roman irrigation projects brought fresh water to cities and also increased agricultural production in arid parts of the empire. On the Italian peninsula these public investments helped to support an urbanization level of 30 percent, at a time when some 95 percent of the world's population lived in the countryside.

Heating techniques in private villas and public baths, public construction of forums, theatres, porticos, and markets made urban living pleasant for the well off and tolerable even for the poor. The empire brought in food and labor from many points to feed a city of Rome that was some 1 million strong. Only Chinese cities hundreds of years later matched this figure, and Europe would not see such urbanization for almost two thousand years.

As had the Greeks, Romans depended on slave labor, at a time and in an era where virtually all societies practiced some form of slavery. In both Greece and Rome slaves worked as household servants, performed heavy agricultural labor, or took on skilled artisanal tasks, all economically important but what the upper classes considered menial labor. But slaves in Rome also had a degree of market freedom, in many cases permitted to work for wages and pay a percentage of what they earned to their master. There was a shifting line between the enslaved, the semi-free, and the fully freed. Many of the enslaved were manumitted, some 10 percent over a period of five years.[21] Freed slaves still owed a debt of obligation to their former masters, making them ideal for delicate tasks requiring loyalty and discretion, as for example managing the legal or financial affairs of noble families. And even though the enslaved may have numbered in the millions, a substantial percentage of the labor in the Roman world was procured through a free labor market. Much of the agricultural land was worked by free tenant farmers paying rent or by sharecroppers.[22] This was, in short, not a society that believed in or practiced much equality, with political power, education, and most of the wealth reserved for the tiny elite at the top and many unfree people at the bottom. That was certainly a limiting factor for innovation, a society that did not activate the potential talents of most of its people, though as we will see innovation could still well up from below, from the day-to-day activities of farmers, artisans, and traders, who might be slaves, serfs, or humble free peasants.[23]

While the words "Roman Empire" suggest war and conquest, we should also remember that Rome was situated in the center of a vast Mediterranean-Near Eastern world. This was, in the words of historian J. G. Manning, an open sea, connecting numerous places and diverse cultures, making them part of one dynamic economy. Besides its historical contacts with Greece,

Rome also drew on the stores of knowledge from Egypt and Persia. Romans learned from them how to master the trade winds so they could sail from the Red Sea into the Indian Ocean, bringing Rome into trade relations with Arabia and India. Roman trade brought in pepper from India, exotic spices from the Far East, along with Chinese silks, ivory, and tropical hardwoods.

The empire also spread Greco-Roman knowledge, innovations, and cultural practices. Screws, gears, presses, waterwheels, improvements in metallurgy, glass production, and clocks, as well as abstract knowledge residing in libraries in Alexandria, Antioch, and elsewhere infused future innovative civilizations, as we shall see. Wealthy Romans acquired land in the provinces and either moved their or managed their lands as commercial enterprises. Meanwhile people at the further reaches of the empire acquired citizenship status and moved to Italy, creating a more ethnically heterogeneous population.[24]

Rome's extensive geographical reach enabled it to generate specialized production improvements in what was still the world's main economic sector, agriculture. Olives and olive oil were staples of the ancient world's diet but producing them in quantity to meet Roman demand required a number of innovations. Taking advantage of Rome's long-distance connections, Spain emerged as the empire's major olive producer. New, more efficient screw type olive presses in North Africa, meanwhile, maximized the amount of oil that could be extracted from the crop, while investments in irrigation also increased olive production in this region.[25] Similar advances were made in the other diet stables, notably wine, which also came from Spain and saw its production increase through use of the efficient screw press. In fact, by shifting acres to wine and oil production, Romans actually increased the available calories they could extract from the soil even as the population grew. The production of oil and wine and their transport into the population centers increased demand for ceramic carrying vessels, as kilns began to dot the countryside.[26]

Given the vast size of the empire and the million or so souls who needed to be fed in the capital city, pressure on food production was significant. So, in this agricultural society, improvements in agricultural production were a mainstay of innovation. Besides wine and olive oil, Romans also increased the productivity of their main source of calories, wheat. Wheat was grown in Egypt, the main Mediterranean breadbasket of the time, and other places, using irrigation, water control, fertilizers, and handheld threshing devices, all of which were undergoing continual modification to improve output. But one crucial focus for innovation was in the conversion of wheat to grain by the milling and grinding process. Here the Romans made a key breakthrough that would, later, spread across much of Europe—the water wheel. Wheels turned by water were deployed extensively in the Roman world, which saw the invention of the cog gear to transmit the rotary motion of the waterwheel to the millstone, which did the grinding.[27]

As in Greece, many of these innovations came from the work of unknown artisans and agricultural toilers, though at least some, notably the water wheel, were studied and written about by intellectuals such as Archimedes and Vitruvius. In other cases, these small, incremental innovations also led to major technical breakthroughs that have stayed with us to the present day. Glass, for example, had been made in many earlier cultures but around the 1st century BCE Romans figured out how to blow glass. This greatly increased the speed of production and lowered costs, as well as introducing new techniques for forming and shaping glass products. The knowledge of glass blowing rapidly spread, especially to the peoples north of the Italian Alps. Meanwhile the increase in productivity led to Roman glass items and artifacts circulating all over the empire. Items that had been difficult to make and rare to find, such as translucent glass for windows, now became common in ordinary use.[28]

The Vital Few

Rome and Greece both exhibited the characteristics of high innovation societies: Education and learning, openness to new ways, ideas borrowed from other peoples and adapted to domestic needs, and vast connections spanning a significant portion of the known world. These societies were not, by our standards, democratic and free, given their heavy use of slave labor and the political power resting in the hands of a tiny elite of citizens, with little investment in human capital beyond the upper social strata. But during their height, both Greece and especially Rome, had a high degree of political stability, which in the case of Rome was effectively extended across a vast empire in ways that encouraged trade, migration, and exchange. What these societies could accomplish needs to be appreciated in the context of the times, and in that context, some of what they were able to do was extraordinary. Take the development and expansion in olive oil production in Rome. This vital resource served many purposes. It was the primary fat in the diet, the main source of fuel for illumination, and an all-purpose lubricant. It was used for cleaning the body, prescribed as a medicine, and served in religious rituals and ceremonies. Total consumption must have been on the order of 125 million liters per year, requiring the harvesting of some 34 million trees and the use of 6 million amphorae to carry it all in numerous journeys along Roman roads and in ships moving back and forth across the Mediterranean, voyages financed by credit and managed by merchants and commercial partnerships.[29]

Still, it is also important to remember that compared to innovation today, which is happening at an ever-increasing pace, the rate of change was slower and the types of innovations possible were more restricted. This is particularly so when it came to raising labor productivity, which is crucial to high per capita income growth. It seems it took the human race quite a bit of time to get to what we would consider merely a primitive life. Indeed, by our standards, there were some rather crucial things missing from ancient technology, most notably power in the form of energy.

Human muscle supplemented by animal power, mainly horse, oxen, donkeys, and camels were the main energy sources in this world and would remain so for the next two millennia. Waterwheels used by the Romans were low-power, low-torque devices. The different power sources available could provide between a fraction to about one horsepower. This is a far cry from the horsepower and BTUs unleashed by coal, oil, and other mineral energy sources starting in the nineteenth century. So how can we claim that history demonstrates humans to be highly inventive, and innovation to be central to the rise and fall of civilizations when we have already covered tens of thousands of years and this is all there is to show for it?[30]

A little perspective can help here. If we were to reduce the time of human presence on earth to a single year, the very earliest tools appeared roughly January 16. But it took until December 12, nearly the middle of the last month of calendar, for even the more sophisticated, specialized stone tools to make their way into human hands. Agriculture started on Christmas Day, December 25. The Bronze Age commenced December 28 and Columbus set sail on December 31. Men landed on the moon just before midnight on New Year's Eve. So, we humans have been really inventive, thinking deeply and making things in a conscious systematic way for only a tiny fraction of our existence. We are, as it were, still in our infancy as innovative beings. Put another way, we have made incredible changes and progress in a relatively short time. Over the "recent" past of a few thousand years, innovation has been driving massive changes in human life and making and unmaking civilizations.[31] It seems highly unlikely that innovation is going to stop being a force to reckon with any time soon. Innovative societies will still be the centers of economic, political, and military might, the creative centers of art, culture, and value, over the long run.

The time scale of innovation is not linear either. As noted earlier, at any given moment, the majority of devices, technologies, methods of production, products, and artifacts are not new and cutting-edge, but incumbent, older models.[32] It's the rare product like the iPhone that can entice people to upgrade every few years. And more recently the time for the "next big thing" in consumer electronics has stretched out into years, maybe decades, compared to not so long ago when it seemed every year something new and fantastic was released. This is totally normal because over time the possibilities for revolutionary breakthroughs in any one product or industry are bound to decrease. Sometimes they disappear. Take the standard paperclip, the so-called gem design of a single wire forming two loops, one inside the other. That was patented over a century ago. Many inventors have tried to come up with something new, different, better. And they have all failed. It seems there simply is no way to design a better paperclip than what we already have.[33]

Paper is another invention that has had remarkable staying power. As a paper trade, I can tell you this is something I give thanks for every day. Here is a product whose origins lie some two thousand years in the past, yet for many uses there is still nothing better out there. For some fifty years people have made predictions that we will soon "go paperless" in a digital world, and yet paper books are *gaining* in popularity today.[34] Even as some tasks today are carried out purely electronically, others continue to be done best on a physical medium. It seems, for example, that today's "born digital students" actually prefer and do better reading from printed textbooks. Experiments also show that they retain more by writing out their notes longhand on paper, rather than typing them on a computer. Many replacements for paper have withered and died. Historical archives and libraries are today accumulating all sorts of optical and electronic media and software that can no longer be read or played back because the technology has become obsolete. Meanwhile, paper in books and documents can last centuries or even millennia.

All this is a reminder that putting out something radically new is hard work and is not going to happen at regular intervals. It takes time and cannot be predicted easily beforehand. Just as we need lots of people encouraged to be innovators—society should draw on all of its human talent because we don't know who the next innovator will be—we also don't know when the next radical breakthrough will happen. Maintaining the conditions that spawn innovation is crucial to being ready for the next big thing. Many an inventor right now may be toiling away on a fruitless quest to make something new or better that simply cannot beat what is already out there. That's why it is so important to encourage creative thought, to get as many people as possible in a society thinking like innovators, to provide the education, experience, connections, and resources to let them be creative and try their hand, even if many will fail. It is the only reliable way to promote innovation we know of.

History shows that when this is allowed to occur, when many minds are working and converging on a set of problems, there are likely to be more and faster solutions. The more diverse the innovative base, the greater the output. It is one reason why throughout history, we find simultaneous inventions happening. Both the English genius Isaac Newton and his equally brilliant German counterpart, Gottfried Leibniz, converged on the invention of calculus at almost the same moment. Alexander Graham Bell invented the telephone, as we all know, but he had to literally race to the patent office ahead of his rival, Elisa Gray, who came up with the same technology at the same time. When we see this sort of simultaneous innovation, often across different societies at the same time, that's a healthy sign that innovation is being promoted.[35]

With our move through pre-history and the ancient past we have now seen how innovations have been central to making human life as we know it: Cities, civilizations, intellectual, artistic, and political thoughts and pursuits. Innovation centers like ancient Greece have flourished when they could master the combination of creativity, connection, and trade with other people, and the tools of finance, business, and commerce that allowed good ideas or improved methods and techniques to find a place in society. Over time, once powerful centers of innovation and creativity have declined, as did ancient Egypt, Babylonia, or Greece. Others rose in their place and often took from and adapted the creations of their predecessors, as the Romans did from Greece and Egypt.

Many of these innovations, it is true, came in the form of buildings, monuments, public works, religious artifacts, and temples. They were not necessarily productivity enhancing, though some, as with agriculture and trade, contributed to economic growth. Still, many of the innovations, in astronomy, mathematics, even in what we would consider pseudo sciences such as astrology, along with the painted vases, the temples to the gods, the stadia for sports, the water works, were life enhancing and value adding for the people of these civilizations. We should always remember that art, pleasure, religion, and the everyday comforts of life are important vectors for innovation. Even now, these are a major part of what makes our lives pleasant and livable.

Ideas, practices, knowledge, and technique were moving, flowing, merging, and coming from one part of the world to another. They were flowing in and out of the great center of innovation in the Far East, China, across Asia, India, and into the Middle East and the Mediterranean. And they were moving from the ancient worlds of Babylonia, Assyria, Persia, Egypt, Greece, and Rome into what would become the next great innovation civilization. It all converged in an unexpected location in the Arabian Peninsula, giving rise to an entirely new civilization that would begin to generate the next great wave of innovation. Let me take you there, to the land where I was born and raised, to Egypt and the Islamic Civilization of the Middle East.

CHAPTER 2:

Innovation in Islam's Golden Age

Secular and religious education went hand-in-hand when I was growing up in Egypt in the 1960s and early '70s. Both my mother and my aunt were teachers. My mother taught Arabic, and from her we learned to think independently and understand the Muslim faith. My father was an art professor, a painter, and a musician. His father was also a scholar and taught at Al-Azhar University. Founded in Cairo in the tenth century by the Fatimid Caliphate during the Golden Age of Islam, it is said to be the oldest university in the world. Even today it is a thriving center of Islamic learning and Arabic literature. My great grandparents on my father's side made their fortune in the cotton trade but lost everything during the Great Depression of 1929. That is why education was so important to them. They knew that if their children were educated, they could make it in this world. The synergy between my mother and father was powerful, and they instilled in me a profound love of knowledge and the arts and the belief that I could be anything I wanted to be if I applied myself. My uncle was also a key role model for me as well. Although he wanted to be a physician, his father encouraged him to become a mechanical engineer; he then landed a top job in the United States at Bechtel and became very successful. I wanted to be like him. As I will be showing you, I have followed all these examples that taught me the core values of being innovative through education, applying those lessons learned, and executing the very best ideas.

Part of my education was religious. I was expected to attend religious classes after school and read and recite the Quran. It is the sacred text of the Islamic faith, but it also imparts the value of knowledge. Seeking knowledge is a sacred duty. In fact, knowledge and scholarship have been revered by Muslim society since its inception, thanks to the Prophet Muhammad's teaching that "the ink of scholars is more precious than the blood of martyrs." Not long after the birth of this new religion on the Arabian Peninsula in 622 C.E., the rulers of the new empire (known as "caliphs") ushered in a new Golden Age of Islam. They were remarkably committed to learning, and in the seventh century made elementary education compulsory for boys and girls who were taught the basics of Arabic grammar and how to read the Quran. *Madrasas,* or religious centers of education, were attached to mosques and served to educate legal and spiritual leaders, and also offered support in mathematics. Book writing and production flourished, and the gathering and transmission of knowledge among contemporaries and between generations was supported by the powerful caliphs.[1]

The goal of education, Martin Luther King, Jr. once said, is "to teach one to think intensively and critically. Intelligence plus character—that is the goal of true education."[2] While education can teach you skills, it must also build your character. Starting with family, teachers, and spiritual leaders, we learn the fundamental values that will guide us on the journey of life. Innovation is always about finding ways to add value. We can do this by drawing upon the core values we have learned, the transformative experiences that have shaped us, and by exchanging this knowledge with others. Since innovation means going beyond what is common, accepted and routinely practiced, moving into areas unknown and taking on new risks or gaining new experiences, people need some place to begin from, something to ground them as they venture out into the unknown. Values often provide this platform as well as a basis for exchange with others, who have different values. If people only exchanged what they already had and shared what they already knew, little innovation would be possible. We can see this process in operation as we look at the next great center of innovation, the Islamic world during its golden age from the eighth to the thirteenth century.

The Golden Age of Islam was one of the great eras in the history of innovation. Islam formed a culture of learning, creativity, and commercial and technological invention that rested upon but at times also surpassed the ancient Greeks.[3] A number of factors reflected in our innovation model coalesced under the ruling caliphates to make this new golden age possible, including: A profound hunger for ancient and new knowledge; patronage of scholarship and a commitment to all forms of learning; a tolerance of other religions and the acceptance of other cultures; the unification of the realm under one official language (Arabic); the creation of a strong administrative state and the infrastructure to run it efficiently; the promotion of business and trade both within the empire and outside its borders; and a search for useful new technologies to improve the well-being of the many peoples under the caliphates' rule. Trade was crucial to the growth and development of the vast Islamic empire, bringing a host of new people, ideas, and technologies into the realm. Islamic leaders also welcomed those of other faiths and passionately sought out the intellectual treasures of their new subjects. In most civilizations they conquered, they allowed indigenous cultures to retain their own administrations, religions, and cultural heritage.[4]

The armies of Islam retraced the path of Alexander the Great as they forged their new empire and vast trading network. Their territory eventually stretched from the Middle East, across North Africa, into Europe in the West and on to parts of India, Central Asia, and Southeast Asia in the East. The spread of Islam was only halted in Europe when Charles Martel turned the flank of the "Saracens" (as Europeans called Muslims) at Tours in 732, pushing them back behind the Pyrenees into the Iberian Peninsula, where they formed a new colony in southern Spain called *al-Andalus* or Andalusia. Likewise, only the powerful Chinese empire resisted their drive to the Far East. During this golden age, the Muslim world grew larger than the Hellenistic and Roman worlds together, and its vast trading empire was more extensive, more varied, and more powerful than any other society had achieved in the past.

With this extraordinary expansion, a broad array of ethnic and religious communities came under their control, including large urban populations of Persians, Aramaic speakers, Syrians, Jews, and Christians. Intellectual centers of scholarship flourished throughout their empire, providing access to a wonderfully diverse body of cultural knowledge Muslims were eager to absorb. They restored the ancient ties between the key historic centers of civilization, bridging Hellenistic learning from Greece (and later Alexandria) with Sumerian, Persian, Indian, Chinese, and Egyptian wisdom. They forged an intellectual melting pot that began to thrive throughout the span of their empire, and promoted the free, rapid flow and exchange of ideas and scholarship, alongside, goods, credit, capital, and the instruments of trade and economic exchange. Only rarely in history does a society create such a flourishing of creativity and innovation. The Islamic Golden Age was one of those.[5]

A Culture of the Book

As the inheritors of the classical traditions of Greece, Persia, India, and Mesopotamia, the caliphs pursued an unprecedented program to gather, translate, and disseminate this ancient learning. During the seventh century, the Umayyad Caliphate initiated the movement to translate most of the corpus of the ancient Greeks into Arabic. This effort then gained momentum under the Abbasid Caliphate in the following century when it became a regular state-sanctioned activity. The third Abbasid caliph, al-Ma'mun (813-833 C.E.) built the House of Wisdom (*Bayt al-hikma*) in Baghdad in 832 C.E., a remarkable library and scientific center staffed with linguistic experts, scribes, and scholars who made translations of Greek, Pahlavi, Sanskrit, and Syrian treatises into hand-written Arabic books. Most of the translation industry centered in Baghdad, which became the new capital in the eighth century. This search for ancient and new knowledge and a love of new literature like *The Thousand and One Nights* spurred the birth of a culture of the book in Islam that helped to educate, enlighten, and entertain the masses.[6]

Bureaucratic necessity also fueled the Muslims' advances in communication and information dissemination throughout their vast empire. Caliphs from Baghdad to Cairo used paper lavishly for their decrees and documents, to organize payments and taxes, register the army, and keep the treasury flowing smoothly. To advance and disseminate the new translations and service its bureaucracy, the rulers of Islam needed a more efficient form of communication that did not rely on papyrus or the labor-intensive processing of animal hides into parchment. Muslims learned papermaking technology from the Chinese in Central Asia during the eighth century and developed their own inks, dyes, and glue to manufacture paper books. And while the Chinese used woody fibers from such plants as hemp, jute, and bamboo to make their paper, Muslim manufacturers changed the process by using linen rags that were readily available from the large urban populations that were filling the cities. They improved upon Chinese techniques for beating fibers and prepared the surface of their paper by sizing it with starch, thereby creating a strong yet supple new product that was improved over the following centuries to be finer and whiter.

Much less costly than parchment or vellum and more durable and easier to manipulate than papyrus, paper radically reduced the cost of information and communication. The decision by Islamic rulers to employ it triggered its acceptance across the Islamic world. Thus, religious and secular, and sacred and scientific, knowledge could be communicated over a wider territory and to more people. In addition, unlike papyrus or parchment, it was impossible to scratch or alter paper without leaving a trace, which facilitated the provision of authentic documents fundamental to trade, government, and the implementation of Islamic law. The new communication technology also provided a major stimulus to trade in agricultural goods, which was powering the medieval Muslim economy. Merchants throughout the empire regularly used paper for bills, payment orders, and other documents that kept the economy booming and interconnected across vast distances.[7]

Muslims built their first paper mill during the eighth century in Samarqand, a Central Asian city at the western end of the Silk Road. Samarqand had thrived as an important center of commerce for centuries and became famous for its paper production. Before long, this technology spread rapidly across Muslim-controlled Iran, Iraq, Syria, Egypt, and North

Africa into Andalusian Spain which served as a gateway for the introduction of this pivotal technology to other parts of Europe. Recent scholarship has overturned a tendency by historians to disregard this seminal contribution of the Islamic world to the transformation of Western civilization. In fact, paper was just one of many ways that the Islamic world's great outpouring of innovation would eventually stimulate the innovation culture of the West. But that story comes later.[8]

In 794-95 C.E., the Abbasid caliph Harun al-Rashid hired Chinese workers to develop a paper mill in the magical new capital, the "Round City" of Baghdad. The design of the city was inspired by caliph Abu Jafar al-Manur's love of the Greek mathematician Euclid, and it was constructed within a perfectly circular wall one mile in circumference, 98 feet high, and 145 feet thick at the base. Baghdad paper became greatly prized and was sold in the Suq al-Warraqin, a stationers' bazaar in the southwestern district of the city lined with over a hundred stalls that also sold books. Within forty years, Baghdad, with a population estimated at one million, was the largest city in the world.[9] Glamorized in the *Arabian Nights*, the city was perfectly situated between the swift waters of the Tigris and Euphrates that flowed into the Indian Ocean, providing the waterpower critical for paper manufacturing. Arabs began to harness the powerful force of hydraulics as never before to serve their new industry. The use of the water wheel was one of many pivotal technologies they had learned from the ancient Greeks. In fact, like papermaking, the use of the water wheel was a vital innovation that helped propel the growth of Islam. Muslim hydrology brought agricultural prosperity through the empire and was also introduced to Europe via Iberia.

While paper was a crucial breakthrough, the Islamic world did not adopt the printing press. Although the Chinese had developed moveable type in the eleventh century, and the technology is said to have been known to Islam by that time, Muslims continued to copy books by hand. They only began to print them nearly a millennium after they introduced papermaking. Many Western historians have argued that the Islamic civilization made its worst mistake by not adopting the printing press until the eighteenth century, which served to isolate their world from the mainstream of knowledge. Still, even so, the Muslims' incredibly efficient paper business and positive attitude toward books and book-learning triggered an explosion of scientific and literary creativity in a broad range of subjects in the medieval period.[10]

Book bazaars became a regular feature of city life and elite patronage of authors by the rulers and the wealthy grew commonplace, spurring new scholarship. Lavish sums of money were heaped upon authors and book translators. The mosque formed the center of this book economy, and even poets published their works there. Before long, great libraries were constructed to house these books, some of which allowed the public to freely partake of the new learning. They were built by the caliphs and wealthy citizens, and others were attached to mosques or the mosque schools. Where the Great Library at Alexandria had once been the center of Western knowledge, it was gone by 600 C.E., a victim of fires, decay, and neglect. In the seventh century, the Umayyads opened the first library of the golden age in Damascus, which featured Greek and Christian works on alchemy, medicine, and other sciences. But it was under the Abbasids in the following century that patronage proved to be a major stimulus to the creation of these libraries. In another part of the Islamic empire, Egypt, Fatimid sultans also loved books and amassed vast collections. Al-Aziz, the second Fatimid ruler, is said to have had forty rooms overflowing with books. He possessed 18,000 volumes on ancient science alone. The library of Shiraz in the tenth century was said to be housed in 360 rooms. Enormous private collections became commonplace, often numbering in the tens of thousands of volumes. In Muslim-controlled Iberia, a culture far more advanced than any other in Europe emerged. The Islamic library in Cordoba contained 400,000 books by the tenth century. The *madrasas* of the mosques held their own collections as well, and many were open to the public. All Muslim sects understood the value of public libraries to spread the knowledge of Islam. There were 30 *madrasas* in Baghdad alone, and 150 in Damascus by 1500. One Egyptian *madras* founded by al-Qadi al-Fadiz in the thirteenth century boasted some 100,000 volumes. By contrast, in the fourteenth century the Sorbonne Library at the University of Paris contained a mere 2,000 manuscripts, and the Vatican library had only 2,257 by 1455.[11]

The ruling caliphates, religious leaders, and wealthy citizens filled these massive libraries with copies of translations of Greek and other classical learning, as well as manuscripts written by contemporary authors of Islam. Islamic scholars were the first to make direct translations and comparisons between Greek and Indian mathematics, Chinese and Persian astronomy, and Greek and Indian medicine. They explored how these ancient ideas corresponded with one another and with their own religious worldview. They were not simply caretakers and appropriators of ancient knowledge, as the Western world believed until scholarship in the past several decades proved otherwise. "Philosophy is drawn from the Muslims," the thirteenth-century English philosopher Roger Bacon wrote. A Franciscan friar and one of the earliest Western proponents of the scientific method, Bacon admired the Muslims for their intellectual innovations. Arab authors added extensive commentaries to the corpus of the Greeks, sometimes based on their own original scientific studies. Astronomy, alchemy and chemistry, geography, medicine, pharmacology, mathematics, optics, and agricultural science flourished under them, producing giants of scholarship that would profoundly influence Western civilization in the centuries to come.[12]

Tolerance

Tolerance under Islamic rule was of critical importance to the flowering of knowledge and innovation in this golden age. The new urban multilingual, multicultural, multi-religious milieus of Baghdad, Damascus, Cairo, Seville, Cordoba, and other major cities stimulated the routine exchange of ideas and technologies. A broad range of ideas was tolerated and even encouraged, and no single dogma was imposed. Caliphs and other prominent bureaucrats attended and supported lively gatherings of Christians, pagans, Jews, and Muslims that featured intellectual discussions of the books they produced. "It is within this culture," argues the science historian F. Jamil Ragep, "that the value of knowledge—whether religious, practical or theoretical—was promoted, partly to deal with this burgeoning quantity of texts and ideas from a variety of sources and partly to conform to various Qur'anic and prophetic injunctions to seek knowledge from whatever source."[13] Indeed, far from being an inward-looking or exclusive religion, particularly under the Abbasids, Islam in this period welcomed non-Muslim residents. Much of the scholarship and knowledge transfer in the Golden Age was in fact performed by Jews, Christians, and Persians. Under Muslim rule, the Jewish people fared especially well. They had been badly treated by the Christians in Byzantium, but prospered under the Muslims who allowed them to continue to practice their faith. Many also converted to Islam, and shared their advances in astronomy, medicine, engineering, math, agriculture, and literature.[14]

From its inception, Islam forged a special relationship with Christians and Jews and considered them "Peoples of the Book." Just as Muslims had the Quran, Christians and Jews also had their own sacred texts that formed the foundation of their communities. They were respectfully called the *dhimmi* (covenanted people) and granted religious freedom, provided they paid a special tax. Muslims paid a different form of tax. Christians and Jews intermarried with Muslims frequently, further bridging ties within these communities. There were, however, restrictions. Christians and Jews were forbidden to proselytize Muslims, build new temples or churches, or publicly display or celebrate their religion in any way. Still, the Jewish people flourished in Andalusia and elsewhere in the Islamic world. As a protected minority, they participated in unlimited opportunities in the booming commercial environment, trading across the Mediterranean and importing products from the Far East. They undertook large agricultural projects, and joined the educated classes to improve their status.[15]

Religion and the Pursuit of Science

It might be tempting to argue that highly religious societies like Islam cannot be innovative societies. Religions may be conservative, fearful of change. They may emphasize transcendent spiritual values over material ones. They may attune people to the study of texts and scriptures rather than to mechanical or scientific arts or to business and trade. Some religions are even antithetical to trade and money-making. Money-lending was denounced in the Quran and Islamic legal literature (and in Christian texts too). To some degree the widespread adoption of Christianity in the old Roman world ushered in a period of intellectual and material decline along these lines. But as with the case of Islam and as we shall see later with Christianity, Buddhism, Confucianism, and other religions, there need not be a conflict between innovative, creative, inquisitive thinking, and religious pursuits. In fact, religious, scientific, as well as political roles often overlapped. Ibn Rushd (later know as Averroes in the West) was a great Islamic natural philosopher who also served as a judge specializing in religious law, initially in Seville and then in Cordoba in Andalusian Spain. He argued that both religious and natural philosophy were valid forms of knowledge.[16] When Islamic mathematicians developed trigonometry in its modern form, the need to find the precise direction of Kaaba in Mecca (which must be faced during prayer) formed the impetus for these studies. Indeed, religions *can* inspire invention and creativity.

The sciences pursued by Islamic scholars were closely linked to the moral and religious thought of Islam in this era. A large number of Islamic thinkers, important theologians, and philosophers held that the knowledge gained by studying nature and natural philosophy was useful to the understanding of God. With astronomy in particular we see how religious motivation could inspire innovation. Religiously-committed scholars made great strides in advancing knowledge of astronomy, and they employed geometry and trigonometry to make their calculations. Mathematics served the needs of commerce, civil society, and religion. In Egypt and Syria an important new, mathematically-based profession emerged: the timekeeper, who was attached to the mosque and specialized in the astronomical science of timekeeping. His roles as religious official and mathematician/scientist overlapped. The timekeeper of the Umayyad mosque, Ibn al-Shatir (d. 1375), also worked in the Maragha Observatory in western Iran, which was constructed following the sack of Baghdad in 1258 by the Mongols under the patronage of Hulagu, their ruling leader. Hulagu staffed the observatory with Ibn al-Shatir and a team of Muslim astronomers and mathematicians. While they did not develop the heliocentric system published by Copernicus in 1543, they did improve the Ptolemaic system that modeled the position of the sun, earth, and planets in the heavens. According to Toby Huff, "The Arab-Muslim astronomers criticized and perfected Ptolemaic planetary theory with the result that they produced significantly improved planetary models…." The planetary models of Copernicus formulated 150 years later were mathematically equivalent to those developed by the Muslim astronomers and mathematicians of the Maragha observatory. This has led historians to ask "'not whether, but when, where, and in what form'" Copernicus gained knowledge of the Maragha models.[17]

Knowledge of the stars, phases of the moon, seasons, and celestial phenomena such as comets and eclipses were considered useful for two reasons. In Islam, as in other religions, important events and festivals are marked by their occurrence in the calendar, moveable feasts that change every year. Thus, it was important to have skilled astronomers who could plot their exact occurrence year by year. In addition, the Muslims' five daily prayers were to be said within certain time intervals, which had to be calculated according to the altitude of the sun. The science of timekeeping became quite advanced under Islam, and relied upon numerical schemes, geometric constructs, and trigonometric calculations. By contrast, Europeans during this era could not count hours, had no clocks, and were incapable of making much-needed reforms to their calendar.[18]

Many people at the time also believed in astrology and thought that the stars and zodiac foretold events and yielded favorable and fortunate (as well as dangerous) times to perform or undertake certain actions—wage war, start a journey, have a child. These same beliefs were operating in China as well, another society that invested heavily in knowledge of astronomy and astrology. In both places, astrology provided additional motivation for the refinement of mathematics and astronomy. However, although Islamic Neoplatonic philosophers earned recognition for astrology by identifying divine determination with the constellations, scholastic theologians rejected it because they believed that a causal connection between the stars above and earthbound events contradicted the doctrine that God is the exclusive and immediate creator of all events.[19]

Astronomy and even mathematics served at times as handmaidens to religion, providing strong arguments for their vital importance to and acceptance by the community. As the historian Tamim Ansary has recently explained, "In ninth and tenth century Iraq (as in classical Greece), science as such did not exist to be disentangled from religion. The philosophers were giving birth to it without quite realizing it. They thought of religion as their field of inquiry and theology as their intellectual specialty; they were on a quest to understand the ultimate nature of reality." But even though a knowledge of astronomy was required for the determination of the correct times of prayer and the precise direction of Kaaba in Mecca, orthodox religious circles did not, in general, favor the astronomical sciences.[20] In fact, the flourishing of science that took place during the Islamic Golden Age would decline as religious orthodoxy asserted itself more strongly.

A growing orthodoxy in Islam worked against the development, spread, and application of new knowledge, threatening the innovative possibilities of the flourishing empire. Religious authorities grew increasingly suspicious of the ancient sciences, and those suspected of unorthodox views were often persecuted. If they were believed to be engaged in heretical thinking and owned large libraries, the libraries could be confiscated and destroyed if they were found to contain books on these subjects or works on astrology and witchcraft. Some studies have shown that even during the Golden Age, there was a high degree of secrecy and concealment by scholars pursuing the study of the natural sciences. Even though scientific inquiry was generally tolerated, and at times encouraged by the ruling elite, it was never institutionalized and formally taught in the *madrasas*. Scientific studies were pursued outside the colleges, and to specialize in one science, students moved from city to city seeking experts who taught them privately.[21]

Cracks in the utopian vision of a harmonious Muslim blending of piety, learning, and justice were already beginning to bubble up to the surface as scholar-theologians and philosopher-scientists seemed to be moving in competing directions by the eleventh century. A growing chorus of pious voices began to condemn the pursuit of reason, philosophy, and the natural sciences. These intellectual arguments often resulted in violent and bloody clashes, which paralleled the loss of political stability in Islam as a whole as its golden era began to wane.

The religious orthodoxy was most offended by mathematics and geometry in particular. The tenth-century mathematician al-Sijzi wrote that in his region it was lawful to kill "geometers." He and others argued that these kinds of sciences created pride in human accomplishments and took the practitioner's attention away from God. And yet these efforts to suppress the work of scientists and mathematicians failed to impede the robust cultivation of these forms of knowledge. In line with our model of innovation, Islamic philosopher-scientists continued to keenly observe the world around them, critically compare their own observations with those of the ancients and publishing their findings.[22] But the conflict with religion and the growing power of orthodox-minded clerics was a sign that the flourishing of science and innovation in the Islamic world had an end date.

Practical Innovations

Still, the practical ramifications of this new scholarship in math and science were not lost amid these growing religious tensions in the Muslim world. Jabir ibn Hayyan and other Islamic experimenters made significant advances in the area of chemistry. Like astrology and astronomy, chemistry and alchemy were closely aligned, and would continue to be in the Middle East and Europe through the Renaissance. In the search for ways to create gold and transmute one metal into another, alchemy provided a powerful impetus for learning and innovation. Among the results of Jabir's work was the alembic, or pot still, which produced alcohol. Although distilling would have its most famous application in liquor, alcohol was also an important chemical for experimentation as a solvent. The Persian physician Rhazes recorded his advanced knowledge of Arabic chemistry. The rise of chemistry in Islam produced soda, alum, copperas (aluminum sulfate), nitre, and other salts. Many of these products were used in a thriving textile industry of the Middle East.

"Muslim civilization," wrote the historian Maurice Lombard, "was based to a considerable extent on textiles." High-quality silk, wool, and cotton clothing and furnishings were produced in workshops throughout the empire. Fabrics often were used as presents, wages, and rewards. Cotton cultivation expanded dramatically in al-Jazira, which was then exported to

Mosul, Baghdad, Akhlat, and other Armenian textile centers. The Muslims borrowed the central Asian technology of irrigating their cotton crops with underground channels, which in turn supported its acclimatization in northern and southern Syria, regions that became the main suppliers of cotton for the entire Mediterranean world.[23]

Islamic medicine likewise flourished under the strong patronage of the Abbasids. The most influential Greek writers translated by Islamic scholars were Dioscorides, Galen, and Rufus of Ephesus. Their humoral system of pathology would dominate medical practice in the Islamic empire and subsequently Europe through the seventeenth century. In fact, when scholarship in Europe began to emerge in the twelfth century, the extensive works of Aristotle and Galen were recovered from Arabic sources that had been interpreted, and at times, challenged and disproved by Averroes, Avicenna, Rhazes, and many others. Avicenna's *Canon of Medicine* became a standard European text until the 1600s. Medical knowledge and patient care in Islam reflected a rich tapestry of cultures and traditions. Magical and folkloric practices proliferated together with Hellenic medicine, forming a medically pluralistic milieu. Jewish, Christian, and other medical practitioners operated side-by-side with Arabic doctors. The Bukhtishu family of Nestorian Christian physicians based their medicine on the Hellenic Greeks and served the caliphs in Baghdad for eight generations.[24]

Innovative treatises on ophthalmology led to an increase in ocular surgery during this era. Islamic writers on surgery also modified surgical instruments and techniques originally pioneered by the Greeks. And Arabic writers made great strides in pharmacology, much of it diverging from the earlier Hellenistic works. The broader and different geographical world of Islam brought physicians into contact with a host of new drugs unknown to the Greeks, including camphor, musk, and sal ammoniac. Anatomical writings, however, remained conservative and in line with Hellenic observations. According to historian Emilie Savage-Smith, "Learned Islamic physicians produced a vast quantity of medical literature on their own, in which they imposed a logical and coherent structure on the earlier Greek medicine while developing a more precise scientific vocabulary. They also added an extensive pharmacology, more elaborate notions of medical pathology, knowledge of certain new diseases and disorders, new therapies, and some new surgical techniques and instrumentation." Once Europe began to undergo a dramatic political, social, and economic recovery during the eleventh and twelfth centuries, they imported the Greek medical traditions—with important, innovative additions—from the observant Muslims. Indeed, even during its economic decline, the Islamic world continued to influence the development of medicine in the West through the Renaissance.[25]

In contrast to the Christian world, where monasteries of the medieval period provided relief to the sick and poor, urban hospitals were a major Islamic achievement. The caliph Harun al-Rashid opened the first Islamic hospital in Baghdad late in the eighth century, and soon all the major urban centers had them. These hospitals provided treatment to a variety of patients including the insane and the aged. Wealthy citizens employed their own private physicians (Muslim, Christian, and Jewish) who treated them at home. Especially in the large cities of Baghdad, Cairo, and Damascus, evidence indicates some medical instruction took place in these early hospitals, but not in any formalized way. Most medical instruction was conducted through private tutoring or through self-learning.[26]

Despite the skepticism toward the field by conservative clerics, mathematics also made great strides during the Golden Age of Islam. Arab mathematicians are credited with inventing trigonometry. They studied the Greeks' invention of geometry, the Babylonians' concept of place value, and the Indians' pivotal concept of treating zero as a number and decimal arithmetic. The ninth-century mathematician Muhammad ibn Musa al-Khwarizmi, who was attached to the caliph al-Mamun's House of Knowledge in Baghdad, then integrated all of these breakthroughs into a cohesive system and invented algebra (derived from the Arabic word *al-jabr*). This new systemization would form the very basis of the field of modern mathematics and was also employed by other scholars to make additional breakthroughs in astronomy and create the highly accurate sundials necessary for religious as well as secular timekeeping. This new Arabic-Hindu numeral system would gradually replace earlier forms of notation such as Roman numerals throughout Europe.[27]

A Network of Trade

We can now start to see the various forces that made the Islamic world such an innovative culture in this period. The Muslims brought together old and new learning and borrowed and adapted knowledge and ideas from many cultures. They practiced a religion that was tolerant of non-believers and outsiders. They encouraged immigration and settlement of talented people. They placed a strong emphasis on learning, education, and books. They created a vast, expansive civilization that spread across multiple geographies and had contact with multiple peoples with different forms of knowledge living in different cultures and climate zones. The result was an immense, tolerant world where the exchange of goods, ideas, and knowledge could take place under one roof, so to speak.

The scholarly apparatus of the Islamic world that unified multiple cultures and traditions of knowledge had its counterpart in the equally strong ties of trade, urban expansion, and transportation. Trade flourished under a single language and a single monetary system. Major urban development throughout the Muslim world also profoundly impacted the growth of trade engaged in by a wealthy class of merchants who dominated caravan traffic and spearheaded the economic expansion of the empire. The prosperous city of Samarqand stood at the nexus of the trade routes coming from India and Persia. It is estimated that its population reached 500,000 during the late ninth to tenth centuries. During their peak development, Cairo and Cordoba also had a half a million residents. This rapid urban growth and expansion of trade gave rise to a higher standard of living among the wealthier classes, creating ever-rising consumer demand and the increasing consumption of luxury goods. Trade in the cities provided a critical means of contact and also a way to bring into use various products and practices and to exchange them with other people. Merchants and trade, for example, played an important role in the transmission of chemical knowledge to Islam. The *Hu* merchants were Persian and Arabic and travelled the famed Silk Road to trade with the Chinese. Through this Asian contact, they learned the principles of Chinese alchemy which led to its proliferation in Islam and to the discovery of such chemicals as caustic alkalis (the word alkali is derived from "*al-qili*," which is Arabic for sodium carbonate). Islamic merchants exported many of these new chemical products as well. A chemical knowledge brought home by the *Hu* made its way to the West through merchants as well.[28]

After the capital of Islam moved from Damascus to Baghdad after 750, there, along the Tigris, its people had access to the Indian Ocean via the Persian Gulf. Islamic law and custom provided a legal framework for traders of many stripes in a vibrant international commerce that moved goods, money, people, and ideas between East and West. Despite formal prohibitions on charging interest and other necessary commercial practices, in fact the law and religious and legal institutions were quite pragmatic and flexible. They bent to accommodate economic growth and opportunity. Muslim traders used letters of credit, partnerships (*mudaraba*), and created dense networks of trade where participants engaged in lending and borrowing. Many of these techniques would later find their way into Italy and be taken up by the city-states of the Renaissance.[29] Arabs, Syrians, Persians, Ethiopians, Bengali, Yemeni, Muslim, Jewish, Jain, and Nestorian Christians all participated in the vast Indian Ocean trade diaspora. They carried cloth, precious metals, and silver coins from Europe and the Middle East to India, Southeast Asia, and China, and brought back the high valued goods of spices, pepper, silk, and porcelain from Asia and India. Each trading group managed its own affairs, often families of merchants, but they also worked across lines at key ports such as Aaden. Different groups specialized in different functions: Jains in credit and finance; Guajarati in the carrying of trade from India to the Far East; Muslims and Hindus in the trade on the Malabar Coast. Often groups connected and aligned themselves through mixed marriages to cement trade alliances. As the saying went about a merchant, "If he dressed in a Javanese costume, he looked like a man of Java." The same held for Thais and Indians. It mattered less what the merchant's "original" identity might be: Interconnections, intermarriage, and toleration for cultural differences were crucial to sustaining the process of exchange. From the Silk Road and over the Indian Ocean, from the Persian Gulf and from Samarqand in Central Asia, goods and information flowed into Baghdad.[30]

The Islamic trading network also provided connections from the Middle East to Europe and the West. Goods made their way up the Red Sea, into the Nile, through Cairo, into the Mediterranean, across North Africa, over the Straits of Gibraltar, into Andalusia and Western Europe. The caliphates had created a vast trading area with established routes that ran to China, where Muslim traders were in port and inland cities. That trade network ran through central Asia as far north as Scandinavia. While Europeans had lost access to the Indian Ocean after it was closed by Muslims in 700 C.E., they traded through Egypt for highly prized eastern goods, like silk and spices. Overland trade brought silk, porcelain, paper, and cotton textiles from Asia and the Middle East in exchange for furs, amber, and slaves from Northern Europe, where Vikings met Muslim traders at Kiev Rus (Ukraine).

As with ancient Greece and Babylonia, the Arab Islamic trading world developed instruments of debt and credit, joint-stock ventures, and banks. Under the wide umbrella of Islam a trader could draw or make payment on banks that ranged from Cordoba in Spain to China. They even developed a new means of bank payment, the "sakk," a Persian word that came into English as "check." Such financial practices and institutions would only later make their way to Europe, starting with the bank of the crusading Christian Knights Templar who borrowed the same model from their religious enemies.

Trade abroad stimulated the economy at home. In Baghdad, Basra, Kufa, Samarqand, and other cities of Islam, silks, spices, sapphire, ivory, ebony, pearls, camphor, aloe, teak, sandalwood, lead, glass, and other commodities, both elite and ordinary, passed through these ports, accumulating wealth. Within the extensive Islamic world from Spain to Morocco, to central Asia and Persia, the wealth stimulated production of all sorts of items: turbans, veils, cotton cloth, bracelets, yarn, iron, oils, fox furs, taffeta, rope, cheese, dates, carpets, incense, walnuts, almonds, pewter ware, and soap. The last, especially bar soap, became one of Islam's innovations to the world, a product of both the knowledge of chemistry and the religious injunction to keep clean.

Accumulating wealth for the upper classes, expansive economic relations and the commitment to preserve and enhance knowledge, often appropriated from multiple cultures, made Islam a center of a variety of important breakthroughs that it would eventually pass on to the rest of the world. The Golden Age of Islam also corresponded with one of the great moments of creativity in China, under the Tang and Song dynasties, something we will hear about later. Here too Islam played a key role in bringing the innovations of the Far East westward. China, pressured by the Mongols on their western frontier in the tenth and eleventh centuries, responded by building a vast navy, with iron nailed hulls, lateen sails, and sternpost rudders, which greatly improved control and maneuverability and tacking against the wind. The lateen sail passed to India, which had extensive trade relations with China, was picked up by Arab sailors along with another Chinese breakthrough in navigation technology, the magnetic compass. Arab scientists also refined the early Greek designs for the astrolabe, a device of celestial navigation crucial for finding latitude. These innovations were introduced to Europe in later centuries, with the result that it would rise to challenge the Middle and Far East in trade and technology.[31] But Europe had far to climb from the depths to which it had plummeted during the so-called "Dark Ages."

The Decline and Fall

When the Roman Empire fell to the barbarian tribes in the fifth century, knowledge of the ancient Greek, Egyptian, and Babylonian societies was lost in the western quadrant of Europe. Illiteracy rose and agricultural productivity essential to sustain population growth, specialization, and trade declined across the western Mediterranean and Europe.[32] Low agricultural productivity discouraged creative thinking. Famines and inadequate caloric intake made for a much more conservative and cautious approach to life in post Roman Europe. Indeed, it is worth remembering that in any pre-modern society, food always comes first. The English word "lord" for example, derives from the Anglo-Saxon "hlaford" or keeper of loaves, a meaningful name in a place where bread was the staff of life. Only when caloric security is adequate do people venture into other things.

The end of the Western Roman Empire did not mean the end of all European civilization, though. In the East, the Roman Empire continued, now under new management as the "Byzantine" empire centered in

Constantinople in modern- day Turkey. It would endure for another thousand years. But the old Roman world had also changed in an important way: It adopted the new religion of Christianity. Under the emperor Justinian, a new orthodoxy descended, one that was closed to non-Christian learning or ideas. Scholars, translators, and transcribers of knowledge soon left the Byzantine world, finding a more receptive home in Persia where they carried much of the learning, science, and knowledge from the ancient world with them into what became the Golden Age of Islam, as we have just seen.

The Latin-speaking parts of the old Roman Empire and its one-time colonies in northern Europe lost touch with this fount of learning, science, and knowledge. Without Rome, roads, armies, state administration, and trade connections all deteriorated. Territories fractured into small principalities and minor warring states, causing illiteracy to rise and the production of basic agricultural staples to decline. Low agricultural productivity meant low, and in some cases, declining population and contributed to that innovation stifling insecurity.[33] So, as the Muslim world adapted and built on the ancient world's knowledge and commercial trade patterns, and as the old Roman culture continued in the East around Constantinople, Western Europe devolved, for a time.

By 1200 C.E. that time had passed and Europe would begin a long climb economically, militarily, scientifically, and technologically that would make it the next great innovative society. That story lies in the next chapters, but first we have to explain why the Golden Age of Islam came to an end. After 1200 C.E. the Islamic world, while still important and extensive, started to lose the competitive and innovative edge it had exhibited over the previous five centuries. What went wrong? If we look at the factors that promote innovation: Education, extensive cross-cultural contacts and immigration, openness to learning and a lack of religious orthodoxy, vigorous trade, a mild state that provides security, law and property rights, we can see that a number of these factors weakened in Islamic society as the centuries passed. In other cases, it was not so much that the Islamic innovative culture declined as other places, notably Europe, began to build up stronger institutions, taking the innovation process to an entirely new level. Consider Islamic education. There were schools, *madrassas*, yes, but these were primarily for religious instruction and they did not have the independence from the state that European universities were able to obtain. Secular learning and natural science were distinctly secondary. Students who sought secular knowledge worked closely with a scholar and so had to travel to those places where science was being taught. There was nothing like the emerging European university that brought together many forms of knowledge in a self-governing body of academics. Similar patterns existed in the professions and disciplines, such as law and medicine. These were not so much self-governing guilds of experts who exchanged knowledge as family-based enterprises handed down to succeeding generations.[34]

There was, even for a thinker as dazzling as Averroes, no sense of a single, unitary form of truth that cut across nature and religion and was available to all peoples and classes. This concept, as we will see, was a hard-won victory for science and philosophy born out of the Christian church in the later Middle Ages. But when it occurred, it helped to provide a basis for the Scientific Revolution—universal knowledge available to all. Indeed, after 1200 C.E., if anything, Islam returned to a more orthodox form under the influence of the theology of Al Ghazali, who argued that philosophy was "un-Islamic." Even paper and printing, to which Arabs had contributed so much, came under attack. The new technology of printing, invented in China but rapidly developed in fifteenth- century Europe, was not accepted by the Islamic world for centuries afterward. Then of course there were simply the fortunes of history. In 1258 Mongol invaders sacked Baghdad, burning libraries and destroying manuscripts and books. It was said that the river ran red, not so much with blood but with the ink of destroyed books.[35]

In societies that do not cultivate and maintain tolerance of different opinions, leadership in innovation can decline. This happened to Islam at the end of its golden age. As I discovered myself as a teenager, even in societies that prize learning, religion can have a stifling effect if it is too concerned with conformity and orthodoxy. When I was thirteen, I was very religious, but pretty rebellious. I stood up to the Muslim clerics in my mosque and challenged their understanding of the faith and was critical of their religion. For this, they kicked me out, which triggered in me a crisis of faith that lasted for three or four years until I could come to terms with religion in my own way. In societies that do not cultivate and maintain tolerance of different opinions, leadership in innovation can decline. This happened to Islam.

Innovation centers can also arise in other places, places that may borrow from the once flourishing cultures of innovation and start their own path. That is what happened in medieval Europe as the most innovative centuries of Islam came to an end. At the very moment the strengths that had brought forward Islam's golden age were declining, new conditions were emerging favorable to innovation in Europe. In contrast to the more fragmented polity of Europe, the Islamic empire had a strong central state that did not permit private merchants to flourish as they were starting to in Europe. Private ownership of property was circumscribed in Islam, but secure property relations are a key institution for innovation. Over time, the state consolidation of power actually increased in the Islamic world with the rise of a state and military elite class, further undercutting merchants and private actors. In contrast to Europe, Islamic law did not recognize the town as an independent political unit, and strong independent towns and cities ruled by merchants were a key part of the dynamism of entrepreneurship that Europe would exhibit.[36]

A new model of learning, thought, and innovation was on the horizon in the West. From a part of the world that had barely subsisted on the fringes of the wealthy and successful civilizations of Islam, India, and China, cut off from the lucrative Indian Ocean trade, out of touch with both the advances in science and technology coming from those civilizations as well as even the older learning of Hellenistic Greece, Europe would emerge as the new center of innovation in the world. At first it would start back in the Mediterranean, in the old Roman-Greek geography of Italy and Greece, the places that had contact with the wider Middle Eastern-Asian network. But it would spread to western and northern areas, places that had been long regarded as the home of barbarian tribes. Ironically, an important stimulus to the rise of Europe was the contact it had with Islam.

CHAPTER 3:
The European Miracle

Growing up in Egypt, I dreamed of going to Europe. During the 1970s, Egyptian college students often spent their summers working there. I was studying accounting and business at Cairo University when I met a student who had just returned from working in Europe and he really felt the experience had broadened his horizons. So I told my father that I also wanted to work in Europe during my summer break, and he suggested that I contact my uncle who worked at the United Nations in Vienna and stay with him. But I wanted to make it *on my own*. Since I was nineteen going on twenty, I felt pretty independent and had always found a way to make my own money. In Egypt I worked in a pasta factory and even sold sugar on the black market during the war with Israel. My mother fought with me constantly over this, but there was something about taking risk that was in my blood, unlike my two brothers.

I took the train to Vienna, but fell asleep on the way and ended up in a town I had never heard of called Graz. The second largest city in Austria, it has a long tradition as a seat of learning, with six universities and some 60,000 students. One of the oldest, Karl-Franzens University, was once home to Joseph Schumpeter, the father of innovation economics. When I got off the train I met a fellow Egyptian selling flowers. He invited me to stay with him and help him sell. I didn't know a word of German then, but man, could I sell! During the summer I also hitchhiked around Europe, took trains, though I had little money. Still, I loved traveling and getting to know people so was willing to live the homeless life for a time.

Being a solo traveler teaches you to observe, and also to make your own decisions on the spot. For instance, one evening I ended up in Belgium looking for a place to stay. I had slept on beaches, the railway station, I even tried to camp out on a warship in Venice. In Brussels I decided to try a small mosque I found. Knocking on the door and speaking in French I said, "I am coming to God's house." Even though I had some issues with the clerics in Egypt, there was still the kernel of faith lying dormant within me. "What do you want?" the very cross imam demanded. "I would like to pray and sleep in the mosque tonight," I answered. "This is not a hotel!" he shouted, sending me away in the pouring rain, soaked to my skin. I left angry as hell. Suddenly a red Russian Lada pulled up next to me, and the driver offered me a ride. "I am heading to the train station," I told him, and hopped in the back. The two men in the front were drug dealers, it turned out, and the two women in the back were prostitutes. They took me to a bar where the women plied their trade, fed me, and gave me a place to sleep for the night. It was a kindness I never forgot. How ironic, I thought, God turns you away and the devil takes you in! Never again would I forejudge people. In the Middle East we were taught not to judge people on how they looked or dress, but after this incident I really came to see that all people are the same, though when confronted with problems everyone has a different reaction and finds their own solution. That is one reason we are all potential innovators.

I loved my new life in Austria and didn't want to go back to Egypt. After experiencing the extraordinary freedom of European society, I loathed the idea of returning to Cairo University, which completely stifled any independent thinking or expression whatsoever. But my parents demanded that I return home to finish my degree. Although I acquiesced and did finish my studies in Egypt, I never really attended classes. I just sat for the exams. I graduated in 1983, did the mandatory year and three months in the military while working eighteen hours a day in a four-star international hotel restaurant as a receptionist and guest relations specialist. That also helped me to hone my skills of observing and understanding people from other cultures. There is no better place for learning about people than the hospitality trade. Then, at long last, I returned to Austria to work and get my Master's degree in business—this time, with my parents' blessing. Back on my own in Graz, I attended classes and sharpened my skills in English, German, French, and Spanish while working as a waiter in different cafes and jazz clubs that were frequented by the most educated students. I learned a lot working in those trendy cafes and smoky, boisterous clubs. Going to Austria turned out to be one of the most important, transformative decisions of my life. It would put an indelible stamp on the development of my personality, teach me about the power of observing and understanding people from other cultures, fuel my desire to travel the world, and—perhaps most importantly—help me learn to think independently and keep an open mind. Europe was for me an education.

Education in Europe also plays a key role in the continent's top ratings in today's global innovation indices. Four European universities now rank in the top ten of 1,000 institutions worldwide, part of this region's long and powerful tradition of supporting independent thinking that stretches back to around 1100 C.E. when universities opened their doors in Bologna, Paris, Pisa, and Oxford. Back then, students from all over Europe traveled along perilous routes far from home to attend these new institutions, seeking out the best teachers.[1] Like those students in the Middle Ages, I flourished in the European style of education that encouraged freedom of thought—a critical ingredient in the formula for innovation.

According to the Global Innovation Index of 2018, European nations are among the most innovative in the world. With Switzerland ranking first, followed by the Netherlands, Sweden, and the United Kingdom, seven of the top ten are in the European Union (EU). By far, Europe also has the highest HDI (Human Development Index) rating in the world based on the annual United Nations survey that grades nations by such factors as life expectancy, gross national income per capita, and years of education. The region's strong educational systems, great diversity, and collaborative, cross-border initiatives also contribute to its formula for innovation, giving birth to such institutions as CERN (the European Organization for Nuclear Research) in 1954, one of the most respected scientific research centers in the world. But Europe is not without its challenges. A brain drain has plagued the EU, with many of its top scientists fleeing to Silicon Valley especially after the Great Recession due to lack of entrepreneurial opportunities in their native countries. One recent study even claims that some 50,000 French nationals have immigrated to Silicon Valley. Critics have labelled Europeans as followers rather than leaders in entrepreneurship, its executives as decidedly risk-averse, and claim that start-ups are hobbled by inadequate sources of venture capital. For all its current problems, though, Europe has a strong history of achievement in innovation that dates back to the Middle Ages, followed by the Renaissance, and the Scientific Revolution that laid the very foundations for modern science and the Industrial Revolution that forever changed economic and material life.[2] To understand how Europe's innovation culture developed, let's explore the historical precedents that opened the door to breakthroughs in science, technology, law, government, commerce, and finance—in fact, nearly every aspect of society.

The Institutions of Innovation

As we saw in the last chapter, the Muslim world was rising to great heights during its Golden Age while Europe was fast asleep. But when Islam was making its greatest scientific discoveries, its social order started to decline just as slumbering Europe was starting to awaken. Under siege for hundreds of years by Germanic tribes, Huns, Magyars, Muslims, and Norsemen, Europe had lapsed into an age of darkness beginning with the fall of Rome. Only clerics knew how to read, and peasants toiled in the fields from dawn until dark to try to keep their families from starving to death. But key advances in agricultural technology combined with new, favorable weather patterns began to generate an abundance of food and a steady uptick in population. It has been estimated that European population nearly doubled from approximately 38.5 million to 73.5 million between 1000 and 1340 C.E. This agrarian dynamic also freed people to engage in new commercial activities. Urbanization was well under way and towns blossomed once again.

Money flowed into the hands of Europeans for the first time in centuries, and some amassed great wealth.

In addition to increases in population and agricultural productivity, a technological revolution was underway by the eleventh century triggered by brand new sources of power, such as the water mill and the windmill imported from the Middle East. There were other critical factors at work launching Europe's rebirth too. These included the development of institutions that empowered individuals to speculate and act freely, like the universities, guilds, banks, and city-states. Europe also drew on the inheritance of the foundational works of the ancient Greeks and the scientific and mathematical works of Arabic-Islamic authors. And in Europe a new, powerful class of merchants made advances in finance, forged international trading networks, and built a market-based, pre-capitalistic economy. Let's look first at the rise of the universities in Europe to see how they helped empower free thinking across society.

One of the critical factors promoting innovation is a society's institutions. Organizations, laws, governmental structures and regulations, civil and voluntary bodies, and commonly accepted rules and practices have the potential to either promote or stifle innovation. In this case, the particular institutional form of the European university played a positive role in shifting the region towards an innovative new economy. Here Europe diverged from other cultures. The colleges of China, for example, mainly prepared students to take the harsh examination that formed the path to careers in the massive state bureaucracy. The madrassas of the Muslim world were primarily religious institutions. Neither of these societies institutionalized instruction on the natural sciences which formed the core of the medieval European university curriculum, together with moral philosophy, metaphysics, and the liberal arts of grammar, astronomy, music, geometry, rhetoric, and logic.[3]

A new form of critical, rational, independent thinking arose in medieval European universities that would transform the very fabric of the region's governmental, educational, and economic institutions and help pave the way for the Scientific Revolution and the rise and development of modern science itself. This remarkable new creative spirit midwifed both an institutional and intellectual transformation, giving birth to very modern and unprecedented ideas about the nature of the earth and the universe, theology, law, and even man himself. It emerged from the study and debate of Latin translations of ancient Greek writings and key Arabic works on mathematics, medicine, optics, and astronomy, as well as a new interpretation of ancient Roman law. Chinese inventions and technologies introduced through the Islamic world also played a pivotal role in the transformation of Europe from a very stagnant backwater to a roaring tidal wave of knowledge and innovation that would encompass the globe starting in the fifteenth century. So, how did this "European miracle," as some scholars have dubbed this revolution, come to be?

During this period, universities gained extraordinary new powers to organize internally, set the curriculum and standards, and to act as a single unit rather than a collection of individuals. In contrast to other societies at this time, European universities were free from direct state intervention.[4] It was their very detachment that enabled them to serve as incubators of science and new knowledge. These educational institutions achieved their independence because a legal revolution was sweeping through Europe, one that paralleled and fueled the rise of the new university system. It was based on simplifying, modifying, and transforming ancient Roman law. This legal revolution was pivotal and fundamental to the transformation of European society as a whole, one that led to the reconstruction of all manner of legal issues and entities, including feudal and manorial law, the laws governing cities and towns, commercial regulations, and laws affecting individuals. There was no parallel development to this legal revolution in China, India, or Islam at this time, so in this case, as with the rise of autonomous universities, cross-cultural forces were not fundamental to these distinctly European innovations. Europe had pioneered important new features to the innovation model.

It was also not just a revolutionary legal system and the new style of university that distinguished the West's institutional structures from elsewhere. Europe created a whole series of these sorts of self-governing corporate entities. Monasteries, for examples, were separate from the church proper. They carried on a highly disciplined style of life and inculcated a strong belief in the virtues of work and self-sufficiency that made them not only places of the spirit, but also centers of innovation. Monasteries developed and improved waterwheels for milling grain and drained swamps to reclaim land for agriculture.[5] Different orders specialized in different technologies. The Cistercians built and maintained the dykes in the Low Countries and used water-powered machines at their abbeys. They had running water, which at the time was very uncommon even in European cities. The Carthusians dug deep wells for water in France (the first at Artois, from which we get the name artesian well).[6]

Likewise, cities were self-governing units. Separate from the estates of the king or prince, incorporated cities could rule themselves independently, regulate markets, and determine who could live and work inside their walls. Such free cities played innovative roles as incubators of new networks of trade and commerce across Europe, from Italy to the Baltic. In a similar manner, mercantile and craft guilds were formed beginning in the tenth century, and they too enjoyed a private, civil status as little monopolies, and served as a major source of learning, knowledge, and the transmission of critical skills among artisans and craftspeople.

The Birth of Secularism

These institutional structures served Europe in another way. They became the conduits through which Europeans gained access to the knowledge of the ancient and Muslim worlds, the sort of knowledge they had lost for hundreds of years during the so-called Dark Ages. Islamic learning made its way into Europe through the great translation movement of the twelfth and thirteenth centuries coming by way of Andalusian Spain (the one part of the West under Muslim control), as well as Sicily and northern Italy. Within a century, Latin translations of the Aristotelian corpus and major Arabic works became available in the West. Ibn al-Haytham's work on optics, the algebra of al-Khwariz, the medical writings of Galen and Hippocrates, Ibn Sina's medical canon, Euclid's *Elements*, and Ptolemy's *Almagest* all became standard university texts that would dominate European scientific thought for the next four centuries.

The great synthesizer of thought in the European Middle Ages, Thomas Aquinas profoundly influenced generations of university-trained scholars through his writings proposing that there was no contradiction between the study of the natural world and religion, or between what today we might call science and faith. Earlier Christian church fathers like St. Augustine had placed knowledge of the natural world on a distinctly lower plane than religion. With Aquinas, the pursuit of knowledge of the world, both human and natural, no longer contradicted religion. As the West embraced this new scientific worldview that treated the universe as a rationally ordered system, a "world machine," it certainly posed a threat to Christian teachings. But, unlike the case of Islam during its Golden Age, the Europeans made this unique secular, scientific outlook fundamental to the official and public discourse of higher education.[7] Although the church had supreme authority in religious matters, it now had thinkers who were also open to secular knowledge and encouraged investigations that revealed the unity of religion and nature.[8]

European philosophers, led by St. Anselm and Peter Abelard and culminating in the work of Aquinas, developed the dialectal method of reasoning to carry out this new work. And the universities provided the fertile ground as incubators of the rational dialectical tradition. Through dialectics, thinkers used reason and bounced hypotheses off each other to arrive at the truth. Dialectics greatly increased the scope of reason, and could be applied to religious texts, the law, or to the study and analysis of nature.[9] The capacity of humans to discern cause and effect relationships and the search for underlying laws of truth as opposed to God's mysteries opened the doors to later generations of scientists, as we will see. Although these new principles of thought were set in motion before the Scientific Revolution of the sixteenth century, they formed the precursors of modern science with their emphasis on reason, regularity, laws, and an investigatory approach to the world.[10]

But it was not only the lofty debates of university scholars that helped transform Europe into an innovative society. The case of the Franciscan monk Roger Bacon is illustrative of the complexity of the age, where various forces and institutions were giving rise to different forms of thinking and empirical experimentation. Following his training at Oxford University, Bacon taught there and then at the University of Paris. He collaborated with another Oxford scholar, Robert Grosseteste, who wrote an important work on optics called *De iride* (On the Rainbow). They undoubtedly read the Latin translation of Ibn al-Haytham's seminal eleventh-century work on optics (*Kitab al-manazir*, which also profoundly influenced Kepler around 1600) and Ptolemy's *Optics*. Back in Oxford Bacon set up a laboratory to conduct empirical studies that demonstrated how ocular refraction defects of the eye could be corrected with lenses. The first to record comments on the use of lenses for practical purposes, Bacon published his findings in his *Opus Maius* (an encyclopedia of science c. 1268). His work gave rise to a new industry in Europe, eyeglasses. Sometime around the end of the thirteenth century, a Florentine priest is believed to have invented the first spectacles. By 1301 Venetian guilds had regulations governing the sale of eyeglasses. This breakthrough led to the Italian manufacture of thousands of pairs of glasses shipped across the world by the early 1400s.

Bacon himself was not always shown the appreciation due a scientist and inventor. As an avid practitioner of alchemy and collector of books on magic, he received the nickname Doctor Mirabilis. Religious authorities in Europe were not amused, however. Bacon was rejected by his own order, the Franciscans, and then imprisoned for his radical beliefs. In this case, we can see the influence of the universities in paving the way to innovative thinking, the importance of ancient Greek and Arabic-Islamic science which set a precedent for his breakthroughs in optics, the building of networks for collaboration, the tension between the church and practitioners of suspicious forms of inquiry, the creation and spread of new knowledge through handwritten texts leading to the practical invention of eyeglasses by another man of the cloth, and the powerful role of the rising guilds in making this new invention a marketplace success by regulating Italy's sale of these new products internationally. Europe's "Dark Ages" were not completely over when it came to secular learning, but intellectual values and university practices were clearly changing in ways that were making Europe an increasingly vital place of knowledge and learning.[11]

Borrowing and Inventing New Technology

As Europe was rejoining the wider world, it gained access not only to abstract knowledge through the universities and books copied by hand, but also to specific practical technologies and inventions through very powerful cross-cultural currents. In particular, it absorbed what had been invented in China, as well as in India and the Middle East. The most prolific historian of Chinese science, Joseph Needham has claimed that "the river of Chinese science flowed into the sea of modern science" through the transmission to Europe of such extraordinary developments as the magnetic compass, papermaking (and possibly printing), gunpowder, mechanical clockwork, iron-casting, stirrups, and the efficient horse-harness. While artisans whose names have been forgotten were often the architects of the practical knowledge that led to such ingenuity, they were often transmitted by Islamic and European merchants doing business together along the Silk Road. While the European mind was being shaped by philosophers and theologians, ordinary farmers, sailors, artisans, and merchants became the "mindful hands" of innovation. In the fields, on the docks and boatyards, Europeans were borrowing significantly from other cultures and adapting these techniques, devices, and knowledge to suit their own needs and conditions.[12]

This new knowledge spread through the guilds as well as by handwritten treatises in the vernacular that were circulating throughout Europe before the arrival of a watershed invention in the history of innovation: The printing press. The printing press was born from the confluence of many advances, some borrowed from other cultures but then transmuted in Europe. From 800 to 1500 C.E., the people of the Muslim world had spread their knowledge of papermaking throughout a large portion of Eurasia and North Africa. "Had they not mediated between the cultures of the Far East and the Far West," argues historian Jonathan Bloom, "Europeans would probably have remained ignorant of paper…until the first European mariners reached Far Eastern ports in the sixteenth century." Muslims established papermaking factories in southern Europe (Spain and Italy) during the eleventh century, and by 1500 or so much of Europe was producing a paper that was lighter and significantly cheaper—although less durable—than parchment. The

Italians in particular were enormously successful in this industry due to technological improvements as well as aggressive marketing tactics. They controlled waterpower more efficiently to power stampers, utilized brass wire to form molds, and watermarked their paper to ensure its quality to buyers.

Finally, borrowing practices, devices, and ideas from multiple cultures, a silversmith named Johann Gutenberg built the first practical printing press using movable type. With his training in metals, he understood the importance of replacing soft woodblocks (initially pioneered by the Chinese in the eleventh century) with more durable metal type to make his press more practical. Precisely how printing technology made its way to Europe is not clear. But one thing is certain: The print revolution that would unfold following Gutenberg's invention fundamentally transformed European society. As with most breakthroughs, his press did not change the world overnight. But by the fifteenth century, hundreds of entrepreneurs benefitting from a new degree of legal autonomy uniquely European launched printing enterprises. By 1500, with improvements and rapid diffusion of the technology, there were an estimated 15-20 million copies of books in print.[13] Books were being sold in markets, at fairs, and across the continent by book dealers. Going well beyond bibles to print and reprint and all sorts of secular writings and novel texts that would astound readers or attract sales by enticing people with things that had not been seen before, the book not only spread existing knowledge but also stimulated the development of new types of knowledge.[14]

Books were diffusing so fast that already some thinkers were concerned about how to separate good knowledge from rubbish, and worried about an information overload, oddly prescient of our own era.[15] At the same time, the availability of more writings of more diverse type and tastes encouraged the spread of literacy and the refinement of reading practice. Europe was *ready* for printing because its people profoundly embraced the new spirit of open, unfettered inquiry, in a society bursting with creative new ideas that needed to be expressed—and shared—in business and commerce, math, the arts, architecture, religion, literature, science, and medicine.

While Gutenberg is credited with the invention of the printing press and many innovations in the process (including an ink for metal printing and the special mold he used for casting), it was undoubtedly the cumulative product of collaboration between various craftsmen and scholars from different cultures over centuries. In addition, Gutenberg never got wealthy off of his press and died nearly a pauper. Embracing early modern capitalism, others made it commercially viable—a key component of the innovation process—and catapulted it into a thriving industry that made all forms of learning accessible to the general public for the first time. With the transference of learning from isolated, rural monasteries to the universities and other urban centers, the pursuit of new knowledge became accessible to the common man as never before. Together with the rise of the universities, the widespread availability of books in the vernacular (fueled by the Protestant Reformation) triggered a European revolution in literacy unlike anything the world had ever witnessed. In fact, China, India, and the Middle East "did not fully close the literacy gap with the West until the end of the twentieth century," argues Toby Huff, "and even then, the gap was not closed in most parts of the Muslim world." Europe launched the daily newspaper in the 1640s, whereas China introduced newspapers two centuries later.[16]

By the late Middle Ages, as the Islamic world had grown less open to innovation, Europeans were surging ahead in all kinds of creative endeavors that were transforming the very fabric of their society. Islam's paper industry withered, and printing was not adopted there until the eighteenth century. From the late Middle Ages to modern times, Europe firmly took the lead as its culture and military strength began to dominate the world. As we have seen, the separation of church and state, the revolution in literacy, new technologies and the growth of scientific inquiry, the rise of institutions like universities, and a revolution in the law and government were all crucial to this development. Powerful interdependent, intellectual, scientific, and socioeconomic forces were unleashed during this great awakening of the European mind that would firmly place this region on a path of ascendancy and dominance that would endure for centuries.[17]

Cross-Cultural Networks of Trade and Discovery

The movement of ideas and inventions into Europe and then across the different societies of Europe reflected the deep connections made between that continent and the outside world via trade networks. These lines of commerce linked it to long-standing trade networks in Asia, the Middle East, and North Africa by the eleventh century. Such contacts were vital to bringing new products, technologies, ideas, and practices home. The growth in commerce was fueled by an abundant food supply and population boom. As people became more secure in their food supply, they were more willing to make, trade, and buy all sorts of shiny new things.

Although Europe had never been completely isolated, the wealthiest Europeans were now able to travel, exposing them to new delights like silks, sugar, and spices. The Crusades were also bringing Europeans into contact with foreigners, which not only stimulated an appetite for exotic goods, but also cross-fertilized ideas and practices, opened doors of trade, and established new kingdoms and principalities in the wake of the Roman collapse. Likewise, with the Muslim expansion into North Africa and Spain, and then the later push of the Muslim empire into Macedonia, Hungary, and Austria, Europe was positioned as something of a crossroads of peoples and empires. It was also a diverse and fragmented place, compared to the empire of China where one dynasty succeeded another and a strong central bureaucracy reigned supreme. European fragmentation added a measure of creative potential spurring different regions to specialize and compete with each other. Divided rather than unitary rule offered some advantages that would promote innovation.[18]

Cross-cultural connections between Europe and the Middle and Far East had begun with the economic and commercial growth of southern Europe. Italy in particular benefitted from its proximity to the East and long-standing relationship with that part of the world reflecting its strong seafaring tradition dating back to the Romans, the Greeks, and before them, the Mycenaeans, the Cretans, and the Phoenicians. By the eleventh century, Italy had become the economically advanced part of Europe, remade by a mixture of peoples coming into the old Roman homeland. And it was never totally united under a single ruler due to ongoing competition between the Emperor and the Papacy. Continual incursions by Muslim forces fueled the flames of factionalism and cultural competition, as did significant activity and influence by the Byzantine Empire along the Adriatic. What most characterized medieval Italy was the emergence of strong republics—city-states—as relatively autonomous economic institutions. Along the coasts the seaports of Amalfi, Pisa, Genoa, and Venice began to dominate trade between Western Europe and the Byzantine and Muslim empires, competing fiercely with each other for this lucrative business. The empires in turn handled the trade between the Western world and the Far East—India and China, Southeast Asia.

Europeans had no direct access to the Far East, for the rise of Islam had cut them off from the Indian Ocean.[19] But Europe was finally able to tap into the highly profitable overland trade after the Mongols conquered China and reestablished the old Silk Road. Quite happy to trade with anyone, the Mongols protected commerce, reduced banditry, and limited the extraction of tribute, tolls, and taxes by individual states, all of which lowered the cost of trade and transport.[20] Western merchants were also welcome in Egypt and other parts of the Muslim world, where savvy traders persuaded them to pay top price and accept less than the top-quality goods due to their relatively weak bargaining position.

The Italian city-states positioned themselves as the suppliers to Europe of some of the world's most highly sought-after goods: Sugar, cotton, gemstones, honey, wax, dyestuffs, nuts, soap, and spices of all types, especially pepper from the Malabar Coast of India. Pepper commanded so high a price that it served as money in Genoa.[21] What could Europe provide in return? Europeans shipped wool, iron, tin (from the famous mines of Cornwall), wood and lumber, silver, fish, wheat, and furs. The trade was complex, with merchants on both sides stopping at one port then another, offloading some goods, taking on others, until the circuit was complete. While it was difficult for Europeans to maintain a positive balance of trade against the wealth and diversity of goods produced in the Far East, they had access to one "commodity" that had special value to their counterparties in Egypt: They became the primary suppliers of slaves between the Christian and Muslim worlds.[22]

Whether commodities arrived from the East by land or sea, Europeans did not control the ports and markets. The trade relations that Genoa, Venice, and other Italian city-states established with the rulers of Egypt, Baghdad, and Constantinople were therefore vital for commercial access. Over the next several centuries, Italian merchants would put considerable effort into maintaining these trade networks through a complex brew of diplomacy, military intervention, and business acumen. They also competed with and fought each other, especially arch rivals Genoa and Venice. From this rivalry and the imperative to trade with people of different cultures, religions, and values, critical commercial and financial innovations began to emerge from medieval Italy, many of which have endured until modern times.

Because the Italians had not adopted the manorial-feudal system of agriculture common in the rest of Europe, conditions in the Italian cities were far less restricted by tradition and the conservative hierarchy of agrarian society. As self-governing entities, they allowed wide participation in political and economic life by a large segment of their people. Not democracies in the modern sense, they still were more open to the ambitious and non-aristocratic than were other parts of the world. Those who made enough money could participate in the governing structure of the cities and even, more rarely, get a chance to enter the rarefied inner circle of elite leadership.[23] Like Amazon and Apple today, which both set global records by recently reaching a trillion dollars in market capitalization, Italian merchants formed a new power elite, and ruthless families like the Medicis of Florence and the Sforzas of Milan took the place of the feudal landlords and their military aristocracy. Driven by finance, trade, and commerce, Italian cities put business first and developed a political apparatus to support private enterprise, including all trades and occupations that related to commerce and shipping.[24]

Where the Italians were most innovative was in business organization and finance, especially the latter. Creative and accessible financing can make life easier and more predictable for the average person—credit cards to promote consumption, mortgages to buy big ticket items like houses, innovative new payment systems such as PayPal and Venmo to make transactions smoother, instantaneous, and more reliable. Today blockchain technology may be upending traditional financial practices in commodity trading, banking, and other financial sectors. Financial innovations and good financial systems are a crucial but often underappreciated part of the innovation process.

In medieval Italy, entrepreneurs greatly benefitted from brand new ways to access venture capital to launch their enterprises. They devised a number of innovative financial practices that placed them squarely at the forefront of the European-Middle Eastern trade and also allowed them to cultivate the booming internal market in Europe. For example, to conduct business over long periods of time and long distances, they came up with the *commenda*, a sort of joint-stock company where people could invest in maritime trade without actually having to undertake voyages themselves. Reminiscent of similar devices found earlier in the Muslim empire, it allowed merchants to mobilize capital from multiple sources. Investors could put their money into different commercial ventures, thus diversifying and reducing risk. Long-distance trade was perhaps the riskiest business around, though also potentially the most profitable. Individuals and groups could pool funds to buy into *commenda*—even women, who under Roman law could make contracts in their own names.[25] The *commenda* also formed just one variant of a host of new business practices Italian traders deployed for these purposes. They also had *compagni* (companies or extended partnerships) as well as traditional family partnerships like those of the Muslim world.[26]

One reason the Italians could sustain these sorts of business relationships was because they had invented an improved system of accounting—double entry bookkeeping. Single entry accounts had been used in trade in many parts of the world for centuries, even longer. But the double entry system allowed the manager to see profit and loss immediately, which proved to be an advantage when trade voyages lingered over long periods of time and involved multiple exchanges. More importantly, though, it provided a means of control, a way of detecting mistakes or fraud—something especially useful in the growth of complex partnerships and long-term company structures. Italian port cities also supported whole new classes of professionals, such as notaries, who provided the legal services to write and officially sanction contracts.[27]

Credit has always been an important lubricant of trade and the Italian innovations here spurred the growth of the European market-based economy. Through letters of credit, a traveling merchant could draw on the accounts of bankers and merchants in the various port cities he would be visiting, the letter writer providing assurances that the loan would be repaid. Versions of letters of credit were used in many parts of the world before Italians adopted them. But the Italian traders then took it a step further and developed the bill of exchange. The bill of exchange was even more ambitious because it allowed a trader to borrow money in one currency and repay it in another without carrying various currencies with him as he travelled. Just as important, bills of exchange provided a means to hide interest charges in the rates of exchange between the different currencies, thus avoiding Christian restrictions on interest and usury.[28]

European merchants, money changers, and other financial actors also turned into bankers, providing another source of loans and credit. New banking practices emerged first in Venice and Florence and soon spread to other Italian cities, and then later to cities of northern Europe. With the quickening pace of commerce, more people had greater need to store their money safely, preferably with someone who could be trusted to return the funds when needed. One group in particular became the entrepreneurs of banking. This was the money changers, that is, specialists who held various coin and currencies and stood ready to convert one into another on the spot. Money changers were found all over the ancient world and are mentioned, rather negatively, in the Bible when Jesus drove them from the temple. But regardless, in every market center, town square, and yes, temple, church or wherever people gathered to do business, money changers set up their tables, or *bancos* in Italian. Soon they were being asked to take and hold the funds of others. Over time, they accumulated significant amounts of money, and since all the depositors did not necessarily want their funds returned at the same time, it was possible to loan out the excess reserves. A major financial innovation, fractional reserve banking was born out of the financial arrangements of medieval Italian trade.[29]

Italian merchants and financiers were true innovators, and their practices spread widely across Europe. In the Middle Ages even the crusading Knights Templars became international bankers. But Europeans were able to introduce these new financial practices and institutions because they could improve upon of what they had learned from their extensive contacts with other cultures in other parts of the world. Just as European agricultural improvements built off of technologies from China, so, too, did financial innovators draw on and modify existing practices from other cultures. Risk, finance, credit, means of exchange, all sorts of financial mechanisms and devises and methods were prevalent in the Muslim world, India, and China, where many of the Italian-European practices originated.[30] Thus, unlike the universities and new legal system, European innovation in business and finance was not so much a radical departure as a series of adaptations and improvements upon what had been learned from other people, other cultures. The strong links Italians had formed with Byzantium, the Mongols, Arabs, Egyptians, Persians, and others gave them access to a wealth of commercial ideas and practices. This cross-cultural contact made the Italians the key business innovators of medieval Europe and the inventors of early modern capitalism.[31]

In addition to these critical financial developments, Italian merchants also made innovations in long-distance trade that allowed them to extend their contacts further around the known world. Both Genoa and Venice established merchant colonies (*fondaco*) in the Byzantine capitol of Constantinople, where they managed much of the trade in and out of that empire. Once the Mongols reopened the Silk Road, Italian adventurers made their way across central Asia and set up operations in both mainland China and the island of Formosa (today Taiwan), in some cases ousting or besting their long-established Muslim competitors. The most famous of these Italians, of course, was Marco Polo and his father. But papal ambassadors, friars, and envoys of European kings also travelled the road to China, and Polo's book was translated into multiple languages. Today, the Chinese are pioneering a monumental new Silk Road through the Belt and Road initiative to expand their trading network around the world over land and sea. I do not know if the Chinese are drawing on their own successful history with the Silk

Road for this project, but it certainly fits with patterns we have seen, where connections and contacts outside of one's own culture are taken to be vital for innovation and entrepreneurship.[32] As a commodities trader, I can tell you that the market is always interested in reducing the charges for transactions and improving the efficiency of exchange.

Italian advances in trade and finance also became available for others within Europe to emulate. If borrowers and adapters of financial practices and techniques from one part of the world, Italian merchants were the innovators for other Europeans, bringing to them practices they had not known before. This is a good example of the dual sides of innovation. It can involve incremental changes to existing practices and also radical breakthroughs. The difference has to do with who is doing the innovation. When something is new to a person, group, or culture, it can be a radical transformation in that context, even though it may well have already existed and been familiar to other people in a different place. Just like today, much of innovation involves such cross-cultural connections that bring new practices and inventions to different cultures and societies.

Take, for example, the impact of the spinning wheel on Europe. Although the precise origin of the spinning wheel is unknown, it may well have been borrowed from technologies from India where cotton was indigenous. Some scholars believe the spinning wheel was invented in India sometime between 500 to 1000 C.E. Others argue that it probably originated in China, where it was described in literary sources from the Han Dynasty and pictured as early as 1210 C.E. Towards the end of the thirteenth century, spinning wheels and other types of textile machines appeared suddenly in such Italian cities as Lucca. Perhaps some Italian merchant carried the designs home from China or India in his saddle-bags. The introduction of the spinning wheel and the fulling mill into Europe triggered a dramatic increase in cloth production without a parallel rise in the labor force involved in the process, an innovation made possible because of the connections Europe had with the rest of the world.[33]

The rise in cloth production had a stimulating effect on trade across Europe as well. Europeans sold their cloth through creative and colorful new "Champagne Fairs" outside of Paris. These meeting points of exchange were made possible by the actions of governmental authorities, who were very interested in having such commerce take place on their land. Local authorities protected buyers and sellers against fraud by providing guards, ensured the integrity of weights, measures, and currency, and set up notaries to handle contracts and courts to settle the inevitable rowdy disputes.[34] The Fairs were eBay's of their times. The market is always interested in reducing the charges for transactions and improving the efficiency of exchange. This happens through advances that either increase speed or cut down costs, and sometimes eliminate the middleman all together. Merchants and traders who want to stay in business and survive this process have to innovate and adapt by changing their business practices to suit the needs of their market. That is exactly what the Italian merchants did in the European cloth market. Soon the Champagne Fairs were things of the past, as Italian merchant companies moved directly to the main economic centers of northern Europe, such as Paris, London, and Bruges. Agents and correspondents of Italian trading firms went to these cities to carry on business, instead of meeting periodically at the fairs.[35] The center of the wool trade was Bruges, the key port of northern Europe before its harbor silted and turned it into a jewel box tourist town that it is today.[36] As they had in the Middle and Far East, Italian merchants set up communities and enclaves there and used their command of sophisticated banking and financial instruments to dominate the trade. In many cases, they became part of and intermarried with the local population, further cementing their ties in trade, much as the Jews had done in the Muslim world during the Golden Age of Islam. Back in the home cities, investors and partners carried on the other end of the business. With their mastery of bills of exchange, banking and credit, promissory notes, long-term joint-stock companies and partnerships, and their critical connections throughout the Mediterranean and the East, Italians were simply too well-positioned to be outcompeted by local merchants. They provided the links that connected the two Europes, North and South, from Venice to Vienna, from Cologne to Bruges.[37]

Following the Italian model, other cities also began to organize into effective ports of trade to gain access to some of this lucrative trade. Those along the north Atlantic employed many of these same financial and commercial innovations, and enjoyed a level of autonomy and independence from the feudal world that made them highly competitive. These Hanse cities (sometimes called the Hanseatic League) were able to displace the traditional traders in this part of Europe, the Scandinavians.[38] In Northern Europe another innovation emerged: Stock markets, providing a more formal and efficient way of lending and borrowing funds. Multiple cities developed effective stock markets after the seventeenth century—Antwerp, Amsterdam, London. The first of these, the Antwerp Bourse, attracted bankers and financiers from all over Europe, making the city for a time the center of the European international economy as the Italian cities lost their competitive edge and began to slip into decline.[39]

The Black Death

Europeans had much to be thankful for by 1300: Good weather, good harvests, good fortune, and good business were all lifting them out of darkness and poverty. But the pathway to growth, innovation, and prosperity is often fraught with setbacks, and Europe was soon struck with a series of hammer blows. The first was self-inflicted, though unintended. Famine struck Europe about 1300. After several centuries of good weather and intensive cultivation of new land, the region's population had grown significantly, fueling trade and production. But once the population pushed past the carrying capacity of the land, all it took was one bad harvest and millions faced starvation. Between 1315 and 1322 several years of bad weather led to multiple crop failures, and after 1350, colder weather patterns and too much rain in the north and droughts in the south had dire consequences.[40] An underfed population was ripe for the effects of the new epidemics sweeping along trade routes.[41]

Now Europe began to feel the harsh, punishing side of nature. It came in the form of bubonic plague. Here was another case where the very thing that had helped lift Europe out of its stagnation turned against it, in this case trade. The Silk Road and the China trade that had connected Europe to the East became the conduits for devastating diseases. On the ships and caravans that flowed between West and East were rats, and on the fur of rats, fleas, and in the blood of fleas, bacilli that caused bubonic plague. The plague, or Black

Death as it was more commonly known, devastated Europe between 1347 and 1351, killing at least 30 percent of the population and in some cases as much as 60 percent. The Black Death also hit China, India, the Middle East, the whole Euro-Asian land mass, plus parts of North and East Africa. In the most concentrated cities of Italy, mortality rates are believed to have reached 80 percent. To combat the spread of this lethal contagion, Venetians implemented quarantine on ships arriving at its ports from infected areas. The word "quarantine" derives from the Italian words *quaranta giorni*, meaning 40 days. Although this practice had been employed for centuries in China, Byzantium, and Europe, the Venetians were the first in the world to institutionalize this important public health measure that would protect populations until the nineteenth century when the germ theory of disease revolutionized public health practices.[42]

The waves of plague soundly knocked back European population levels, and with them, trade, commerce, and production. It took some two centuries for the region to recover. Diseases like the plague and starvation also had political repercussions, leading to peasant revolts that erupted across Europe. And as the poor and working classes challenged the authority of the master-landlord class, serfdom declined significantly by the fourteenth century, changing the structure of European society forever.[43]

While Europe was convalescing from nature's assaults it was hit yet again, this time by political and military turns of events. The Muslim world, itself in significant disarray and decline from its golden age, was invaded and taken over by Turkic people from Central Asia. They were Muslims too and they soon controlled the centers and capitals of Islamic civilization and established themselves as the new caliphs. These were the Ottomans, and by 1450 they had charge of a vast empire that stretched from India and Pakistan to Spain. They pressed into the Mediterranean, challenging the Italian city-states in a series of contests that did not finally end until the 1700s.[44] When Ottoman troops captured Constantinople in 1453, overwhelming the Christian Byzantine Empire, they shut off European access to the Silk Road.[45]

History can be fickle, though. Just as Europe suffered unexpected reversals from diseases coursing through the routes of trade, decimating hard-won population growth, adversity in the loss of trade led to unexpected innovations that proved highly favorable in the long run. So, if one danger a society faces in remaining innovative is an overabundance of easily available natural bounty—the so-called resource curse that has made parts of the Middle East too easily dependent on oil revenues—hard times can spur creative action. The resourceful response of Europe came from its non-natural resources: Its human capital and trade connections built up over the previous centuries. These proved invaluable in setting the region on a path of innovation, discovery, and, finally, large-scale economic revolution that produced the second great macro invention in human history—industrialization. It all started with winds, currents, and sailing ships.

Mastering the Seas

Gradually, over the years, Portuguese sailors mastered the winds and currents of the Atlantic. Although we do not know exactly how these advances occurred, they were spurred by skilled boat builders who had devised new ship designs and sail systems. During the preceding centuries, European boat builders had developed the round ships—the galleys of Venice and the cogs used in the North. These square-rigged ships with stern rudders could hold more cargo and travel longer distances than traditional galleys. They also sat high enough out of the water and were large enough to carry armaments and mount cannons, adding military-inspired advances such as castles for defensive and offensive purposes.[46] Adapting the triangular lateen sails initially pioneered by the Chinese by the first century, they gained greater maneuverability and the ability to tack against the wind, enabling them to move up and down the Atlantic using prevailing wind patterns. Europeans improved Asian technology, adding better rigging and heavier ropes that allowed the sails to be manipulated even on larger ships.[47] Portuguese sailors also adapted new methods of navigation, particularly out of sight of land. The Chinese had invented the magnetic compass and Islamic astronomers had improved the astrolabe and related devices for finding latitude by learning the angle of the sun and stars. With these technologies plus better charts and maps and regular timetables, Europeans discovered how to sail the ocean year-round, regardless of wind, cloud, or fog.[48]

Iberians were well positioned to take advantage of the streams of knowledge and technique flowing from the East, as they had been part of the Islamic empire until 1492 when the last Muslims were ousted from Spain. Just before they were expelled, the sailor Vasco da Gama pulled together these improvements in ships and sailing, knowledge of the seas and stars and experience in the open waters of the Atlantic to pioneer a new route around the horn of Africa and into the Indian Ocean. Cut off from its traditional trade routes to the Far East, Europe had devised a new way in, and the Portuguese began to establish trading outposts and factories (meaning a place where factors of merchants hung out while they bought and sold wares) along the pepper coast of India and further afield toward the spice islands of Indonesia.

Pepper, nutmeg, and other Eastern spices were highly desired, valuable commodities that took up little space and added little weight to ships, making them relatively inexpensive to transport long distances. They were products of great desire, almost like drugs, that brought the flavors of the orient to the bland diets of Europeans. For Christians, they may have even brought a taste of paradise, or what they imagined paradise was like, so redolent these spices were of biblical lands.[49] Indeed, some theologians even suggested that paradise was located to the East.

These sorts of powerful, evocative emotional appeals can provide powerful motivation for innovation. For merchants it made the risky and costly trip around Africa and into the hostile waters of the Indian Ocean well worth the effort. For princes and kings, the Eastern trade could be taxed easily and effectively—people would still buy the produce even with a tax penalty. Controlling this trade provided both economic and political benefits. Taxes could be used to support navies against rivals and increase the leverage one's own merchants had in the trade. Not surprising, given the high profits of this lucrative Eastern trade, other European nations soon followed the Portuguese—the Spanish, the Dutch, the English. After da Gama, Europeans engaged in a fierce competition that greatly expanded their role and presence in the Far East. Being open to ideas and practices from foreign cultures, competition, and rivalry, and seeking creative solutions to problems can produce startling innovative outcomes. And sometimes the consequences of those innovations are unpredictable. They may yield positive consequences that the innovators themselves never dreamed of. That is exactly what happened to risk-taking Europeans during this Age of Discovery.

The same breakthroughs that propelled the Iberians down the coast of Africa and into the Indian Ocean also sent them across the Atlantic to an undiscovered realm: The New World, the Americas. Here, too, technologies that had circulated around the Mediterranean and Eastern trading worlds came together in a new invention—the carrack. It was a full-rigged ship deploying the inventions of the previous generation—fore and aft sails, stern post rudder, the ability to tack and maneuver, capable of carrying cargo in bulk as well as artillery, and ready to set sail wherever Europeans wanted to go.[50] When a mariner from Italy who was well versed in the latest sailing technologies and knowledge, much of it gleaned from the Middle East, approached the King of Spain with an idea of stealing a march on the Portuguese in the Eastern trade by sailing west, it triggered a global revolution. Columbus's voyage would have repercussions that reshaped the world—especially Europe's place in it.

The Ghost Acres

Columbus's voyages revealed the exotic lands of the Americas to Europe and the rest of the world for the first time since pre-historic people crossed the land bridge over the Bering Straits at least 13,000 years earlier. The voyages launched a global system whereby people, goods, capital, technologies, ideas, practices, in short, all of human culture could move back and forth across the entire world. One of the first things that moved, unfortunately, was disease. With a much larger population and landmass, and a highly evolved trading network, Eurasians had been exposed to many more germs than their New World counterparts. The result, as with the Great Plague of the fourteenth century, was a series of devastating epidemics that wiped out a huge portion of the native populations of the Americas. From known killers such as smallpox, typhus, and cholera, to seemingly mild childhood diseases such as measles, the peoples of the Americas lacked immunity. As a result, populations in North, Central, and South America declined by as much as 90 percent. One of the most deadly weapons in human history, disease allowed Europeans to conquer or dominate the New World civilizations and societies and begin to repopulate them with their own people.

These tragic outcomes had important ramifications for European economic life. Following the exchange of germs, all sorts of other plant and animal life moved across the Atlantic, what historian Alfred Crosby has aptly called the Columbian Exchange. New food crops, notably maize, manioc, potatoes, and tomatoes, made their way to Europe, Africa, and Asia, greatly enhancing the food potential of those regions. Likewise, European and Asian crops, such as wheat, barely, and rice, travelled to the New World, along with European livestock—cattle, pigs, sheep—that did not exist there before. World population grew as a result of the products of the Columbian Exchange.

There were, however, negative consequences as well, ones that we must recognize as antithetical to innovation. The worst of these was slavery, notably the capture and kidnapping of West Africans to labor on the lands being occupied by Europeans. With the reduction in native population, the vast and fertile lands of North and South America lacked an adequate labor supply. Over time, immigration of Europeans would make up for this shortage, but before that happened, slavery filled that gap. Slave labor in turn bought out of the Americas valuable minerals such as silver from the Andes and turned the lands of the Americas into growers of global commodities, the most valuable of which was sugar. Sugar was another highly desired "drug like" product that found a profitable market among European and other consumers. Indeed, with the lands available to grow cane and the labor of Africans, sugar production rose so dramatically that its price fell fast, making sugar perhaps the first global consumer product.

European governments, competing with each other for the lucrative Asian trade and for the riches of the New World, supported private ventures and devised new business entities, the state companies. The most famous of these were the British East India Company and its even larger rival, the Dutch East India Company. But a whole series of unique government-supported ventures marshalled private capital backed by military protection and state support to bring silver out of South America, furs out of Canada, settle colonists in North America and Mexico, and control the spice and pepper trades of the Far East. Such imperial ventures, with often violent clashes between rival European nations and sometimes brutal conquests of native peoples, would mark the period between 1400 and 1800.

Overall, the Columbian Exchange provided Europe with something extremely valuable. This was not the minerals, the gold and silver that the conquistadors had come seeking after Columbus. True, they eventually found their way into global trade, particularly silver from the rich mines of the Andes, where massive quantities went to Spain. In the short term, this mineral wealth made Spain wealthy and powerful, but only in the short term. In the same way that abundant mineral wealth like oil can undercut the willingness of a country to innovate, so the great silver hoard simply passed into and out of Spanish hands to pay for goods from the Far East. A substantial percentage of New World silver ended up in China. And Spain gradually fell behind the parts of Europe that were making the innovative transition to industry.

Where the New World bounty did help was in providing what historian Kenneth Pomeranz has called the "ghost acres" that allowed Europe to overcome one of the key roadblocks to industrialization—adequate food and other necessary commodities. The calories unleashed by the Columbian Exchange, as well as the valuable inputs to production that could be extracted from the New World—lumber for ships, meat and leather from cattle, cotton for the mills—helped Europeans overcome an important economic constraint. To make the leap from agriculture to industry, societies have to move people off the land and into cities where they perform nonagricultural labor. But take too many people off the land and you risk not having enough food or other agricultural materials to supply the urban workforce, which after all cannot feed itself. The ghost acres of the Americas took care of this problem. It freed Europe to experiment and innovate new ways of production.[51]

While these developments provided Europeans the opportunity to move to a new stage of economic development, they were not the sole cause of that great breakthrough of industrialization. As Daron Acemoglu and James Robinson have argued, empires bent on extracting wealth for the few have come and gone throughout history, and such wealth and resources do not guarantee a culture of innovation that continues to fuel economic growth, a culture that endures. It takes a culture built on a combination of new institutions and new or renewed connections of trade and exchange to fuel both growth and entrepreneurial innovation. With its dominion spanning the world, Europe had forged the first truly global commercial network, with its trading posts, colonies, ships, and companies spreading to the East into India, Indonesia, and the ports of China in one direction and its settlements, plantations, and mines to the West in the other. This global web with Europe at the center was the product of a complex and interconnected series of innovations in institutions and government that replaced feudalism, decreased the power of monarchs, and resulted in independent and commercially autonomous cities; in agriculture, shipping and navigation, engineering, medicine, science and astronomy; and in trade, business, and finance. "All the money, all that entrepreneurial energy, all that urban diversity, all those sovereign entities in such close proximity competing for grandeur, eminence, and reputation generated a dynamism unprecedented in history," argues Tamim Ansary. Imagine holding a printed book in your hands for the very first time. What a marvel it must have been! Or sailing across the world through barely charted waters and seeing Native Americans proudly standing along the shoreline. Or learning that the sun, and not the Earth, was at the center of the solar system.

Europeans had essentially destroyed their old society and understanding of nature and were forging a new one that was ushering in capitalism. They had created a social order closely bound to the concept of change and the acceptance of risk, to disruption of the status quo and accepted methods of doing things. As the famous Austrian economist Joseph Schumpeter explained, innovation "is the process…that incessantly revolutionizes the economic structure from within, incessantly destroying the old one, incessantly creating a new one. This process of Creative Destruction is the essential fact about capitalism."[52] Europeans had created a flexible, highly competitive new environment in which people welcomed and hotly debated new ideas—and celebrated success. This socio-political framework would endure for centuries. While we have seen that from about 1100 to 1700 Europeans forged the basis of a promising innovation culture, another revolution was on the horizon that would give greater form to that emerging ecosystem. For that we have to look inside European societies during the eighteenth century, and here we will see that the extensive links that the region had made to different parts of the world as well as the connections among its many different cultures gave it access to knowledge, techniques, ideas, and human capital that would spark a wholesale technological revolution.

CHAPTER 4:

Innovation in The Industrial Revolution

The stage was set. Europeans had formed powerful new institutions, created more representative governments, and forged a market-oriented society. An emerging innovation culture was fueling breakthroughs across society and laying the conceptual, methodological, and institutional foundations of modern science. Empirical methods of understanding nature led to advances in sailing and military technologies that enabled imperialistic Europeans and those descended from them to dominate most of the world's commerce. A new class of merchants was generating significant wealth that unleashed the desire for all kinds of new goods and inventions, and encouraged artisans to devise new labor-saving technologies. These advances were freeing people from working on the land, and the population was rebounding from the devastation of the plague which had shaken the very foundations of the feudal order. Europeans stopped making things by hand in their homes or in small shops and began to migrate to the growing cities in great numbers and work in factories running power-driven machinery that manufactured all manner of things faster and more efficiently. What soon followed was a massive upsurge in the productivity of labor.

The Industrial Revolution began to unfold, first in England around 1700, and then across Europe. Like the agricultural revolution ten thousand years earlier, it changed almost every feature of society. Alongside agriculture, industrialization was the greatest "macro invention" in human history. Perhaps only writing, book printing, and the Internet are near the same level.[1] And industrialization became the basis for a new type of innovation, a more conscious, organized model that made innovation a prerequisite for any society that wanted to be and remain successful.

Industrialization involved the substitution of machines and mineral sources of energy for human or animal muscle power. Through new technology (a word coined during the Industrial Revolution) and new ways to organize production, less and less effort was needed to make more and more. This seems rather commonplace today in a world where we expect our economies to grow at a healthy rate (and become concerned when they do not grow fast enough). Likewise, we expect to be able to produce more and more with less and less, so that overall income per person rises. But these expectations were both new and unprecedented in 1700. Only after the start of the Industrial Revolution did per capita incomes and labor productivity rise substantially and consistently.

In the past there had been moments of growth, with the aid of trade, improvements, and innovations, but only a small percentage of the population reaped much benefit. For the most part, growth simply meant people were better fed, lived longer, and had more children (and those children were more likely to survive childhood). Important results to be sure, but this also meant that the increase in income and production were "eaten up" by a rising population. The vast majority of world population throughout history had lived much as people in the poorest societies live today—on about a dollar a day.

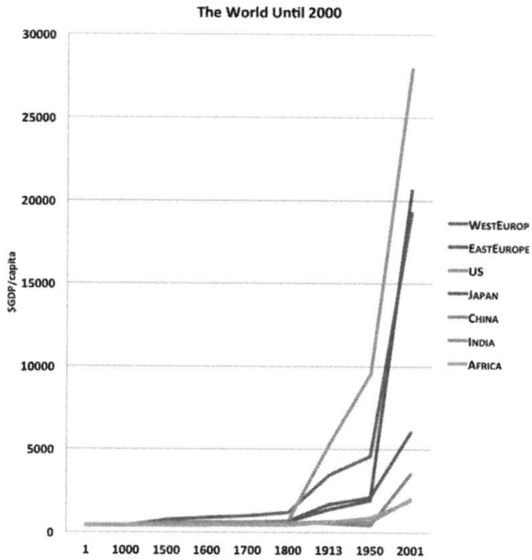

Source: https://ourworldindata.org/economic-growth

Over time, these same improvements and techniques have stretched into many realms of economic life—into services, finance, retailing, and consumption, and into the vast infrastructure of the information economy. Not only that, but the same processes of improvement and innovation also hit agriculture. So, we can use the term "industrial" in the broadest sense, both then and now, to include the ways that humans are able, through technological invention and the knowledge gained from the sciences of biology, physics, chemistry, and other disciplines to substitute artificial technique for human muscle power, and today for human brain power as well! As we will see, the miracle involved an interaction between different cultures, with individual inventors, artisans, and farmers, business organizations and public institutions such as universities, governments, and markets all taking a hand. But this is not surprising because our model of innovation includes all these factors, and we have already seen similar combinations leading to innovation in the past.

This is also a story with surprising twists and turns, not the straight road sometimes laid out by theories that have one stage of the economy moving effortlessly to the next: An agrarian to industrial to service economy, for example. In fact, it was something that did not have to happen at all, and something that might well have transpired in places other than Europe. So, perhaps we shouldn't call this the *European miracle*, but the miracle that first occurred in Europe. Indeed, it is not even clear that, should the world be plunged into another dark age of lost knowledge, we could recreate this great macro innovation from scratch. The other side of that coin, though, is that once an innovation is made, it is learned, and as it is learned it can be transmitted to many other societies. Everyone can benefit from innovation, especially the macro ones.[2]

The coming together of factors and forces, chance and fortune, provide a perfect illustration of the model of innovation I have been stressing. The macro innovation of industrialization was also the product of many incremental advances that had to occur before the *big* breakthrough was possible. There is an important lesson here, which shows why I put so much emphasis on making connections across culture and activating as much of the innovative potential of people as possible. Sometimes the most consequential changes follow from small steps forward that pay off slowly and have unanticipated effects. This is the reason why societies should strive to build the socio-political framework that drives an innovation culture dedicated to the improvement of existing or the development of entirely new products, services, or organizational business models. Those that do will succeed in propelling long-term growth, improving standards of living and quality of life. And because you never know what breakthrough will be crucial, or when and where it will occur, people from every level of society should have the same opportunities.

How did it Happen?

By 1700 England had already obtained a premier position in trade, commerce, and finance. Its navy was the strongest in the world, allowing it to take over or push aside its European rivals in the scramble to control territory in the Americas and the Caribbean. English merchants, along with those from the Netherlands, France, Denmark, and other parts of Western Europe, spun extensive webs of commerce that brought goods from the Far East and from the New World to their citizens. These commercial ties provided the sorts of connections that assured that Europe, and England within Europe, was well positioned to both learn from and exchange with the major cultures and civilizations across the globe—in China, India, Egypt, Ottoman Turkey, Africa, the Americas. Much innovation relies on the ability to synthesize, make comparisons and analogies, and modify what is learned from others.[3] The exchange, trade, merchant networking, and sharing of information that linked England to Europe and to the world were thus important preconditions for the big breakthrough. Indeed, since much innovation involves less formal knowledge and science and more on what can be passed between people or learned in practice, these sorts of informational networks may have been even more important than books. Until about 1700, England was largely a skill importer from Europe and elsewhere. It acquired knowledge and technique in smelting, forging, in making glass and pottery, guns, watches, and instruments, knowledge which had moved from Italy to Spain, to Northern Europe, often originating in the East. After 1720, England became an exporter of skills and knowledge as it devised the first machines of the Industrial Revolution.[4]

The first hint of how the balance of innovative power was changing came in agriculture. In even the most economically prosperous parts of the world, from Northern Europe to China, between 75-80 percent of the population still labored in the fields. England, along with the Netherlands, Denmark, and Norway, were the first to change that. Borrowing techniques from the Netherlands, English landowners set out improving their land and the organization of their estates into larger farms, so that it required less and less labor to feed their people, with greater and greater agricultural efficiency.[5] They may have been helped even here by a generous immigration policy—a key part of the formula for innovation—as England accepted Protestants from Flanders and France who were suffering under Catholic kings.[6] Today, the most innovative societies rely on global collaboration and the work of immigrants for success. Neither the Manhattan Project nor the American space program would have succeeded without the participation of scientists who had emigrated from Europe, like the German aerospace engineer Wernher von Braun. The International Space Station has eighteen countries participating, with the United States, Russia, and Europe the major partners;

the Square Kilometer Array radio telescope project scheduled to be completed in the early 2020s has eleven member countries. Switzerland, regarded as a world champion of innovation, has recorded one of the highest rates of international co-authorship in the world. And in 2016 Europe adopted "scientific visas" to promote cross-border movement of science researchers. And in Silicon Valley more than 50 percent of start-ups have at least one foreign-born founder.[7] But the roots of such transnational learning and cross border ties can be found much earlier as well.

Aside from an innovation ecosystem that welcomed immigrants, there were two other preconditions that existed in England that paved the way for the birth of the Industrial Revolution. First of all, by 1700, England's highly productive agriculture, and the "ghost acres" from its overseas American colonies, meant that its workers were better fed and healthier than those elsewhere. It could even export food to other nations. [8] The colonies of the empire provided all sorts of benefits to the mother country in terms of resources from the fertile lands, as well as new markets for an expanded range of British manufacturing. Improved agriculture released labor from working in the fields and sent it to cities. England was almost one quarter urban, rising to 40 percent by 1850, compared to France at 14 percent and Germany at 5 percent.[9]

A second precondition was motivation. Innovators respond to opportunities. We call this the demand side. It is especially important in moving from ideas to actual execution of those ideas. Perhaps the greatest inventive genius in history, Leonardo Da Vinci filled notebooks with extraordinary designs for such marvels as the submarine and helicopter, but he did not actually build many useful devices because the technology and materials to create them did not exist in the 1500s. In fact, the real executors of innovation were for a long time those anonymous farmers and shipbuilders who gave Europe the heavy plough, the waterwheel, and the round ship, men and probably women too, focused on the practical realities of mundane life, responding to needs and opportunities in their immediate environment. But those responses were achieved by an organized, purposeful, systematic approach to work and learning that typically led to small and not very dramatic changes, which eventually added up to significant improvement in life and technology. Likewise, one of Europe's great medieval technologies, the cathedral, was created by master builders and masons who responded to opportunity put out by the Catholic Church, slowly but surely refining and improving building techniques and technology.

Innovation need not be the product of singular genius. In fact, if you want continuous improvement that adds up to a major change, you need the ongoing work of many individuals, who piece by piece can build a technological revolution. Take, for example, the development of the steam engine. School children learn that James Watt invented the steam engine, yet it was Thomas Newcomen who fabricated the first device in 1712. Watt improved upon Newcomen's work and successfully marketed his upgraded steam engine. But neither would have made that breakthrough without the work in the preceding century of the Anglo-Irish chemist, philosopher, inventor, Sir Robert Boyle, who unsuccessfully used the explosion of gunpowder to power an engine piston. Of course, this first attempt completely trashed the cylinder, which had to be cleaned after each firing! But this is how incremental advances in knowledge occur, sometimes over a significant amount of time. The creative innovator exploits the advances—and failures—of others.

At the same time that James Watt and Thomas Newcomen were developing their engines, a shortage of labor was creating a *major* demand for workers due to the devastating effects of the Black Death on the European population 250 years before. For those who survived that epidemic, the years that followed were surprisingly good, at least if one were a worker rather than a landowner. Shortage of labor after loss of population drove up wages. The good times did not last forever, of course. With fewer people to feed and higher wages, food was more abundant, leading to a recovery of the population that drove wages down again.[10] Still, compared to India and China and other parts of the world, Europe had fewer people and higher wages. Europe's population would not return to its 1300 level until 1800.[11] Higher wages tilted European innovators toward labor saving technologies, technologies that could dramatically improve productivity and hence lead the way of transition from an agricultural to an industrial society.[12]

This was particularly true in England, where the Industrial Revolution first took root. High wages induced innovators to search for labor saving technologies. In fact the first famous machines of the Industrial Revolution all had this characteristic. These included a host of machines for textiles, which even in the Middle Ages had been one of the world's major industries. People need to be fed, but after that they needed to be clothed, so textiles were always a major part of the economy. Hand spinning thread and hand weaving cloth was a laborious process that involved many hours of work for both men and women. Improvements such as the spinning wheel and vertical loom helped, but when these activities could be mechanized through powered spinning machines (the famous spinning jenny, jenny short for engine) and power looms, productivity shot up enormously.

Before the Industrial Revolution the center of cotton textiles had been India, where fiber was grown and where the large Indian labor force spun it into textiles. After the British developed the machinery of textile production, Britain quickly outcompeted and all but devastated the long-standing Indian textile business, using cheap cotton imported from their colonies in America. India, soon after, came under complete British rule and lost its old manufacturing industries. Innovation in industry had changed the world balance of power, both in India and elsewhere as machines for doing work, technologies for working metals, and new sources of artificial energy allowed the replacement of human effort with more efficient machine power. Across the globe the nations that moved quickly to industrialize—much of western Europe, North America, parts of Latin America, Australia, and New Zealand—became the new centers of wealth and power, displacing the near and far East and Africa below the Sahara.

Much of this transformation was made possible by a series of interlocked breakthrough innovations and continuous improvements in earlier breakthroughs.[13] The English inventor Richard Trevithick recognized that greatly increasing the pressure of the steam engine would permit a smaller, and more economical design. High pressure steam engines were deployed on boats, leading to the steamship by the early 1800s. Trevithick, meanwhile, put steam engines on wheeled platforms that ran on iron rails, the first railroad. Railroads provided the world's first fast and inexpensive means of overland transport. In the past, only water transport was cheap enough to move bulky goods any distance; carriage by horse and cart over unpaved roads quickly became too expensive. With railroads, moving goods in bulk overland was now possible, a transportation revolution that knit together the nation. England developed the world's most well integrated and seamless national market as a result, allowing for still more division of labor and greater market efficiency. This has been a common pattern in history, where a new technology not only improves productivity but challenges existing technologies to keep up and improve themselves, a process that greatly expands the value of the original innovation to society.

Building a railroad, for example, required cheap metal for the rails and for the bridges that would have to cross rivers. Soon improvements in the production of ferrous metals reduced the price of iron and steel to meet that need. Henry Cort in the 1780s developed the puddling and rolling process that allowed mass production of wrought iron. Then in the 1850s, Henry Bessemer invented a method to mass produce steel, a far more durable alloy of iron, but one that had throughout history been difficult and expensive to produce. Bessemer's converter reduced the time it took to produce steel from a day to less than an hour and dropped the price from £40-50 to £7 per ton. Using steel rather than iron rails meant that railroad companies could build bigger locomotives and pull longer trains, dropping the price of transportation still more.

Meanwhile as with other breakthroughs, the Bessemer steel making process provoked further innovations, notably the Gilchrist-Thomas lining added to the original Bessemer converter. This limestone lining neutralized phosphorous in the iron ore. Phosphorous made for low-quality steel, but rich deposits of iron ore throughout Europe contained high levels of phosphorous. By neutralizing it, Gilchrist and Thomas permitted steel makers to tap these plentiful supplies.

As with the steam engine, innovators began to emulate and improve on the British breakthrough, not just in England but across Europe and across the Atlantic as well. In America, William Kelly patented a process nearly identical to Bessemer's, reflecting simultaneity of common knowledge and problem-solving capabilities that continue to occur across economies today. Germany developed the Siemens-Martin open hearth, a furnace that could take in scrap metal and low-quality ores to make steel, supplanting Bessemer. The famous American steel magnate Andrew Carnegie adopted the open-hearth process and improved steel making until he was the world's lowest cost producer by the end of the nineteenth century.[14]

As steel became available for many uses, metal workers were able to produce new machinery of far greater durability and precision than was possible with wood or even iron. In particular, the Industrial Revolution was led by machine tools, which are the powered cutting, stamping, and shaping devices that can be used to make other machines. So innovators developed lathes, grinders, drills, and presses that could turn out precision metal parts at greater speed and lower cost than humans working with hand tools could ever do. The machine tools allowed for the production of a diversity of new goods by industrial methods: Guns and armaments, clocks, steam engines, spinning jennies, and later of course automobiles and engines, or today semiconductor chips. The same machine tools could be adapted to all manner of goods and products, a process that economist Nathan Rosenberg called "technological convergence." Important breakthroughs in one sector, like textiles, could ripple through the economy and industrialize many other sectors, greatly increasing overall economic productivity. The evidence shows that this is exactly what happened in England, as technological convergence gave the first mover nation a competitive edge over even its nearest European rivals in production of manufactured goods.[15]

Much of the early phase of industrialization involved heavy industry, the making of commodities and goods that would serve as inputs into other production, where the final goods to the consumer were made. Steel, coal, railroads, steam engines, and spinning jennies were not so much final products that the average person bought but producer goods that made the production of consumer goods cheaper. However, England also developed a vast consumer goods sector as well, in part because it was so successful in reducing the cost and improving the productivity on the producer side. Clocks and jewelry, pottery and ceramics, pianos and furniture and a host of other household items and luxuries were all were turned out in abundance and at lower cost than before in industrial England. These products were available to middle-class consumers, in England and abroad. Increasingly, demand for such goods would stimulate further improvement to lower the cost and make consumer products available lower down the economic scale. Industrialization was a complete transformation that had buried itself deeply into people's everyday lives.

England's Tangled Bank

Macro innovations are important because they open up a whole new range of economic possibilities. They are radical breakthroughs. They also change attitudes toward work, industry, and technology, setting minds to the task of still more innovation. The Industrial Revolution was thus also an intellectual revolution. By the time the first machines were being put into service in England, thinkers such as Andrew Ure, a Scottish physician and chemist, and Charles Babbage, who conceptualized the computer even before we had electronics to make one, were lauding the great improvements and productivity possible by replicating or replacing the movement of human hands and arms with machines.[16] They began talking not just about a machine or two to augment human capacity, but a whole factory system that would radically, and continually, transform and improve production. Innovators need to imagine a possible new future so that they can go beyond what is already known and practiced.[17] This sort of entrepreneurial creativity benefitted from thinkers, writers, and promoters who gave voice and image to new ideas of production.

As industrial innovation gained advocates and promoters, so too did the idea that a division of labor and specialization could make nations wealthier, if only governments would allow, indeed encourage free trade and open markets. The execution of industrialization in England was spurred by such policies, removing tariffs, encouraging market prices in agricultural goods, promoting improvements in product design and patents. Just as the Industrial Revolution was unfolding, dreams of a self-regulating market economy were finding their advocates in men like the chemist and minister Joseph Priestly, who identified the element oxygen, and most famously the philosopher Adam Smith, who wrote the bible of capitalism, *The Wealth of Nations*, in 1776.

Government policy can help promote innovation in a number of ways, including providing access to education, protection for intellectual property and innovations so inventors can profit from their work, and a stable macroeconomic environment. In the early Industrial Revolution, though, not all of these factors were yet in play. For example, people were better educated by 1800 than they had been in the past, with the spread of literacy, printing, and books. But England was actually not the best educated society in Europe, and not significantly more literate than other places. Unlike today, formal education did not yet play a significant role in the economy. Likewise, England had instituted a number of mechanisms to encourage innovation by allowing innovators to profit from their work. There was a functioning patent system, and the government gave prizes, premiums, and lifetime annuities to individuals who made important breakthroughs.[18] But a few examples aside, much of the early Industrial Revolution did not actually depend on patents or monetary incentives.

Formal education and patents would grow more important over time, but initially, the key to British industrial success was something more general—an innovation culture that was open to new ideas, new knowledge, and a system for spreading those ideas across different industries. Britain's upsurge in manufacturing ability came from the efforts of many anonymous inventors who toiled away making improvements in mechanization and labor-saving devices, and building up the knowledge and skills that would be applicable to many other sectors of the economy over time.[19] In fact, much of the work was not even done by people who called themselves inventors, let alone scientists or intellectuals. Much was carried out by nameless, skilled mechanics and craftspeople.

Although England had a strong and extensive engagement with the Scientific Revolution of the seventeenth and eighteenth centuries with such brilliant, highly educated, elite scientists such as Isaac Newton, Robert Boyle, and William Harvey, many of the key inventors were neither especially well-educated nor part of the scientific establishment. This is true even of the more famous figures. James Hargreaves, inventor of the spinning jenny, and Samuel Crompton who revolutionized textiles with his even more sophisticated spinning mule, the ironmasters Henry Cort and John Wilkinson, machinists Henry Maudslay and Mathew Murry, none had more than basic schooling and literacy. In fact, Hargreaves may well have been illiterate. But they all had done on-the-job learning as apprentices.[20] During the Industrial Revolution, much as today, the strength of these innovators derived from their observational skills and ability to translate what they observed into new products, techniques, processes, or machines that customers desired, much as we have stressed in my innovation model. As Peter Drucker has argued, "go out to look, to ask, to listen.... Successful innovators use both the right side and left side of their brains. They look at figures, and they look at people. They work out analytically what the innovation has to be to satisfy an opportunity."[21]

And as we move down from the famous inventors to the mechanics, craftspeople, apprentices, and fitters, we find an even less elite group. They are the ones who worked with the machinery and observed its flaws or found avenues for improvement. They did not possess the sort of knowledge that you got from books and plans but the sort you learned with your hands, hands-on knowledge, acquired by observation, trial, error, and analysis. Most of their improvements were never patented. There was a lot of human capital in this Industrial Revolution, to be sure, but most of it was in this artisan class. This was also the sector missing in places like France, which was as or more advanced in formal science than England.[22] The society that can draw broadly and deeply on the creative talents of its people has the edge because so much of innovation involves less dramatic but crucial improvements that must go on continuously. On-the-job and vocational training continues to be an important part of the European educational system today, along with corporate mentoring, and is driving advanced manufacturing capabilities in such powerhouses as Germany. The most successful European nations, it seems, are the ones who have not forgotten the lessons of the early Industrial Revolution.[23]

The capacity for observing, learning, analyzing, and doing thrives in subcultures. In decades before industrialization, skills had been cultivated in apprenticeships and by guilds. Young men (they were almost always men), who learned a trade or craft as apprentices then moved across Europe as journeymen, thereby transferring skills and knowledge as they went. It seems this sort of fluidity of movement and knowledge was not as common in other parts of the world, for example China, where a strong state and bureaucracy regulated the acquisition of knowledge and its application in service to the government, not the competitive market for talent. The men and sometimes women who built, installed, fixed and fitted and tinkered with the machines often congregated in cities, where information could be exchanged readily. They met informally at coffee houses and public houses. These meeting places were like today's garages, and once again coffee houses, that stimulate so much innovation in Silicon Valley.[24] Micro communities of artisans and apprentices were interested in sharing what they knew, especially because in many industries such as steel or machinery, it took the combined efforts of a number of skilled workers and craftspeople to make a successful product. Craft communities also fanned out across the landscape, seeking new opportunities in rival cities and eventually outside of England, where they spread the knowledge of industrialization to the rest of Europe.[25]

Would-be inventors in the Industrial Revolution also engaged in self-education. They frequented mechanics institutes, technical libraries, and trade schools, all of which proliferated in this period.[26] There were by the 1820s schools of the useful arts, clubs to disseminate the latest scientific discoveries, and philosophical societies that drew in not just the elite but the middle class and working mechanics. These proliferated in Britain's commercial, financial, and manufacturing centers like Liverpool, Manchester, and Edinburgh, at a time when universities themselves did not emphasize practical training.[27] If high levels of formal education were not necessarily required, this sort of continual investment in lifelong learning and education was still valuable, as it allowed innovators to see what others were doing, to find out about the latest technique, machine, and discover what insights from science might have to offer. With its high level of urbanization, England also provided lots of places where this sort of learning and applying could go on, and with the freedom to move and settle without internal restrictions or medieval ties to the land, such people could spread and share what they knew with others.

We often focus on competition as an important stimulus to innovation. And in industrializing England, with its increasingly free, liberal markets, there was plenty of competition among firms and individuals engaged in the early innovation process. As we will see in a bit, there was also increasing competition between England as the first industrial nation, and its neighbors in Europe, who suddenly had to fear they would fall behind economically. But there was also a lot of sharing, as happens today in sectors innovating rapidly. We often like to borrow from Charles Darwin and evolutionary theory the idea that the economy runs on the principle "survival of the fittest." But Darwin also noted another feature of a successful ecology—interdependence. He called this "the tangled bank," a healthy ecology of different species whose existence mutually supports each other. They do so by in part by constituting a food chain, but also by maintaining a healthy general environment, a balance of chemicals in water and fertile soil in which plants can grow and animals thrive.[28]

This ecological interdependence, which the world only rediscovered with the ecology movement fifty years ago, is another way to think of a healthy economy. Innovators have to draw on others to complete their objectives: Designers need skilled fabricators to carry out their designs, and fitters to make the products actually work in real world conditions. The makers of final products need a strong supply chain, including the designers and builders of the tools and machines that are necessary to mass produce the final goods. Such interconnections we have seen at different moments in the past, but the machine era, the industrial era has really made it clear how important it is to have all the parts working together. A healthy innovative economy has a fluidity of knowledge, so that innovations work and can move across sectors.[29] This was what England was first able to achieve.

England's tangled bank benefitted from a wealth of interrelated producer industries, such as coal and steel, textiles and machinery, machine tools and a wide range of other machines they were used to produce.[30] It included those artisan communities and mechanics who traded knowledge with each other. But there was finally a third factor. England, though the first mover in this great new venture of industrialization, was ready and willing to borrow ideas, knowledge, technique, and technology from elsewhere, including other parts of Europe. In fact, in many ways the strength of innovation in England lay in its unique ability to execute ideas that others had come up with first. English inventors and industrialists executed on a mass scale ideas and designs in ways that the original creators had not been able to.[31] Continuous papermaking machines, the Jacquard loom for weaving complex designs, the Leblanc soda making process for the chemical industry, Bertholett's bleaching process, the first gas lighting systems, the linen spinning machine, and the process for canning food were all invented outside of England, often in France, but had their first application and their development in the United Kingdom. By the nineteenth century a common European proverb claimed that for something to be perfect, it may be invented in France but it must be worked out in England.[32]

Openness to other cultures was a hallmark of English innovation, which makes England's current unease with its relationship to Europe and its leaving the EU warning signs of long-term trouble ahead for the island nation. These recent developments stand in rather stark contrast to how England actually built its industrial culture. During the eighteenth- and nineteenth-centuries, significant learning and borrowing across Europe and from the East was fueling innovation. The Protestant immigrants who fled hostile Catholic territory arrived in England with skills in watch making, optics, ironware, among other things.[33] Indeed, from 1500 to 1700 religious wars and conflicts had set a great deal of migration in motion all across Europe, from the north of England all the way to the Levant. Just as in the earlier centuries, the Italian city-states were amalgamations of many different peoples—Greeks, Turks, Dalmatians, Romanians, Germans, Jews--so too was England becoming a receptacle for people bringing knowledge and skills from elsewhere. Religious wars in the Netherlands brought some 30,000 Dutch to England. Another immigration wave swept over England in the sixteenth century as French Protestants (Huguenots) arrived.[34] London's foreign-born population swelled to over 10 percent. Talented craftsmen and smaller-scale machinists and industrialists, some of them immigrants, also migrated to northern English cities. Birmingham in particular became a consumer manufacturing goods center, turning out large quantities of buttons and buckles, teapots, sugar bowls and silverware, screws, locks, iron and brass hardware, candlesticks, snuff boxes, pipes, engraving, glass ornaments, beds, couches, cabinets, cutlery, and children's toys, to name just a few.[35]

Perhaps the most famous example of an innovator who learned, borrowed from, and adapted ideas and practices from elsewhere was Josiah Wedgewood, the famous maker of pottery and ceramics. For centuries Europeans had tried, and failed, to figure out how the Chinese turned out their fine, gleaming, translucent porcelain. The Dutch had come close with their Delft-ware imitations in the seventeenth century and eventually the Germans would achieve quality hard porcelain in 1710, though knowledge of the technique was largely kept secret. Wedgewood began by producing more humble earthenware, often imitating classical Greek or Italian designs, and soon had an active clientele from the middle classes who craved what had once been luxuries solely for the wealthy. He mimicked the high-end imported Chinese porcelain, freely borrowing styles, designs, and images from across Europe, the Middle East, and Asia. Just as importantly, he innovated in marketing, with stores, showrooms, endorsements from royalty, illustrated catalogues, free shipping, and special sales. Wedgewood, a name synonymous with English housewares, was a great borrower of designs and cultural motifs from others.

Industrialization Moves Abroad

By the early nineteenth century, England had all the earmarks of a highly innovative society. It had pioneered one of the great macro inventions in history—industrialization—involving the use of complex machines to replace human labor. It had quickly become the richest nation on earth, and had begun building what would be the greatest overseas empire in history. It produced two-thirds of the world's coal and half of its iron and cotton.[36] Its middle class was larger and more urban than any other comparable nation of its size and had access to more and more consumer goods. London was the largest city in the world by 1825, surpassing Beijing (it would take New York another century to beat London). And it was a center of finance, banking, insurance, and foreign trade, a true global city. But innovation also stimulates imitation, and England, while the first industrial nation, was not destined to be the *only* industrial nation. Its wealth and strength soon attracted competitors, the first of them coming across the English Channel from continental Europe.

Many nations believe they can maintain their innovative edge by keeping secrets and excluding others. The question of how much borrowing China does from American science and technology continues to be a thorny and contested issue today. England too thought it might be able to keep the secrets of industrialization at home, but this proved impossible, and indeed would have been counterproductive. There was a long tradition of knowledge and technique flowing across the continent, so lots of potential for creative borrowing and mixing. Since the late seventeenth and eighteenth centuries, a period often identified with "the Enlightenment," Europe had been building an astounding array of institutions to create, share, and disseminate knowledge. Most nations of the continent founded or expanded their universities. Encyclopedias, periodicals, exhibits, and displays of the latest scientific advance proliferated, all with an emphasis on the way society might be materially and morally improved. Kings and their courts patronized the creative classes, and commissioned translations of foreign works to acquire knowledge that their own people lacked.[37] There was a "diversity within a wider unity" in Europe that may have helped to not only spread industrialization but also provided a fertile environment for continued improvements and innovations as different people observed and analyzed what they learned in different ways.[38]

One reason that Europe as a whole, and not just first mover England, became a center of industrialization, and surpassed its long-time rivals in the Middle East and China, was because knowledge and skills could move across borders. Crafts could span nations when different skills were needed. Textile printing and dying were arts that involved people in London, the Netherlands,

Switzerland, Marseille, and Barcelona. Iron masters exchanged knowledge between England and Sweden. Knowledge and technique flowed in multiple directions. Glassmaking, once a specialty of Venice, travelled to France and England, and elsewhere. The sort of skill in scientific instrument making possessed by a Galileo at one time was soon found in Paris and then London in later times.[39]

Europe had long been a region of intense rivalry and warring states. Britain and its continental peers competed for the prizes of territory and goods from the new world, clashed on the high seas, and fought land wars over religious differences that stretched back centuries. There was as well competition among cities, both within nations and across them, as cities were the centers of trade and commerce and provided an important part of the tax base for military armaments. Indeed, military demand itself provided some of the first schools of engineering to fit the demand for precision skills and manufacturing for weapons such as canons. Normally this sort of military conflict is bad for economies, but it also meant that there was keen interest across the nations of Europe in innovations that might gain a rival an edge.[40]

Britain made efforts to keep its secrets from getting out, including blocking exports of machinery, plans and designs, and strategic technologies. But customs inspectors lacked the technical knowledge necessary to prevent smuggling. And when entrepreneurs were prohibited from maximizing profits through foreign sales, they set up shop in the restricted country and opened factories abroad. Even at the height of the American Revolution, with France and England on opposing sides of the war, steam engine developer James Watt opened a factory in France to make and sell his engines, with a fifteen-year monopoly grant from the French government.[41]

Knowledge also moved with people, notably by immigration. Whereas England had received Protestants fleeing Catholic domination, so did Catholics in Protestant England leave for the Catholic nations of Spain and France. Just as with the prohibitions on plans and machines moving abroad, Britain tried to stop the migration of skilled mechanics while rival European nations sought to encourage the immigration of those fitters and mechanics by luring them overseas with high-paying jobs as managers of their factories and works. British engineers and fitters set up the rival textile factories in France and Belgium and when Russia and other nations started importing French and Flemish textile machinery, it was the British artisans who made even that machinery work. Germany, Sweden, France, and other nations desirous of getting what England already had imported whole teams of fitters and mechanics the use and repair of equipment, putting them on long-term service contracts.[42]

Seeking to catch up with England, nations in continental Europe undertook a more deliberate industrial policy. While the first industrial nation might have innovated spontaneously, the later followers had to learn, master, and build industries to scale quickly if they were ever going to match England's productivity lead. Whereas England did not have to rely on schooling and formal education to industrialize, its followers invested much more in education.[43] Germany began to assemble its system of compulsory primary education followed by practical secondary education and new technical universities, a tripartite arrangement designed to produce higher level engineers and managers as well as lower level but crucial mechanics, fitters, and repairers. Prussia in particular pushed hard for expanded education of its citizens, which seems to have paid off in adapting industrial technology quickly. Germany would lead the way later in creating research oriented universities and strong graduate education programs across a broad spectrum of disciplines, including the sciences, mathematics, engineering, and medicine. France, meanwhile, set its new course in education by opening its famed École Polytechnique in 1795, with écoles for mines, bridges and roads, and conservatories for arts and crafts soon after.[44]

To encourage the transfer of knowledge other nations began to translate and circulate what was appearing in English publications. France's *Bibliothèque Britannique* published between 1796 and 1815 ran to over 28,000 pages of translations and summations, with focus on the arts, sciences, and agriculture. There were even industrial spies who sought to get out of England what was still either secret or highly localized knowledge, though in many cases clandestine efforts were not even necessary. The English Royal Society had corresponding members with whom it shared the latest discoveries all across Europe and popular magazines summarized and distilled the latest scientific findings for any reader. Anyone interested could examine English patents, including detailed blueprints and miniature models, and British engineers often registered their patents in France as well. Foreign visitors were generally welcomed in British factories, mines, and industrial plants, often arriving on pre-arranged tours. In the nineteenth century public demonstrations and trade fairs where new machines were dramatically unveiled or taken on the road to show and astound audiences were a common spectacle.[45]

Knowledge of industrial technology spread fast and far, soon reaching the other end of the globe. It was in fact this desire to catch up quickly that led a new regime in Japan with Emperor Meiji after 1868. The far eastern nation shifted dramatically from isolation to world engagement and imperialism. In the Meiji period, Japanese trade and technical missions went throughout the Western world to learn about industry and technology, translated and transcribed vast quantities of Western science and technical knowledge, and founded technical universities in a rapid drive to catch up. As a result Japan quickly surpassed the once revered Chinese empire as well as the far larger Russian empire and became the dominant power in the region by the early twentieth century.

The late comers also tried to protect their infant industries with tariff barriers and government subsidies. While free markets are ultimately necessary to assure that businesses compete in the most efficient manner possible, in the early stages a follower nation may need a period of protection from competition with already established players. The German economist Friedrich List in particular made a strong case for protective tariffs that influenced German policy in the early years, a policy, as we shall see in the next chapter, he learned from the United States. Other nations playing the same catch-up game, such as France and Japan, also found ways to buffer their new industries from full exposure to competition until they could learn and master the techniques so that they would achieve the same level of productivity. In some cases they either directly owned, or contracted to private entrepreneurs its military arsenals, shipyards, and gun foundries, offering subsidies and private financing, as well as high wages and profit sharing to skilled foreign workers who would immigrate and teach locals what they knew.

A Second Industrial Revolution

Technology does not stay still of course, and one reason that these investments and policies started to pay off was that by the late nineteenth and early twentieth centuries, the world was going through what is often called a "second industrial revolution." Now it was no longer sufficient to be at the cutting edge in textiles or even metals. More scientifically complex industries were on the rise: Electricity and electrical equipment, communications, internal combustion engines and powered vehicles, and perhaps above all chemicals and then later petroleum and petrochemicals. These sectors yielded more to scientific and formal knowledge.[46] While England, like much of Europe, had universities such as Oxford and Cambridge going back to the Middle Ages, it had failed to keep pace when it came to technical learning and knowledge, allowing Germany and even France to become serious competitors and in some cases economic superiors to England by the early twentieth century.

Another reason that the other nations of Europe (and also Japan) could catch up was because they also marshalled new financial resources. As a first mover, England had not needed the higher levels of finance that the later comers required, especially for capital intensive heavy industry. Much of the early phase of industry could be financed with either family money or through relatively small loans from banks or from mortgages and buy-in by local investors, often partners in firms.[47] In other cases, merchants who had made substantial fortunes in shipping, trade, and commerce, might reinvest their capital in the emerging new factories and industries. The first firms, as they learned how to improve productivity, could gradually scale up, improve technology, and finance later expansion from internal profits. But this was less possible for the later comers, who already faced well-established British firms and had to import the most advanced technology and master its workings quickly if they wanted to compete. To mobilize capital, Germany developed what became known as "universal banks," which took in deposits and savings from the population, made loans to business, and also acted as investment banks and venture capitalists for new industrial entrepreneurs. The banks held long-term positions in the firms they financed, and took seats on their boards, providing another scarce but invaluable resource, managerial talent, while reassuring public investors that the firms were sound.[48]

By the twentieth century, industrialization had spread from England to the continent of Europe. France and Germany and a bit later northern Italy became major industrial centers, not only following the English lead but innovating in new sectors. In all, the European-wide phenomena of industrialization meant that there would be lots of mixing, borrowing, improving, learning, and adapting, keeping the pot of innovation boiling on the stove. More participants, intense competition, and a profound sharing of knowledge had fostered what Louis Galambos and Franco Amatori call the "entrepreneurial multiplier."[49] Important innovations push others to keep pace while at the same time transforming societies to take full advantage of the breakthroughs. Governments try to promote innovations that keep their nations competitive, and undertake such policies as strengthening patent and property rights, encouraging more widely available and quality education, promoting and subsidizing science and engineering research, providing the initial public funding for risky but valuable infrastructure projects, and in some cases protecting their own infant industries so they have a chance to grow. Likewise, the financial system reorients itself to take advantage of new opportunities in new industries. Innovation becomes self-reinforcing.

But it was not just in Europe that this ferment of activity was occurring. Many parts of the world came to understand that to be competitive and not fall under the sway of the most advanced nations, they would also have to master the arts of industrialization. Those places that could not or did not—China, the Middle East, much of Africa, India—would not only fall behind economically but would also be subject to domination and colonization of those places that did. So, a variety of competitors to Europe emerged. Some like Russia were right on its doorstep, but many others were oceans away, in what can be called "neo-Europes." These were the places where people from

Europe moved, migrated to, and populated: Latin America, North America, Australia, and New Zealand. Some would succeed, others would falter, and others would have to wait. But one place above all adapted the lessons of industrialization, took them to heart, and by the twentieth century, had become the world industrial leader and the next great innovation society: The United States. This is the story we will take up in the upcoming chapter.

And what about Europe, in so many ways the progenitor of all this? The major industrial nations of Europe have remained of course vastly important economic places and major contributors to innovation throughout the twentieth century and into the twenty-first century. On the other hand, the region's long simmering conflicts, hatreds and rivalries, which between 1815, with the defeat of Napoleon, and the start of World War I a century later, had not been terribly bloody, soon turned more deadly than ever. Europe suffered mightily and lost ground economically as a result of being the center of the two costliest wars in human history. After World War II it rebuilt under the leadership of the United States. And with the formation of the EU and creation of the great common market, it had been doing a great job of keeping up with the still dominant economic power of the United States and the emerging power of twenty-first century China. But Europe also has some work to do if it wants to remain a center of innovation.

Today, Europeans are engaged in an intense global competition to win the race for innovation leadership, yet success varies from country to country and even from one region to another. Although many have maintained their scientific excellence and competitive edge, others like Greece and Croatia lag far behind. The European Innovation Scoreboard of 2018 indicates that innovation performance improved in eighteen member states since 2010, while it declined in ten. Nations know that the design and implementation of a sophisticated national innovation ecosystem is essential to help them drive the economic growth they so desperately desire. They are attempting to integrate policies toward finance, education and skills development, tax, trade, scientific research, technology commercialization, intellectual property rights, labor and government regulations.[50]

The EU is promoting policies at the supra-national level and creating platforms that promote transnational and transregional multidisciplinary networks. Through such initiatives as Horizon 2020, it is investing close to 80 billion euros in research and innovation programs. Policies that promote apprenticeships, mentoring, and student and researcher mobility between member states take advantage of the region's many and varied educational institutions. Individual nations also have their own strategies that strive to link science, technology, and innovation with economic and employment growth, which have been stubbornly lackluster since the Great Recession of 2008.[51] Obstacles to innovation remain, however, and a lack of consistency in efforts to promote entrepreneurship and economic growth shows that innovation can still vary dramatically from one nation to another.

Although *Forbes'* annual list of the World's Most Innovative Companies includes some twenty from Western Europe, none cracks the top ten, which is dominated by U.S. firms. EU firms lack the sort of venture capital crucial for startup ventures, capital which remains more plentiful in the United States. Innovation thrives on the constant transformation of a nation's economy and institutions, but some European firms remain reluctant to embrace risk and breakneck change which characterizes American entrepreneurial culture. Unlike their competitors in Asia and the United States, European industries have been criticized for their slow diffusion of innovations and reliance on local rather than international markets.

Europe's superior educational institutions have contributed to its rankings as top innovators in high-quality science, with the Imperial College of London, the Technical University of Munich, and ETH Zurich among the best in computer science in the world. Still, the EU is still struggling to leverage its assets in ways that generate innovations and new firms. As a result, talented Europeans move elsewhere, contributing to a brain drain. Pure education alone does not necessarily do the trick, as the economist Ruchir Sharma has argued. The most educated nations do not always achieve the greatest economic success, as was evident at the start of the industrial era too. Russia, despite boasting a population with the highest average years of schooling (11.5) and the greatest share of university graduates (6.4 percent), has yet to translate this educational capital into solid economic growth. By contrast Germany, an economic and innovative powerhouse in Europe, actually has fewer college-educated graduates than other, lower performing

EU economies. It is able to build the needed skills in other way, such as through apprenticeships. Institutions and education are important to be sure, but they are the "slow-moving forces" in the global race for economic growth and success. Europe now has many promising innovation clusters that are linking universities, firms, and entrepreneurs and nurturing startups in many of the region's largest cities, such as BMW's Innovation Lab in the U.K., the Accenture Innovation Center and Station F in Paris, and Silicon Allee in Berlin.

Since the Global Recession, much of the world has been suffering through the weakest economic recovery in the postwar era. However, nations forging the right innovation culture will be the best competitors in the "noisy jungle" of the ever-changing global economy. In this environment, Europe will need to rethink its mix of policies supporting its markets, education, taxes, regulations, trade partnerships, and labor and immigration policies so that they are focused on rapid innovation and entrepreneurship if it wants to reclaim its old position as the global innovation leader.[52]

CHAPTER 5:

The Pillars of U.S. Innovation

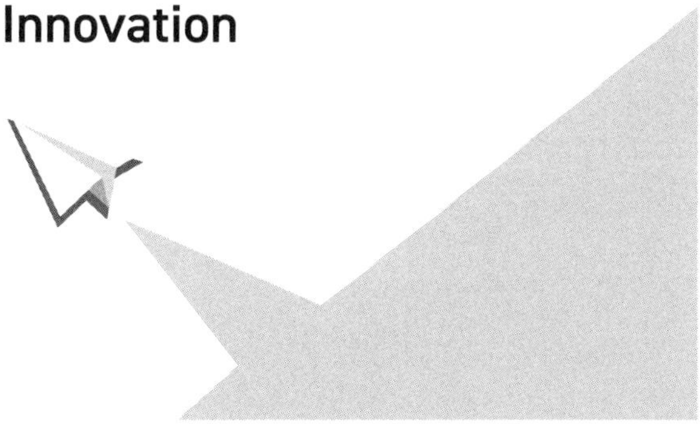

My business in Dubai had been going very well, and by 2006 I wanted to find a way to take it to another level. A friend of mine had just finished a management training program for business owners at the Harvard Business School and he strongly urged me to attend. He told me I needed to be educated. But I had never even heard of the Harvard Business School before. I did know something about America, particularly its reputation for having a strong innovation and entrepreneurial culture, one that welcomed immigrants. Although I decided to go to Harvard to learn how to grow my business, when I got there I discovered something I never expected to find. In my very first class, the professor began to speak about innovation, innovation. What is innovation, I asked myself? Are we here to learn about Samsung, the iPhone, technology? Why do we need to learn about this? But from there I started my journey to think about innovation in the right way. I began to reflect more and more on innovation and how important it is to any country that wants to be competitive, to expand its economy and to stay atop a rapidly changing world. It was at Harvard University in the United States of America that I first began to understand innovation. And that is not at all surprising, because America has been the modern innovation leader for more than century.

This is a history and a record for which America is justly proud. Yet today this proud record of achievement is in danger. No longer does the United States rank at the very top of innovative societies. And while students from across the globe still come to study at U. S. institutions of higher learning, many go home to apply their knowledge and skills in their native lands rather than build their future and their businesses here in America.[1] The problem, as I see it, is that too few people in America really understand the sources of their nation's innovative strength. They are thus in danger of pulling down the very pillars on which the great American temple of innovation has rested. This would be a tragedy, not only for the United States, but for the world. America as a leader has brought benefits not only to itself but to everyone. This is the way innovation leadership works. The most creative and innovative places get to the top, but they provide opportunities, inventions, technologies, and ideas for others to follow them, generating growth across the world. A healthy world economy helps all, but it also benefits the innovation leader, which finds customers for its products, attracts capital and talent from other places, and has the system of resources to continue to lead in innovation.

The American Way of Innovation

America developed its formidable innovation system in the early nineteenth century and by 1900 emerged as the modern innovation leader in such key categories as productivity and manufacturing. It had generated an amazing array of breakthroughs from the telephone to sound recording, to radio, motion pictures, and powered flight. In other cases, it had taken ideas first proposed elsewhere and turned them into mass-produced products. The Germans and French pioneered automobiles and internal combustion engines but America had Henry Ford who made the automobile a product of everyday life. By the middle of the twentieth century, the United States was the envy of the world, and other nations flocked to its shores to figure out what it had done, how it had done it, and how they could emulate the great American system.

The pillars of American innovation were built up over a century, in fact even more than a century, almost from the time Europeans set foot in the

New World. This was in many ways the most amazing change we have seen. In a brief span of time the northern section of North America, starting as a mere colony of England supplying the mother country with raw materials, soon surpassed its parent nation in per capita income, freed itself from colonial status, and began copying innovations from the world leader in technology and then making them even better.[2] It is a pattern that we have seen before and one that we are seeing now with China, as we will examine in the next chapter. But the rise of the United States was, at least until now, the most impressive passing of the mantle of innovation leadership. It is also a lesson that many other countries would like to learn.

So how did this happen? What were the pillars on which America's innovation culture rested? Some of the factors we have seen before. America was an open society, one that drew talent and people from many parts of the world. It also made substantial investments in human capital, in the form of universal (and free) education for its citizens, a strong system of higher education, and high levels of literacy and numeracy. In these ways the nation activated the talents of a large percentage of its citizens, as well as its non-citizen immigrants. But the United States also provided conditions that allowed potential innovators and creative thinkers to execute their ideas and plans. Even more than Britain, the United States had an open and risk-taking financial system that quickly supplied money and credit to innovators and entrepreneurs. Access to capital was even more important and valuable in a new nation playing catch-up than it had been for the first mover, which could start out small and use internal resources to build. A stable constitutional government also helped here, for America was seen by capital-rich England as an attractive and relatively low risk place to invest money. The stable American system of government also provided strong protections for intellectual property in the form of an easy to access patent system sunk into the very fabric of the constitution. By the twentieth century, the United States had added a final factor to its innovation system, one that has grown increasingly important in modern times: Government policies that encouraged scientific and technological research and development and lent support to breakthrough technologies that had great potential but had not yet found a solid market footing.

America, in short, created a deep and complex innovation ecosystem, one that drew on past precedents but also added new features. It supported creative scientific thinkers, allowed commercially oriented independent inventors to profit from their ideas, provided a stable economic environment for investors yet a dynamic and multi-layered financial system to allow risk-takers to get the resources they needed to take those risks. Although a strongly market-based system, America also provided key public goods, ranging from education to infrastructure to land and mineral rights that allowed a broad section of the public to pursue opportunity and bring out their best talents and ideas. America was not an equal society by any means, but it was a place of opportunity as evidenced by the magnetic attraction it had on immigrants from around the world. And those newcomers, continually replenished over more than two centuries, brought the mix of new ideas and new practices that, as we have seen, are crucial to any society that wants to be innovative.

Looking back in retrospect it's easy to identify what was done right (or wrong). But it is much harder to go from identifying what worked to actually *creating* a society and culture that has those desirable features. In fact, just looking at other societies that were founded in the New World at the same time as America shows that even when starting from the same point, only a few will be able to compete in the race. Latin American and Caribbean nations have not established the same culture of innovation that has flourished in the United States, though many have made strenuous efforts to catch up. As we shall see when we unpack the history that made America innovative, one factor above all stands out, a necessary ingredient that can really start the process going—democratic equality. America benefited from its strong roots of democracy, based on the concepts of equality, especially equality of opportunity for free men.[3] At a time when other nations, notably China, are attempting to prove that democracy is not fundamental for innovation to flourish and economies to grow, the American experience is an important one to examine carefully. And taking account of the past and recalling the roots of success are a good thing for Americans themselves to do today. As we shall see, recent developments in the United States threaten to undermine the foundations that have sustained the nation for so long.

Innovation in a New World

North America was not a wealthy place when Europeans first arrived and started to settle there. But it quickly acquired a strong commercial and entrepreneurial orientation, even as a British colony. Colonists from England, the Netherlands, France, and Spain arrived at various times following Columbus's voyages, and settled in various parts of the new world. Their mission was largely motivated by profit. In Virginia, which encompassed a good portion of the southern seaboard of North America, the British were promoting a fully profit-making venture through the crown-chartered Virginia Company.[4] Another corporation, the Hudson's Bay Company, operated in the far north, present-day Canada, where it focused on the lucrative fur trade with Native Americans. Even in New England, a region settled by a sect of highly religious protestant dissenters from the Church of England, profits were not absent. Though their program was an almost utopian one of religious communitarianism, these Puritans, as we have seen with other religious orders, were focused on improving the land and making practical use of nature. They founded new towns and bought and sold land to other settlers. Likewise, in the middle colonies of North America, another religious leader, the Quaker William Penn, took the vast grant of land he had been allotted by the King of England, which he called Penn's Woods, or Pennsylvania, and began to improve it. Penn laid out, in rational, grid-like fashion, his port city of Philadelphia and sold off or gave land to new arrivals, who took that land and started to cultivate grains to sell to the market and ship to other colonies and to England.[5]

This commercial disposition in North America was less a matter of culture, or English origins or even European heritage than it was a function of conditions and institutions, which propelled the region from humble beginnings to rapid growth and eventually to become the place of innovation by the nineteenth century. In fact, the American story provides an almost natural experiment for isolating those factors that we have identified as crucial for fostering innovation. And it provides a clear contrast to other parts of the world that *seemed* to have all of the ingredients for success but ended far behind the United States. That is why cultures and societies rise and fall in the innovation game. Get the conditions wrong and your inherited culture, or early advantages or natural resources, won't save you. The only way to stay ahead is to build a society that allows and promotes continual innovation.

Let's go back to our model and look at some of those key factors and conditions. We have identified education, a strong financial system, a stable government that protects property rights and provides incentives to innovators, and an openness to ideas and to talented people from elsewhere, often realized through a generous immigration policy. Almost all of those features characterized the northern region of the Americas. And, as we shall see, most of them were absent or stunted in the southern region and the Caribbean. The results were clear. In the long term, whatever the advantages one region started with versus another, it was the conditions, policies, and institutions that determined who came out on top. North America actually lacked some of the immediate sources of profit like precious metals and high demand commodities that made South America and the Caribbean attractive and economically successful at first. So, its rapid rise to the top of the New World food chain could ONLY be explained by innovation, by developing new products, new industries, successful firms, embracing the adoption of new technologies, and contributing to the continual improvement of those technologies. It was, as we shall see in the next chapter, the very same pattern and process that China has gone through in the late twentieth and early twenty-first centuries.

Now, let's get one important point out of the way. Both Canada and the United States have some valuable natural resources: Timber, iron, copper, coal, oil, precious metals. And they both have large agricultural sectors producing grain and beef and dairy products consumed internally and exported. So, one might think that it is this natural bounty that explains their success. But Argentina also grows wheat and has even more beef production; the same with Brazil and Uruguay. Venezuela and Mexico have lots of oil. And many places in South America and the Caribbean grew rich in the eighteenth and nineteenth centuries on the great sugar boom or, in the case of the Andes, the great silver boom. But no part of South America developed on the trajectory of North America. Indeed, easily acquired mineral wealth, such as New World silver, once again seems to be as much a curse as blessing. If places do not diversify their economies and become and remain innovative, they quickly exhaust their initial resource advantages. This is an issue we see again and again. Even the mineral wealth of North America required innovative efforts to make nature yield her bounty. There is also an important difference between resources that make the few, an elite, wealthy and those that benefit the many, promoting growth and development across a whole society.

Why did North America Make it, and not South America?

We can see this difference right away when we put ourselves back into the Americas around 1700. Then the smart money would have gone on Mexico or Peru, where silver was to be found, or in Barbados, or Jamaica, which were growing sugar, destined to be the world's first global commodity and even more valuable than silver. Over the course of the eighteenth and nineteenth centuries, demand for sugar skyrocketed. What had been a rare exotic became an item of everyday life. Insatiable demand for sweetness made Caribbean sugar planters wealthy, and sugar became a major source of business profits for Europe's merchant classes. Governments taxed the commodity to strengthen their fiscal budgets and build strong militaries. Sugar also drew people out of Africa, in the form of the horrific slave trade. Together, sugar plantations and the slave trade formed by the eighteenth century probably the largest industry in the world. By contrast, profits from the North American colonies were hardly registering in the minds, and on the ledgers of English, French, and Spanish monarchs and merchants. The northern colonies were minor backwaters with small populations producing some useful raw materials, but not places that made nations (and investors) rich.[6]

Even within North America, the center of wealth lay not with the cold climate colonies, but in the warm South. Like much of South America and the Caribbean, the southern colonies grew plantation crops: Tobacco in Virginia; rice in the Carolinas. Later, these same areas would turn land over to cotton, the next great commodity crop from the New World, eventually rivaling sugar for supremacy. The southern colonies also used slave labor, which was abolished or would soon be in most of the northern colonies. These southern colonies were, up to the American Revolution, the wealthiest and most valuable lands of the northern section of the New World.[7] Yet planation crops and slavery made the few wealthy and did not lead the transformation to an innovative society. For all the wealth and profits plantation economies generated, in the long run the dynamic and innovative parts of the New World grew up outside of those regions, in those places that had been regarded as the least profitable and least likely to succeed. [8]

The North had only one great advantage, an advantage that would become more and more significant over time. It gave opportunity to those who settled there and was a far more egalitarian society. Slave societies of course are by definition unequal, with those enslaved owning nothing, not even their own bodies. In the Caribbean and parts of South America, a relatively small handful of landowners and plantation masters lorded it over vast numbers of enslaved people, creating a society of tremendous inequality. Even the parts of Latin America that did not have slavery were much less egalitarian than North America. In places that retained a large indigenous population, such as Mexico and the Andes, Spanish policy permitted powerful and well-connected aristocrats or successful conquistadors to control large numbers of Indians, up to twenty thousand or more, who had to work for them on giant estates. This feudal-serf type arrangement meant that a tiny land-owning elite had most of the land and mineral wealth and a lot of coerced labor to extract value from these resources. Even after this *encomienda* system was abolished and replaced with private property ownership, the original Spanish grandees became owners of large haciendas. Land ownership remained concentrated and most people worked as landless peasant labor.[9]

By contrast, in North America, many people owned their own land and were able to participate in the market as free individuals. In this still agrarian world, the goal of most families was land and a family farm they could work and manage independent of any lord or overseer. That was one reason for moving to America from Europe. In the Old World most land remained in the hands of lords and aristocrats and most people were tenants or serfs. There was plenty of land and not enough labor to work it in the Americas. The Caribbean, Brazil, and other parts of South America solved this "labor problem" with slavery or with the coercion of the native population. The northern regions, which did have slavery for a time, soon abolished it and instead peopled their land with immigrants from Europe.

At first the immigrants who came to what would be the United States were not exactly free. Many, the majority in fact, came as indentured servants, some 75 percent before the American Revolution.[10] A financier paid their passage in exchange for a contract that bound their labor for seven years, sometimes more. The financier generally sold the labor contract (indenture) to a landowner who needed labor. Other arrivals from Europe came as convicts or were banished as punishment for some crime, often rebellion against the government as was the case for many who came from Ireland. And still others came completely voluntarily because they had few good options in the Old World. This influx of labor provided the energy and muscle to develop the lands and wealth of the North.

In a sense indentured servants are like slaves in that they have to work for others, compelled by law and under the supervision of another. But there was one big difference. While a slave was enslaved for life, as were his or her children, a servant was freed after seven years and his children were never enslaved. Slaves were considered chattel, property, and the owner could largely do what he pleased with them. He could move them to new lands, sell off family members, and use whipping, brutality, even death as a threat and means of control. Indentured servants by contrast had some protections, some limits on what a master could do. Now it might still seem a society where an elite owns most of the land and extracts labor from a much larger group that owns nothing and is compelled to work will become an unequal society, much like the slave plantations. But that is not what happened in North America, because landowners had to offer decent, even favorable terms to get the labor they needed. Seven years of work might seem harsh, but it was a far cry from what slaves endured. Life wasn't easy or luxurious of course, but in one famous incident a group of indentured servants in New England rebelled against what they considered the poor diet offered by their masters. So, a new law specified that servants could not be fed lobster more than three times per week.

The most important consequence of the bargaining position of the servants was that upon end of the contract they were given land, tools, clothes, and other necessities to start a life of freedom. Land soon became widely distributed in the North. Colonies used the headright system. Anyone who immigrated received a grant of land upon arrival, and often those who promoted immigration of others received additional land too.[11] The result was that in North America, in contrast to South America and even to a large extent the southern colonies of North America, land was more widely distributed and wealth much more equal. And that distinction, between equal and unequal, slave and free, set North America on a course that would build the institutions of innovation.

Democracy in (North) America

Over the years many pundits have believed that equal and democratic societies will be more innovative and grow faster than unequal and authoritarian ones.[12] It seems logical. Equality allows more people a chance and prevents an entrenched elite from benefiting themselves at the expense of newcomers and challengers who may have better ideas but lack capital and financing. Equality provides greater scope for entrepreneurship as it draws entrepreneurs from the broad base of the social pyramid, rather than from the small top. And great inequality, where most people own nothing and can barely feed themselves, is liable to leave a huge swath of the population so starved for human and financial capital that they cannot even try. Innovation benefits from having as many people as possible trying to make something new, because you do not know beforehand where the next big breakthrough will come from.

Authoritarian societies are likely to be fearful of innovation, especially if innovations well up from below. Change may challenge the power of the elite, who maintain their position by doling out opportunities and favors to friends and supporters and take kickbacks from the same group—crony capitalism at its finest. They don't want newcomers upsetting this applecart. So, it always seemed that democracy, equality, and innovation should go together, but how? What is the mechanism that links them? This is an especially pressing issue now when China, a communist society and a non-democratic one, seems to be moving ahead rapidly on so many technological and economic fronts. A look at the American experience offers some clues. American had a favorable, perhaps unique combination of political stability, ground in a founding constitution, as well as a strong commitment to democracy and equality of opportunity. While Americans sometimes failed to live up to the ideals—the nation had slavery and suffered a civil war after all—nonetheless it still exhibited the value an open and stable political system can have for innovation.

North America in the colonial period was perhaps the most equalitarian place on earth, more so certainly than its neighbors to the South, including the southern states of America. It was also possibly the most democratic.[13] In fact, it was democratic because it was equal. The economic underpinnings of democracy were its broad distribution of land and resources. Relatively equal incomes and access to resources helped to promote a much more democratic political system. This was not exactly what the founding fathers, who lauded freedom and rights, had in mind. They saw themselves as creating a republic—not a democracy. The well-to-do would provide the leadership and most states after the ratification of the Constitution still restricted voting to those who owned land or demonstrated a certain level of personal wealth. But with land ownership becoming more and more widely distributed more and more Americans, at least those who were white and male, could vote. This broad base of voters from the non-elite, plus the perpetual need to attract immigrants and labor from abroad, encouraged states to abolish voting restrictions. Immigrants were much more attracted to a nation where they could have a political voice, as well as an economic one. As voting restrictions fell, political participation and the percentage of those voting rose. In 1824 just 26 percent of the eligible population voted in elections, but as property and income qualifications on voting were stripped away, that percentage rose to 56 percent in 1828 and 78 percent by 1840.[14]

As the electorate expanded, economic policies themselves grew more democratic. That is, they encouraged innovation and entrepreneurship from the broad base of the population. It is an exaggeration to say that America was simply a land of opportunity. For women and African Americans there certainly was no opportunity. Even for Native Americans and, for a time at least, some immigrants such as Irish Catholics, opportunities could be limited by prejudice or poverty or even laws that barred them from certain occupations. Most men did not rise significantly above the social station of their fathers. The most highly successful Americans came from solidly middle and upper middle-class families to begin with. Characteristic rags to riches stories turn out, on closer inspection, to be less dramatic, more like a move from small town professional to member of the well-to-do merchant class, or from small merchant to wealthy financier, or from skilled mechanic to business owner. That said, America, the northern region of North America, still offered more opportunities for more people than could be found in Latin America or even the southern states, let alone most of Europe and the rest of the world. Most importantly, America had enough mobility and enough opportunity to keep the political system open and responsive to the interests of the non-elite.[15]

Both political parties of the nineteenth century, the Democrats and the Whigs (forerunners of the Republicans) embraced a politics of opportunity. Democratic presidents like Andrew Jackson could start out as landowning frontiersmen, buy more land, and in Jackson's case, slaves to work his land, and take that experience into the White House. His Democratic Party encouraged land sales to ordinary folks and the giving away of resources, even if those lands and resources were taken from the Native people like the Cherokees, who were forcibly pushed out of the way for white settlers. Jackson also encouraged the formation of banks to mobilize capital, state and local banks, and he abolished control of credit and the money supply by the federally chartered Bank of the United States. It was a policy that led to a rollicking and dynamic macro economy, including a significant recession in 1837, but also one that brimmed with opportunity for the ambitious speculator as an unchecked stream of money and credit flowed into the hands of western entrepreneurs.[16] The other side of this economic policy was represented by Abraham Lincoln. His origins were even more humble than Jackson's, though his father owned land and moved west with agricultural opportunity. Through self-improvement and education Lincoln made himself into a successful lawyer. His Whig, then Republican Party encouraged internal improvements, such as railroad, canal, and other infrastructure projects that connected markets, and the building of schools to promote human capital formation, as well as protective tariffs for America's infant industries.[17]

Financial Innovation and the American System

Before the outbreak of the Civil War, an empowered American electorate was voting in policies built around the embrace of innovation and opportunity, and voting out of existence any policies that encouraged control of resources by a small elite or that favored stability and tradition over change. The United States, for example, had a very open banking system. Most banks were chartered by states, and most states put in place "free banking" laws. Anyone could get a charter to open a bank just by applying. Before, each bank had to be approved individually by the legislature, a slow and cumbersome, and potentially corrupt process. In addition, there were many private banks that did not get state charters but merely operated on their reputation with the public. This was a risky but also very lucrative financial system, and access to finance is typically crucial to moving innovative efforts out of the idea or model stage into the market.[18]

By 1840 or so the number of banks and new corporate startups exploded. The U.S. had only 28 state-chartered banks in 1800 but had nearly 700 forty years later, plus an additional 200 private banks.[19] America had more banks per person and as a percentage of GDP than any other country. The contrast with other capital-poor developing countries such as Brazil, Mexico, or Argentina is striking. The U.S. had more banks in 1800 than Brazil did in 1888 or Mexico in 1900.[20] In Latin American nations, which were far less equal and had much less democratic political systems, financial institutions were fewer in number, hard to open, and mainly served the plantation and land-owning elite, an elite that had concentrated political power to prevent any move in the direction of democratic financing. In North America, a proliferation of banks, located in places of almost any size, provided easy access to financing for entrepreneurs.

What is interesting to note is that this openness to finance in America was encouraged even though it was not always the most efficient system. State charters and laws prevented branch banking in many places—policies that in some states would not be rescinded until the 1970s. The fear was that with branches, bigger city banks would soon dominate the financial landscape. Many local banks, on the other hand, would better serve local firms and entrepreneurs, and also offer opportunities for ambitious business people to start their own banks to mobilize capital for projects that would benefit their towns.[21] Branching, however, can be more efficient, as it allows one bank to consolidate and centralize back office operations and thus lower the cost of making loans.[22] But it wasn't efficiency Americans sought in finance, it was opportunity. And the very structure of the American political system encouraged this sort of financial and organizational innovation. Since states made the bank and corporate charters, states also competed with each other for business. This competitive federalism led to easier and easier chartering of banks and other businesses with fewer and fewer regulations and restrictions, much like today where state competition had led some states, notably South Dakota, to ease or erase restrictions on credit cards and interest rates, so that many, indeed most credit cards set up operations there.[23]

America's open banking system encouraged a raucous approach to financing, to be sure. The nineteenth century was filled with bank failures, fraudulent corporations, worthless stock, and counterfeit bank notes.[24] There was no central bank to regulate the money supply, once Andrew Jackson killed off the Bank of the United States. It seems a deep part of American culture to move between openness and speculation, and then take away the punch bowl to reign in the excesses. When the Republican Party took over the White House and Congress after the Civil War, it cut back on the open financial policies of the previous generation, passing laws that ended free banking and replaced loose state charters with tighter federal ones. To encourage bankers to get federal charters, the new laws put a tax on notes issued by state banks. At this time there was no Federal Reserve, so the money supply was created by individual banks issuing their own notes. For a time state banks went into decline, but in a decade or so they had bounced back. American financiers are apparently irrepressible innovators. The state bankers stopped depending on the heavily taxed paper currency and began using something new, the check. With this innovation, they came roaring back.[25] For better or worse America will likely remain a land of financial innovation, which will mean booms and busts and bubbles (not to mention fraud), but also a land of easy financing for innovators to bring ideas to market.

Education for Innovation

Financial capital is an important part of the innovation equation, but human capital matters as much if not more. And the United States quickly became very good at cultivating human capital through its extraordinary investments in education. Although high levels of formal education were not crucial to England's industrial breakthrough, over time industry grew more technical and innovators required greater skill and knowledge if they were to make original discoveries. As studies show, countries that follow a technological leader often need different resources than the first mover if they want to catch up. Education, it seems, was something that America, as well as Germany, leveraged to grow rapidly up to the technological standard England had set.[26] Even in England, moreover, technical knowledge, literacy, numeracy, and self-education had mattered to the class of entrepreneurs, engineers, mechanics, and fitters who made the early stages of industrialization possible. Wide diffusion of these skills and, increasingly, of formal, scientific, and technological knowledge would go even further in the United States in cultivating a broad and deep class of potential innovators. Nations that make skill acquisition and knowledge widely available were more likely to have an innovative population to draw on. Education, which throughout most of the world had largely been reserved for a small elite, became much more democratic in the early American Republic.

In 1870 only about 19 percent of the world's population was literate. Literacy was much higher in Europe. In England, the Netherlands, and Sweden it stood at 75 percent, and France was not far behind. But the United States matched and exceeded those levels. It also stood well above its neighbors in the Americas. Argentina only broke 50 percent literacy in 1900, and Brazil was still at 35 percent that same year.[27] Beyond basic literacy the United States also distinguished itself from most of the world with easy access to primary, secondary, and eventually higher education for its citizens. Some 60 percent of children enrolled in primary schools in the United States in 1840, levels that would rise rapidly until they hit just below 100 percent in 1865. Education was much harder for people to get elsewhere in the world, often requiring fees that exceeded the ability of working class and poor families to pay. In England, even primary schools charged tuition, so not surprisingly only about 20 percent of the British school-aged population enrolled in primary school. Enrollment rates in Latin America were even lower, around 6 percent. And of course education was extremely limited on slave plantations, including those in the southern United States, where teaching the enslaved to read was often illegal out of fear that literate slaves would be better able to plan and carry out rebellions. Only a handful of those held in slavery were even allowed to perform more intellectual forms of labor.[28]

Some of the U.S. educational advantage we can credit to culture, particularly in New England, where the religious dissenters who founded Massachusetts and other colonies brought with them a strong belief that all people had to be able to read and understand the bible. Religious motivation led the early colonists of New England to found schools. Little more than fifteen years after the Pilgrims arrived at Plymouth, they incorporated Harvard University in 1636. Higher education was needed to train preachers, as well as members of the learned professions—lawyers, doctors. Other American colonies followed suit, starting universities soon after the first colonists settled there. Education in America certainly had a religious aspect, but it had a secular side too, as in Europe: A belief in the power of human reason to address the needs of humankind.

Still, cultural motives were not sufficient to explain the extraordinarily broad commitment to public education that America embraced. Schools were free because Americans willingly taxed themselves to build schools and make them available to all citizens, or to new immigrant non-citizens for that matter. As new territories became part of the nation, they set aside land to pay for education. Towns seeking to grow and attract residents (one way to turn low priced raw land into a profitable commodity) offered quality schools free to all who settled there. In America's decentralized and fragmented political system, education was largely a state level concern, not a federal one. But states saw themselves in competition with other states, just as towns did with other towns, and they wanted to attract labor and capital and trade. As with the banks, this sort of competition drove education deeper into American society. Spending money on public education and founding institutions of higher learning was seen as a wise investment. And in America's highly democratic political system, voters were more than willing to vote for free schools for all. A more restricted electorate comprised mostly of the wealthy might have had a lot less incentive to do this, since the wealthy did not need public schools when they could pay for their own education.[29]

One interesting consequence of the American democratic education drive was that America was not in fact a low tax nation. Throughout the nineteenth century America had some of the highest tax revenues per capita of any major industrial nation, and far higher than its South American neighbors. By 1870, tax revenue of the national government per capita in the U.S. hit $11.4. In Europe, only England, Holland, and France collected more.[30] As a percentage of national income, only Peru, Brazil, and Argentina exceeded the United States in the Americas. Americans were essentially willing to tax themselves to build schools and other amenities that they believed promoted growth. They put public funds to many uses, supporting or subsidizing the construction of hospitals, hotels, opera houses, asylums, railroads, canals, roads, post offices—anything they saw as conducive to attracting settlers and migrants and improving the speed of travel, communications, and commerce.[31] Any thought that low taxes are the key to growth or innovation has to reckon with this American experience.

American states and cities could be quite innovative themselves when it came to providing the public basis for private enterprise. When the New York state legislature appropriated funds to dig the Erie Canal, it assured that the vast stream of agricultural commerce from the new lands of the Ohio River Valley would flow to New York City, cementing its place as the center of American commerce and finance. The canal connected New York to the Midwestern grain belt by way of the Hudson River and the Great Lakes, where commodities arrived on New York docks for shipment to Europe and elsewhere. Other port cities such as Philadelphia and Boston lost out. But one rival, Baltimore, struck back with a clever response. Baltimore helped to promote and finance a new technology, the railroad, to make an overland passage to the same markets served by the Erie Canal. The Baltimore and Ohio became one of the first interregional railroad networks in America.[32]

The American willingness to use public funds to develop human and physical capital and to improve the efficiency of the market was a reflection of the nation's egalitarian economy and democratic political system. When people, or at least a substantial part of them, had a voice in the decision-making and a stake in the economic outcome, they were willing to make these investments and pay taxes to do so. By contrast places where a small elite ran things and the majority of the population remained landless, illiterate peasants with little hope for improvement and no political voice were far less willing to pay taxes and make public investments. The wealthy elite with their favored insider status had little interest in encouraging entrepreneurship from those below them on the socio-economic scale. Even when taxes were imposed in these nations, they were paid more heavily by the poor than by the wealthy. In democratic North America, by contrast, voters not only voted to pay taxes, but they created a more progressive taxation system as well.

Industrial Innovation

By the middle of the nineteenth century the United States had in place the policies and the attributes of an innovative society. Although it had started out as a colony of an empire that was itself a leading center of innovation, after the war for independence it industrialized rapidly and caught up to its former mother country. Some of this rapid convergence reflected America's connections of language, culture, and trade, which seems to have help forge bonds of trust between the business people and entrepreneurs (and state governments) of the new nation and capital-rich British investors looking for a place to put their money. America had little trouble attracting foreign investment from the first industrial nation, and it also had good access to the information, knowledge, and technology that its British cousins had already developed.[33] These ties across the Atlantic, if frayed by independence and friction for a time (unresolved issues led to the War of 1812, when the British burned down the White House), also helped to encourage the movement and migration of talented British people to North America.

The best example of this sort of immigration was Samuel Slater. Following a pattern of movement already seen in Europe, Slater, a mechanic in one of the early British textile mills, heard about the interest of Americans in the new textile machines. Knowing that it was illegal to export plans and designs, he memorized as much as he could and, passing himself off as a common farm laborer, boarded a ship for America in 1789. Once in the New World, he struck up a partnership with merchant Moses Brown, who had opened a textile mill in Pawtucket, Rhode Island. With Brown's financing, Slater built and adjusted the machinery and organized and directed the labor of the mill according to experience he had gained in England. For his work in transferring technology, Slater was called in his homeland "Slater the Traitor," but innovation often involves the movement of ideas, practices, technologies, and processes from the place they were first created to societies eager to learn from the leaders.

Americans themselves took part in this innovative process as well. In 1810 Frances Cabot Lowell, a successful Boston merchant, travelled to

Lancaster, England and Scotland to view the new power loom technology of the textile industry. Though not permitted to make sketches of what he saw, he memorized the workings of the machines and brought back the plans in his head. Once again, the movement of technology and innovation travelled through the movement of people, much as we saw with Chinese inventions funneled to the world through Islam. Lowell formed an alliance with several prominent New England backers, notably merchant and financier Nathan Appleton, who provided the funds to build a new industrial town, named Lowell, in Massachusetts. Raised from the ground up, this mill town integrated spinning and weaving into a factory system, a major advance of American manufacturing.[34] The New England region was soon home to other textile plants, and America, with access to its southern- grown cotton, was producing some 112 million yards of cloth by 1830.[35]

Several features of this story are notable for how they illustrate the American approach to innovation. First, they show how a group of successful merchants, though wealthy from trade, was willing to risk their capital in a new technology and a new venture. This sort of entrepreneurial mobility, which was also evident in early British industrialization, is an important part of the process whereby ideas gain financing and organizational and managerial support to move to full execution. In general America did not rely on the sort of financing methods that other places did when trying to play catchup—the universal banks of Germany, the trading companies of Japan. Instead, the American pattern was more decentralized, more competitive, and made use of widely available but locally oriented banks and credit. Secondly, private capital, and indeed people themselves, were willing to leave declining locations or pursue new, potentially higher profit opportunities when they arose. Both people and capital, and ideas too, were extremely mobile in America, which was an important aspect of the innovative spirit of the land.

The Northeast and New England, for example, had originally been agricultural economies. New England farmers even grew wheat, despite their rocky soil, and sold it in an interregional trade that took it to the southern colonies and the Caribbean, as well as to Europe. But once the American Revolution ended and the rich soils of the Ohio Valley across the Appalachian

Mountains were brought under the plough, farmers in the Northeast could not compete and shifted into other things, such as dairy farming. Others simply pulled up stakes and moved to the new lands to start afresh, an exodus that emptied out large sections of New England and New York for Ohio, Indiana, and Illinois and later points further west. This process of agricultural mobility, moving from old land to fresh fertile land, is one reason America has remained part of the global breadbasket. But mobility also helped to allocate resources so that new industries could grow up in the places left behind by the westward movement. It was in the Northeast and in the Great Lakes region of the Midwest that American industry and manufacturing began to flourish.

By the middle of the nineteenth century America was not just catching up with Britain technologically, it was developing its own distinctive industrial and technological culture. It was pushing industrial technology beyond that achieved in the first industrial nation, through a distinctive "American System" of mass production. The American system was defined by a strong emphasis on machine-made parts of standard design, what became known as interchangeable parts. Rather than hand fit in artisanal fashion the individual pieces of a musket for example, American manufacturers turned out machine-made precision parts in large quantities, all standardized so that any one part could be used in final assembly. Barrel, gun stock, gun lock were all made this way and then quickly and efficiently put together. This system combined with Adam Smith's idea for the division of labor (his famous pin factory example, which still used hand production of the pin parts), anticipated the assembly line system finally perfected and made famous by Henry Ford a century or so later. In fact, Ford's automobile factory was as much a continuation, elaboration, and improvement on practices that could be traced back to the 1820s and 30s as it was a breakthrough.[36]

The crucial factor in this system of production was not just the line of assembly, often used to represent the entire process because of its striking imagery, but the preceding process of mass-manufacturing the highly precise parts that made assembly lines possible. To assure this level of precision, parts had to be machine-made: Turned on lathes, drilled with presses, milled, ground, stamped, and bent using machine tools. The British had been the first to develop an extensive machine tool sector, particularly after the advent of inexpensive iron and steel that replaced softer wood for mechanical devices. Americans, however, quickly built up their own extensive and innovative machine tool industry in the nineteenth century, and the resulting devices were deployed in making all manner of complex products: From clocks to typewriters to sewing machines to locomotive engines.

As with other high-level innovations, the American System was soon studied and copied world-wide. American machine tools were regarded as some of the best in the world, and by the mid-nineteenth century American makers were shipping them to many other countries.[37] Germany, Japan and other late following nations took this same path, first purchasing then developing on their own the machine tools to feed their industrial sector and starting mass production factories. Nations that wanted to compete had to stay on top of advances in manufacturing systems and over time, even small innovations and adjustments added up to significant improvements.[38] In manufacturing, for example, the Japanese improved on the American system of mass production in the twentieth century. Firms such as Toyota, originally a maker of looms for Japan's early textile industry, devised the just-in-time system, which improved efficiency of assembly and reduced both time and mistakes on the assembly line. Along with Henry Ford's breakthrough earlier in the twentieth century, the Japanese system was probably the most important innovation in manufacturing history, and it has now been adopted around the world for cars and other products.[39]

An Entrepreneurial Culture

The growth of America's manufacturing economy owed its success to an entrepreneurial culture that could be quite ruthless when it came to financial opportunity and change. Like England before it, America benefited from a strong internal market. Land purchases and conquests from France, Spain, Mexico, and Native Americans gave the United States a continental-sized market by the middle of the nineteenth century. Of course, other nations in the Americas also have lots of land and a big geographical market space, but that alone does not make for a strong internal market. Here U.S. government policy helped. The United States Constitution, through its commerce clause, prevented any state, territory, region, or city from stopping or inhibiting the flow of trade and commerce. Any purely local protection that was designed to favor, say, St. Louis over Kansas City or to prevent products from Massachusetts from reaching consumers in Alabama would be struck down by the courts. While the national government did institute tariffs to protect American manufacturing from external competitors, it did not prevent the internal flow of trade, capital, labor, and goods, assuring that competition between places would be quite fierce. One consequence was that demand for goods was homogeneous in America. That is, for many products consumers in the Northeast, South, or Far West did not demand or expect distinctive versions or exhibit unique patterns of consumption. Any producer therefore could pretty much be assured of reaching the entire population. Add to that the strong commitment on internal improvements that reduced transportation costs and you had an America that even by the mid-nineteenth century constituted a market that few other nations could match.

Government policy also aided this process in another way. As we have seen in the seventeenth and eighteenth centuries, America was land and resource rich but capital and labor poor. Encouragement of immigration and settlement (and also for the South, slavery) helped to overcome the labor constraint. An open and free immigration policy continued throughout the nineteenth and early twentieth centuries. There were essentially no laws governing who could come or how they could come, with one exception: The Chinese after the passage of the Chinese Exclusion Act in 1882. While nineteenth-century Americans had as many prejudices against aliens and neighbors practicing different ways and different religions as any other people, this did not stop or even slow the stream of immigration. The need for labor, both manual and skilled, overcame most prejudice against people. By 1850 annual immigration had risen fast, reaching about 1.5 percent of the U.S. population, the highest level in the nation's history. Over the next half century, the absolute number of foreign-born residents would rise significantly, hovering around 14-15 percent of total population, trailing off after immigration restrictions were imposed after 1920.[40]

The strength of the American System, following the model laid down by England, was the close relationship between communities of technologists, skilled mechanics, inventors, and firms that actually produced and executed their innovations. Even more so than England, America's vast and diversified economic geography created places of networking and innovation, well in advance of Silicon Valley. There was brass valley around Waterbury, Connecticut, where specialist firms made all manner of brass fixtures and hardware. Nearby lay precision valley in the vicinity of Springfield, Vermont, where many of America's machinists and machine tool makers congregated. Providence, Rhode Island housed the American jewelry industry, especially mass-produced and semiprecious jewelry. Trenton, New Jersey and upstate New York served as the pottery sheds of the nation.[41] The American landscape offered many such opportunities for innovators to set up shop and share information and knowledge with others doing the same thing. Through these networks they learned about markets, technologies, demand, sources of supply, skilled labor and the like. They could also draw on needed services and inputs to the final goods, creating a localized and very efficient production chain. It was this pattern that America would repeat again and again, from Detroit's rise as the center of automobiles and automobile supply firms to the late twentieth century emergence of the Bronx as the headquarters of the new hip hop music scene.[42]

By the late nineteenth century, the United States had developed a formidable ability to innovate in all sorts of industries and sectors. It had connected its dynamic financial sector with its high level of human capital and state and federal policies that encouraged innovation and market integration. Innovation valleys and innovation cities provided crucial connections that stimulated competition among firms. It was a Darwinian struggle that only the best could survive but it also replicated Darwin's other important concept, the tangled bank of mutually supportive firms, customers, suppliers, and labor. There was also one final ingredient in this heady innovation culture, one that distinguished the United States from its former parent model of England—strong property rights for innovators.

While patents had not proved substantially important to England as the breakthrough industrial nation, the United States exploited a strong patent system that had existed from the ratification of the Constitution. Whereas most of the innovations in England had been made by first movers who reckoned that patenting only revealed valued information and trade secrets to the public, American innovators were a much more diverse and entrepreneurial lot. English innovation drew heavily upon the skills of employed fitters, mechanics, and technicians, who worked in established enterprises. America established a similar model, as did all follower nations. But America also had a strong group of independent inventors who made use of patent and property rights to protect what they created and earn a profit from it. Not only was patenting relatively inexpensive in the United States, but a number of support mechanisms arose in order to aid in the process. In the early nineteenth century, Philadelphia founded The Franklin Institute. Like other mechanics and institutes found in Europe and the United States it had an educational and informational mission, helping to spread knowledge of breakthroughs in science and technology to would be inventors, especially those who lacked formal education. But it also encouraged those inventors by examining worthy discoveries, holding contests, and awarding prizes to the most meritorious new ideas. Besides offering cash bonuses, the prizes and medals helped to draw the public's attention, and often financial capital, to the independent inventor.[43]

By the 1880s and 90s, patent lawyers and professional patent agents both helped inventors gain patent protection and also promoted a trade and market in intellectual property that diffused innovations and provided a source of profit to inventors. Indeed, U.S. inventors had in some ways the best of both worlds. While the nation's patent system protected them from imitators and copiers, it did not work especially hard to protect holders of foreign patents from U.S. imitators. So, Americans could, on the one hand, gain access to innovations made elsewhere, as in the manner of Samuel Slater or Frances Cabot Lowell. But then American inventors could take their improvements or inventions to the U.S. patent office to secure protection in the American market. This same pattern, of catching up by copying until an indigenous inventive sector is well established, is very much in line with how China has progressed over the past several decades.[44]

Inventing as a Way of Life

In these ways America made the business of inventing broad and "democratic." Almost half of the inventors of the early decades of industrialization had only basic education (though an education that was free and easy to come by in America). Many were engineers, machinists, or full-time inventors. Especially after the Civil War, America became famous for its great independent inventors. Some were native born, like Thomas Edison or Elisha Gray; others were immigrants such as Nicola Tesla and Charles Steinmetz.[45] This is a part of the American inventive landscape that has remained, even as corporations and established firms became a major part of the American economy. Individuals, rather than corporations, filed the majority of patents through the 1930s, and even today, where the vast majority of patents go to for-profit companies, some 9-13 percent is issued to individuals, the second largest category.[46]

With all of these supporting pillars firmly entrenched, the American System proved extremely effective at building a thriving industrial economy. In 1830, the United States was well below Britain and even below Germany in the share of the world's industrial output. Those figures changed fast. By 1880 it had surpassed Germany, despite Germany's own rapid industrialization and was on a beeline to overtake Britain, which it did before the start of the twentieth century. Innovation had transformed America into the world's most industrial nation. It is no surprise, therefore, that around 1900 a spate of books appeared with titles like *The American Invasion* and *The Americanization of the World*.[47]

But just as importantly, innovation also occurred in other sectors, including agriculture and natural resources. Just as today the information economy does not only mean computers and IT but the transformation of a whole host of businesses, ranging from finance and services to even agriculture, so in the nineteenth and twentieth centuries innovation was crucial to American success in a range of endeavors beyond manufacturing.[48] America's great mineral wealth, for example, and fertile agricultural lands were not dramatically larger or better than other places such as Brazil, Venezuela, or Argentina. None of those places grew as the United States did.

And part of the reason was that the United States did a much better job of *exploiting* the natural resources that it had. In developing natural resources, the United States benefited from strong innovation and entrepreneurship that turned minerals and land into actually productive assets. In petroleum, coal, copper, iron ore, zinc, lead, tungsten and many other minerals the United States was the world leader not so much because it had more reserves in the ground, but because it was better at finding and exploiting what it had. One might even say that innovation made the nation rich in the bounty of nature, rather than the bounty of nature making the nation rich.[49]

The Southern Counterexample

We can see the effects of the conditions and policies that promote innovation even more clearly by looking at this variation *within* the United States. The innovative powerhouse of America was in the northern states. There, freedom, opportunity, and democracy were strong, in stark contrast to the southern states. Though politically and culturally tied to the rest of North America, the South had a far different experience when it came to innovation. Like parts of Latin America and the Caribbean, the southern United States lacked the conditions for that combination of democracy, equality, and opportunity that flourished in the North. It held on to its slave-based economy tenaciously, to the point of fighting a civil war to preserve it. The southern commitment to slavery reflected the fact that slave labor was highly profitable—for the owner. It was in fact a perfect example of an economic system that can produce wealth for the few but not for society as a whole.[50]

At one time, before the American Revolution, the slave states were the wealthiest and seemingly most economically advanced part of North America, producing valuable global commodities—rice, tobacco, and eventually cotton. Slave-grown cotton made a small number of very large planter-slave owners quite rich, even as the southern states as a whole fell economically further and further behind the North.[51] The reasons for this pattern are clear: The South lacked the pillars of innovation that were being erected in the North. Southern educational levels were far lower than in the North. The South did not make the investments in railroads and other transportation infrastructure to nearly the same degree as the North, usually content simply to build lines that moved cotton from interior to port. By contrast the northern internal improvements strategy connected a vast internal market and provided the basis for the innovative spaces of a diversified economic geography. Not surprisingly the South had far fewer patents per capita than the North, and the region lacked heavy industry or the machine specialists that the North was developing. These conditions all but guaranteed it would lose the Civil War that soon erupted.[52]

Some southern promoters recognized that the South was falling behind and advocated indigenous industrialization, but slavery stood in their way. The small, elite slavocracy had enough power to restrict spending and investments to those things that enhanced its wealth and position, mainly based on the cotton economy. It was far less willing to provide for the general welfare that would have enhanced human capital across a broad sector of society. There was much less need to attract immigrants to take up land, given that slavery provided an abundant and mobile labor supply. Making the sorts of changes that promoted diversification, education, opportunity, and the like was seen by the slave-owners as potentially dangerous. Widespread education, if available to the enslaved, might just encourage them to run away, or foment rebellion. A society predicated on the violent enslavement of people had to dedicate itself to repression, not innovation and change, for fear that the enslaved would one day rise up. These conditions worked against innovation, openness, entrepreneurship, and creative destruction that can be found in the most rapidly advancing economies.

There was finally one more price the South paid that cost it dearly when it came to innovation. A large swath of the southern population, the African American part, was given little opportunity to contribute its skills, talents, and creativity in the economy. In the North, immigrants may have come as indentured servants or as penniless workers, but nothing stopped the talented from moving beyond their immediate station in life. And even less stood in the way of their children. This was not true for the great part of the working class of southern slaves. However hard life was and however limited the opportunity in the North, it was all but nonexistent for the African population of the South.

How much innovation was lost due to slavery? We can never do a full accounting, but we do have some hints. We know, for example, that the first profitable crop in the South was rice, which came to the New World through the talents and efforts of Africans, who though enslaved still carried their knowledge of the crop from Africa where it had long been cultivated.[53] They were the ones who adapted it to American soil conditions, another case of the small but crucial improvements and changes made by anonymous workers and craftspeople throughout history. All sorts of African cultural traditions have been woven into the fabric of America, from cuisine to music, to crops, even if the people who carried these traditions were largely prevented from profiting from them. We also have a few tantalizing cases of innovation from Africans who, despite being enslaved, nonetheless were able to demonstrate their abilities in the marketplace.[54]

Although many of those enslaved spent their lives confined to labor on large cotton plantations that did not mean they lacked skills or creative abilities. Many were skilled at trades ranging from carpentry to blacksmithing, to boat building, fishing, hunting, and trapping. Others, often women, were able to grow food on small plots of land on the plantation—owners encouraged this as a way to cut down the cost of maintaining their human property—and sell the excess in lively vegetable markets run by the enslaved themselves. Others acquired money when allowed to "hire their own time." When slaves had a valuable skill, at say carpentry or ship caulking, the owner might allow them to earn money by practicing their trade for wages, in exchange for a percentage of what they earned. Simply ordering them to work for others and confiscating all their wages would have undermined incentive to maximize earnings. So, better to split the income. Perhaps there is no clearer example of the American commitment to property rights and its value for innovation than this. Though a slave owner had almost absolute power over those he kept enslaved, down to the right to inflict serious punishment and even death, he could not simply take any property that the slave owned, including his wages from hiring his own time.

When given the chance, and the chances were few, African Americans were able to act as entrepreneurs and innovators just as other Americans. Consider the case of an enslaved man in Kentucky known only as Free Frank. We do not know much about him, including his full name because he was illiterate and was born into slavery. But neither his lack of formal education nor his lowly status stopped him from observing an opportunity, assessing the market conditions, and executing his plan. Hiring his own time, Free Frank used it to mine and sell saltpeter, the crucial ingredient of gunpowder. When the War of 1812 broke out gunpowder was in fierce demand and the price of saltpeter rose rapidly. Free Frank was able to make enough money to begin the slow process of acquiring his freedom and buying the freedom of his wife and children. Once all the family was free, they moved to Illinois, where Free Frank, now free for sure, acquired land and laid out a new town. He called it New Philadelphia, after William Penn's famous city—a new city of brotherly love for free African Americans, and anyone else, could move, settle, and buy one of the subdivided land parcels. He built a church, hotel, and, of course, a school just after the American fashion of real estate development and town building in the nineteenth century. Free Frank in short was a classic American entrepreneur of the era, taking advantage of abundant land, building institutions to attract settlers, subdividing raw land to turn a profit, just as so many of his white counterparts were doing.[55]

This was an extraordinary case to be sure, but we do not know how many other Free Franks were trapped in slavery and never had a chance to put their talents to full use. We do know that the South, and all slave societies, fell behind and remained behind the free and more democratic regions like the North. While the North went through the creative-destructive process of developing new industries and technologies, the Southern slave states were both less innovative and increasingly less wealthy, with such wealth as they had increasingly inequitable. Even after the end of slavery the South remained the least industrial, least technologically sophisticated, least inventive and poorest region of the United States, well into the twentieth century. Slavery, and its attendant social features of violence, inequality, and underdeveloped human capital, was both a moral blight and an economic drag on those places that practiced it.

Expanding the Machinery of Innovation

Over time the United States did not merely take advantage of its early investments and policies promoting innovation, it expanded them, particularly as more and more innovation benefited from higher levels of scientific and technical skill and knowledge. The nation's innovation system by 1900 rested on multiple interlocking pillars: Public and private educational institutions; government agencies designed to promote industry and agriculture; a strong patent system for independent inventors; a buoyant financial sector; and increasingly a highly innovative corporate sector. Let's look at each of these in turn.

After the Civil War the United States developed its famous land grant colleges and universities, which brought higher education and technical training to a broad swath of the population, much as had been done with primary and secondary education before the War. The new universities, open to men and women for low or minimal tuition, not only increased human capital at a time when more and more work required higher levels of technical skills and knowledge, but also provided practical assistance with agriculture, mining, and engineering to the private sector. Over time these universities, University of Michigan, University of California, University of Wisconsin, and as well as transformed private institutions such as The Johns Hopkins University, Harvard, Yale, Princeton and technically-oriented schools such as MIT and Cal Tech, became among the best in the world, leaders in scientific and other areas of research.[56] The open system of immigration encouraged scientists, intellectuals, and thought leaders from around the world to come and live in America as well.

The immediate effect of this expansion of the university sector was that by 1900 the United States had a higher percentage of college graduates than most other nations. The university system also provided a platform for public funding for basic research, the kind that private actors usually would not pay for because it was so basic that it could not be easily commercialized. This work reached into many corners of the economy, showing how "high tech" did not necessarily mean a narrow concentration of innovation on a few new areas. Some of the best examples in the U.S. case, for example, came in agriculture. A combination of state universities and federal and government departments helped to spread scientific advances in farming and technologies such as hybrid seeds. The seed story perfectly illustrates the coming together of the modern forces of innovation in America. Experiments in genetics and crossbreeding at Cold Spring Harbor, a private laboratory funded by philanthropy from industrialist Andrew Carnegie, led to early breakthroughs in hybrid corn, which were further developed at agricultural experiment stations of the U.S. Department of Agriculture attached to universities. Henry Wallace, educated in agriculture at Iowa State University and a future vice president of the United States, produced the first commercial hybrid maize, and founded the Hi-Bred Corn Company (still in business today as Pioneer Hi-Bred) to market the new strains of seeds.[57] Universities, government and non-government organizations, and private entrepreneurs helped to usher in the "green revolution" not only in the United States, but eventually the whole world.

Maintaining Leadership in the Twentieth Century

By the start of the twentieth century, the United States had introduced important modifications of the patterns of innovation that had started in the early industrial economy of England. Most notable was the growing role of large-scale corporations. American firms in the industrial sectors grew into large corporate entities, increasingly owned by multiple passive shareholders and managed and run by full-time, salaried professional managers. These corporate giants integrated multiple stages of production, from raw material to finished product under one roof, or under one corporation at least. By bringing together the stages of production they went one better on Adam Smith and his division of labor. In the factory, labor might be divided for the sake of efficiency and productivity, to be sure, the old American system. But under corporate management all the parts of the productive process were controlled and coordinated, enabling large corporations to increase the rate of output and taking advantage of economies of scale to dramatically lower the price of crucial goods. In the petroleum industry, John D. Rockefeller's

Standard Oil Corporation dropped the price of kerosene (the most important refined product before the automobile and gasoline) by some 90 percent. In steel, Andrew Carnegie did likewise, becoming the lowest cost steel producer in the world by 1900. A bit later, Henry Ford picked up the old American system and integrated the production of car parts and assembly of cars on his assembly line to radically decrease the cost of a car. In 1909 Ford made over 10,000 cars, which sold for $825 each, about $23,000 in today's dollars. By 1925 he was making just under 2 million cars a year, at $260, or $3,600 in today's money.[58]

American corporations and their productive processes were studied, copied, and adapted by all industrial nations, from England to Germany, France, Sweden, and Japan. They marveled at the productive power of what they soon called "Fordism." But it wasn't just one model. America, and other industrial nations, adapted and devised a host of industrial innovations that ranged from large-scale mass production to skilled, specialized production emphasizing changing styles, designs, and market needs. The American economic landscape was vast and varied enough to sustain firms both large and small, industries that ran on large scale and industries that ran at small scale. It had industries where labor was organized and divided on the assembly line, and industries where workers were skilled and experienced mechanics and craftspeople.[59]

In this economy, the talented and entrepreneurial could start out at one place and move to another where opportunity beckoned. Or they could start out in one industry and see opportunities to adapt their capital, skills, labor, and technology to pioneer a new business. For example, in 1893 Frederick Maytag was a reasonably successful maker of agricultural equipment. His most notable product was a self-feeder for threshing machines that greatly reduced the chance of injury or death to workers. Although the company was soon the world's number one producer of this technology, demand for the equipment was seasonal, which meant that Maytag often had to lay off their most skilled workers and mechanics in the slow season. Looking for ways to keep them occupied and employed, Maytag came up with a version of the washing machine, then a new household product.[60] In 1922 Maytag engineer Howard Snyder developed an improved agitator, a design that proved so robust that Maytag washing machines soon acquired a reputation for dependability, so much so that the company gave up farm equipment and moved into washing machines and consumer durables full time.

There is a similar story behind the American pioneering of the airplane at the beginning of the twentieth century. The Wright brothers did not start out with an airplane in mind, exactly. They ran a successful bicycle manufacturing company in Dayton, Ohio, one of those industrial networks that drew together lots of mechanical, engineering, and inventive talent. Bicycles were a new phenomenon, with fantastic public interest and demand. As they hit the market, consumers, men and women, gobbled up the first personal transportation device beyond the horse. Bicycles used the same American system of production of standardized machine-made parts and assembly that had been pioneered in the nineteenth century and would continue under Henry Ford. In fact, some bicycle makers would also transition to automobile manufacturing by developing a number of the important machines and machining techniques needed for the production of automobiles. And for the Wright brothers, knowledge of gears, chain drives, and even aerodynamics, balance and control, led them to their great flying machine breakthrough as well.[61]

One of the great strengths of the American technological landscape was that it contained these multiple points of entry for inventors. Sometimes, an invention led to the start of a new company to carry out and profit from the original idea. This was the case with George Eastman, who invented roll film for cameras, then invented the Kodak, an inexpensive mass-produced camera to use the film, and founded and ran the Kodak Company that made, marketed, and sold film and cameras.[62] Other times, independent inventors were more interested in selling what they created to another firm and just collecting patent royalties for their work. And still other innovators exhibited both traits.

Perhaps the most famous example of the last is Thomas Edison. He set up a virtual invention factory in Menlo Park and then West Orange, New Jersey, where he brought together engineers, mechanics, designers, mathematicians, and those with formal training in physics and chemistry. Much of Edison's work was directed toward solving bottlenecks or problems in existing products or industries—a better stock ticker for Wall Street, a durable filament for incandescent lamps. Other work was directed towards creating products for which demand did not yet exist. So, Edison, often thought of as the solitary inventor, really devised an entire organization focused on innovation. He was as much an entrepreneur and businessperson as an inventive genius. He sought to capitalize on patents by organizing his own companies to market what his mind had come up with. Besides inventing the motion picture camera and projector he started a company to make both the equipment and also to produce early pictures. Likewise, his phonograph was produced and sold by the Edison Phonograph Company. He not only perfected incandescent lamps, but also built and sold electric power generating equipment and set up one of the first generating stations to provide electricity to homes and offices in New York. Edison was not a manager; he usually assigned his patents to the companies he helped to found and, like a venture capitalist, went back to his invention factory to come up with other products that he could sell another day. Like his savvy contemporaries, such as Alexander Graham Bell, Elisha Gray, Elmer Sperry, and Nicola Tesla, Edison was very good at the research and development business, itself a new concept—continual research and work to either develop new technologies or improve or perfect existing ones. [63]

By the early twentieth century, the uniquely American innovation ecosystem was bringing together inventors with a host of other talents in an organizational form that could execute and sell increasingly sophisticated technological products. Just consider one example of how this worked—electrification. Besides Edison, other inventors of the time were also at work on this technology. Elihu Thompson, an immigrant from England, founded with his old high school science teacher the Thompson-Houston Company. The business took off when they brought into it Charles Coffin as CEO. Coffin's skills were in marketing, a crucial skill for successfully launching a new technology. Coffin had made and sold shoes at his uncle's shoe factory in Lynn, Massachusetts, so he was not an inventor, a scientist, nor an electrical engineer. But he grew the company and by 1892 the Thompson-Houston Company, makers and sellers of electric power systems, merged with Edison's own electric company to form General Electric, using financing provided by the famed investment banker J. P. Morgan. Morgan himself had been one of the first customers for electricity in New York at his private residence. Coffin ran General Electric for the next twenty years.[64]

Elihu Thompson, like Thomas Edison, did not play an active role in company management. Both men continued to concentrate on inventing, Thompson ending up with some 700 patents to Edison's 1,000. Indeed, after the GE merger Thompson moved back to Massachusetts and started what became the General Electric research laboratory, hiring a number of brilliant engineers and scientists to work with him, including the German immigrant Charles Steinmetz. The GE story, like Edison's, reveals the way that the United States had by the turn of the twentieth century developed a new and more complex ecology of innovation that brought in organization and a specialized division of inventive labor. This ecosystem drew on the multitude of human resources American society could provide: Independent inventors with practical, hands on skills, trained engineers and mechanics working for industry, scientists employed in industrial research laboratories, and it combined them with investment bankers, professional managers, and clever marketers to both create and bring to the marketplace new or improved products, processes, and technologies. The pillars of American innovation were expanding.

As corporations grew, they added another leg to the inventive table. While independents and startups were crucial for making breakthroughs or founding new firms or even whole industries, existing large firms began to routinize the process of innovation. They diversified into new lines of business, leveraging their technology and market knowledge, and harnessing the talents of their skilled technical people. DuPont, for example, had been started in 1802 by Eleuthera Irenee du Pont, a French immigrant fleeing religious persecution. What began as a family-owned firm producing black powder for firearms and explosives expanded by 1920 into a host of new product lines and industries. Taking advantage of its strengths in chemistry and other branches of science, DuPont was able to move into synthetic fibers, plastics, pesticides, solvents and paints, among other areas. Increasingly science and not just on-the-job skills mattered to innovation, and DuPont like many other corporations opened and funded a large research laboratory hiring men (almost always men) educated at the new American graduate schools in scientific and engineering fields.[65]

Large firms could provide the combination of money, managerial talent, and marketing push that good ideas needed to come to fruition. A significant portion of the corporate "research" budget therefore was spent on development and engineering, particularly process engineering that transformed the first model of a new thing into a mass-produced, low cost, consumable item. Bell Labs, perhaps the most famous corporate laboratory in history, won nine Nobel Prizes for its fundamental research, but it spent about 70 percent of its budget on development rather than research.[66] Developmental work plus production and process engineering were crucial to improving the functioning and lowering the cost of telephone service, incremental rather than radical breakthrough innovations. As a result of improvements in the capacity of transmission systems and the automation of switching systems, however, the United States enjoyed a low-cost telephone system, and American consumers had more telephones than the rest of the world combined.

This pattern was repeated in multiple industries in the United States in the twentieth century. The British scientist Sir Alexander Fleming may have discovered penicillin, but it was a unique collaboration between the American pharmaceutical companies and the U.S. government during World War II that discovered how to mass-produce the first successful antibiotic. Merck, Pfizer, Lederle and Squibb worked together to develop new ways of mass-producing enormous amounts of this new lifesaving drug—646 billion units *per month* by 1945, enough to supply the U.S. and British military forces as well as civilians. Much as in other industries at this time, the intellectual universe of medical science was rapidly shifting and developing strong ties to academia and even government as never before.[67]

It was not necessary to win prizes to be successful at innovation in America. Before World War II, far more Noble Prizes went to Europeans than Americans, though that would change after World War II (in part because of the arrival of immigrant European scientists and intellectuals in America). Meanwhile American education, American inventors, and

American corporations focused much more on practical and commercial innovations.

American Innovation Since World War II

After World War II the United States' position in the world had changed dramatically from forty years earlier. No longer was it absorbing capital from abroad, now it was sending American capital overseas as a creditor nation. During the War, U.S. productive capacity had launched the nation from a second-rate power to the most powerful military on earth as American factories churned out flotillas of ships and clouds of planes, while keeping the Allies fed with American grain. The Arsenal of Democracy, it is fair to say, won the War, even beyond the contribution of American soldiers on the ground.[68] The U.S. aviation industry, far behind the advanced aircraft designs of Britain, Germany, and Japan at the start of the conflict, became the largest in the world and quickly mastered and began mass-producing jet airplanes, a technology originally pioneered by Britain. At the same time, helped by the arrival of many Jewish scientists fleeing the Nazis, the American Manhattan Project produced a fundamental breakthrough with the development of the Atomic bomb.[69] By 1950 the United States was by far the leading industrial economy of the world, with over 40 percent of global output, and its productivity the highest in the world, nearly double that of Great Britain.[70] Following the example of the Manhattan Project, the U.S. developed "big science" projects that drew together universities, government agencies, and large corporations, projects that generated both fundamental knowledge and useful innovations. [71] France, Britain, Germany, Japan and other nations sought to learn and emulate the virtues of this American system of innovation and deal with what they feared was an unstoppable American challenge to their economies.

One of the new features of the postwar innovation ecosystem was a greater role and presence of government. Government had always played a role in innovation, as we have seen. Government set the framework for markets, including property rights, passed regulations on what was and what was not legal, established standards, managed weights and measures, and provided basic public information on matters ranging from geography to population to the weather. In America and other second wave industrializers such as Germany, governments also set up tariffs that protected emerging industries so they could grow without being overshadowed by firms in the early industrializing nations, policies replaced after World War II with a strong commitment to free trade across the globe. Most primary, secondary, and a good portion of higher education was either provided by governments or paid for in indirect ways through private institutions. But now governments, both in the United States and much of the rest of the advanced industrial world, began to take an even more direct hand in sponsoring innovation.

The United States created the Office of Scientific Research and Development in 1941, the Centers for Disease Control in 1946, the National Science Foundation in 1950, and the National Institutes of Health (originally founded in 1887), which provided billions of dollars to researchers to work on basic and applied science, engineering, and medicine.[72] The military gave substantial funding to veterans to allow them to access higher education. It also used its vast budget to procure from private firms, with the help of university researchers, weapons systems. This spending encouraged research in fields such as aerospace, computers, and satellites, among others. The Space Race provided a budget for the development of such technologies too, most notably smaller computers that would be needed on the trip to the moon. For a time, military, space, and more mundane government agencies such as Social Security were the most important consumers of digital computers, providing needed support for this emerging technology.[73] Some of this support had long term, and unexpected payoffs, as innovation, economic competitiveness, and national security came together during the Cold War period. Perhaps the most famous example was the Internet, started with funding from the Department of Defense as a network to allow government-funded university scientists to share scarce computing power.[74]

The growing role of government was one part of what had by the 1960s become the most complex ecology of innovative institutions in history. All sorts of NGOs, nonprofits, and foundations gave money for research or in some cases conducted research and related work themselves. The private Battelle Corporation was a major research contractor, while the RAND

(R&D) Corporation was a nonprofit spun off from an arm of the Department of Defense. Likewise, corporations continued to fund their large research laboratories and firms in many other sectors decided that they needed to stay up to date with the latest in science and technology too, so opened branches to do similar work.[75]

In many ways, the United States in this period was the culmination of a model of innovation that can be traced back centuries, if not to the ancient world, putting in place all the pieces that we have identified as crucial to an innovative society. Through the 1970s the American model of innovation seemed to have peacefully conquered the world. Though few other nations could come close to the U.S. level of R&D spending or the numerous public and private institutions fueling innovation that the United States had developed, most looked to the U.S. as the model they strove to emulate. And contrary to some fears or expectations, innovation did not become fully "corporatized" (nor did it become a government monopoly). Large firms mattered, but so did independent inventors and small startups. The long tradition of industrial centers and districts continued to yield unforeseen breakthroughs, as when Silicon Valley took over as the focal point of semiconductor research, innovation, and production, building a new ecosystem of supporting institutions for innovation. Likewise, unexpected innovators or small firms, like Microsoft, Apple, Amazon, and Facebook, challenged established leaders or led the way to the pioneering of entirely new functions, services, products, or systems of technology.

A Challenging Moment

America's well-established innovative culture, however, came under stress and started showing serious cracks in its façade by the late 1970s. The American economy was changing, and the changes were often painful. In the 1970s and early 80s productivity stagnated, and a depressing combination of rapid inflation, slow growth, and high energy prices shocked the economy. Longstanding firms collapsed or disappeared, with the closure or downsizing of once strong industries and subsequent loss of jobs in sectors such as coal, steel, textiles, and machinery. Manufacturing took an especially hard hit, declining from over 25 percent of all jobs to 8.5 percent between 1960 and 2016.[76] These were painful and costly shakeups as they often led to rapid decline of towns and cities that had hosted these older industries.

History has shown that when nations or cultures are stressed by radical transformation or challenges to accepted ways, they can fall off the path of innovation. But to its credit, the United States regrouped in the decades after 1980 and made adjustments that once again promoted innovation and growth. American business responded by moving out of declining sectors, reducing costs, often by downsizing or offshoring operations to lower wage locations, and concentrating on core functions. Government also innovated by reducing regulations and deregulating industries such as telecommunications, airlines, trucking, and electricity, opening them up to competition. American productivity, which had stagnated in the early 1970s, recovered in the 1990s and 2000s.

Much of the change was mediated through the financial sector. Always a strength when it came to innovation, American finance developed new tools and products such as junk bonds, which were used in takeovers of failing or underperforming firms, selling off or closing the weak units and refocusing on profitability, often under new management. Banks, private equity firms, and hedge funds would use similar strategies to target weak or underperforming companies with acquisitions. Meanwhile venture capital firms provided start-up financing for new ventures, such as the emerging complex of semi-conductor, software, and IT businesses concentrating in Silicon Valley and elsewhere. In the early 2000s vast quantities of such capital went to new Internet startups. Although many of these failed and, inevitably, the boom was followed by bust and contraction, the experience was also a good demonstration of the American model of innovation. Starting as a government project, the Internet was released into the private sector in the 1980s, a pattern similar to that seen in early railroads that started with public investment but then grew with private capital. By the 1990s a variety of government scientists and independent inventors were working on ways to improve the system and adapt it to new uses, developing features such as the IP/TCP protocol and the HTML language that gave birth to the World Wide Web. Robust private sector financing then allowed a host of new ideas, products, and services to be tested in the competitive marketplace. As with the early railroad and other transportation networks, this period of intense growth and experimentation often led to unprofitable investments, overbuilding, and retrenchment, an unruly process to be sure but one that could be highly creative.

Still, the recovery, we can now see, did not fully restore the health of the American system of innovation. Although inflation dropped considerably after 1982, growth in the U.S. economy as a whole has been modest, and at different periods the vaunted American engine of productivity fluttered and stalled.[77] While business profits improved, the benefits of restructuring did not lead to a renewed emphasis on innovation, particularly the high-risk breakthrough innovations that had driven the American economy since the middle of the nineteenth century. Large firms, focused more on immediate bottom line results, began to disinvest from basic and even much applied research, or shutter the vaunted laboratories altogether. In absolute dollars the United States remained far above other nations in R&D spending, but as a percentage of GDP Japan began to best the United States by 1990, Germany by 2010, and China is now not far behind.[78] Government sector and NGO R&D have been flat in real terms since 1980.[79]

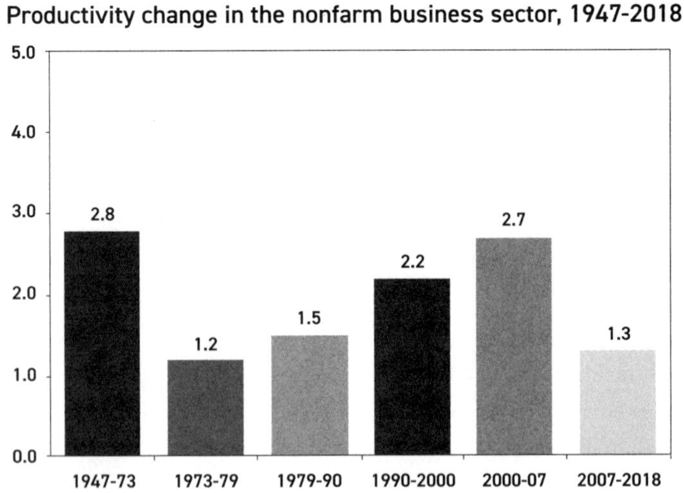

Source: U.S. Department of Labor: Labor Productivity and Costs at https://www.bls.gov/lpc/prodybar.htm

When it comes to innovation, a society can have too little of a key ingredient, but it can also have too much of a good thing. By the 2000s, this seems to have been the case with finance in America. Free flowing capital put pressure on the New Deal-era banking and financial regulations and led to a proliferation of new financial instruments in an era of "securitization." The securitization of mortgages and high levels of leverage and private sector debt caused a global crash in 2007, the worst since the Great Depression. But the longer-range impact of these changes in finance was more and more emphasis on financial engineering and less and less on technological engineering. Financial engineering and in some cases outright manipulation put even more pressure on firms to keep up share prices, cut long-term investments and expenditures for things like research, while draining talent and attention that could have gone to product innovation or improvement. [80]

If America had come to love finance not well but too much, it had lost its longstanding infatuation with the power of education. First at the elementary and secondary levels evidence demonstrated that American schools were underperforming compared to schools in other nations, notably those in parts of Europe and Asia. Efforts to improve or reform American education have met with at best mixed results even until today, as American students still tend to perform in the middle range of students across the world. More recently higher education has come into trouble, with costs to students rising rapidly and state governments less willing to support their universities. It is unclear, though if the source of these problems is strictly a matter of educational policy. American students' performance varies widely by location and socioeconomic class.[81] Students in middle and upper middle-class neighborhoods with good schools and strong funding actually perform quite well in international comparisons, while students in inner cities, poor neighborhoods, and meagerly funded districts do especially badly. Likewise, American higher education institutions are still the envy of the world, particularly at the graduate level. American colleges and universities attract both undergraduates and graduates from around the world. But the affordability and access to those institutions also varies significantly for Americans by socioeconomic class. Private institutions are at the upper reaches of affordability for even solidly middle-class families, and for lower income families private and even state institutions require them to take on substantial debt. Recently those debt levels have risen so high that many students may find it significantly hampers their economic futures, even with the benefits they receive in terms of higher earnings.

America has never been an equal society, though it has often provided ladders and access to opportunities missing in more traditional, rigidly structured nations. This rough equality in fact was part of the reason that America could develop democratic political structures and policies that promoted innovation and change, in stark contrast to other parts of the New World. Inequality, however, is now emerging as a real threat to the American innovation machine. The problems can already be seen in the growing disparity of school funding and university access. More directly, the lack of access to education, jobs, financing, and opportunities is taking out of circulation a larger and larger number of potential innovators who will never have a chance to test their ideas in the marketplace. This is a combination brain drain, frustrated talent pool, and narrowing of the all-important base of potential innovators societies need. We are, as one critic puts it, losing who knows how many potential Einsteins. The lessons from history are clear; one need look no further than what slavery did to a vast pool of potential innovators in American history. The same loss may be happening today due to rising inequality.[82] Shutting down opportunity and restricting the important tools and resources for innovation to the few is a recipe for slowing or even stopping innovation.[83]

In the immediate term, inequality and lack of opportunity may have knock on effects that further reduce the innovative potential of society. Job losses, stagnant wages, and a growing disparity of wealth may be generating a backlash directed against immigrants and immigration. America for two hundred years, and really even more, has depended on a continual influx of people from virtually every corner of the globe. Scientists, engineers, entrepreneurs, artists, musicians, creators of all type have been attracted to the United States for its wealth of opportunities, and its liberal policies that encouraged people to come, settle, acquire citizenship (for them and especially for their native-born children), get access to land, financing, education, and build new lives. This system brought both talented and highly educated people here—from Einstein to Irving Berlin, to Elon Musk—as well as those of humble means who arrived to work. But whatever their origins, immigrants have also had a superb work ethic, as one might expect from people who make a long, arduous, and difficult journey from one culture to another, that has driven them to success beyond what one would expect.

It is very much akin to my own experiences as an Egyptian who moved to Austria and came to study in America. Immigration not only opens you up to different cultures, ideas, and people but it often drives you to do things that the native-born do not do. Only about 6 percent of the American population today, for example, are non-native, naturalized citizens, yet they represent almost 11 percent of the membership of the Fortune 400 richest Americans. Immigrants are twice as likely as those native-born to start new businesses.[84] Shutting down the immigration pipeline can only hurt American innovation. Already the number of students coming to study in American universities is declining and increasingly those who do study here are returning home to India, China, and elsewhere rather than staying to work or start businesses. In fact, Chinese graduates of American universities working in Silicon Valley are going back to China in droves to start their own businesses after hitting the "Bamboo Ceiling" in the United States where they were unable to advance to leadership levels. History has shown again and again that open, receptive societies that learn from other cultures and are open to talented people are key to a successful innovation ecosystem. But, like education, current U.S. policy is causing this crucial pillar of innovation to crumble. This is occurring at the very moment that a new challenger to innovation supremacy, China, is on the rise. China, as we shall see, is offering what could be a new and different model of innovation, one that may leave the United States and nations that have followed its lead, behind in the race for innovation.

CHAPTER 6:

The Rebirth of Innovation in China

It is little wonder that so many Chinese engineers working in Silicon Valley are now being lured back to their homeland. Opportunity abounds. A few years after I started my business in Dubai, I also saw just this sort of opportunity in China to expand my young company and sell paper there. I decided to open small offices in Hong Kong and Shanghai in 1996, but there were many roadblocks to establishing a foreign trading company in China during this period. Although my first efforts ended in failure, and I moved my Asian business to Malaysia the following year, I realized that to succeed in China I had to work hard to understand and respect the values and the many cultures of this vast nation with 55 distinct ethnic minority groups among its 1.3 billion inhabitants. I believe respect of other cultures is the key to doing business *anywhere* in the world. Today, I buy 80 percent of my paper from China, which is now one of the most innovative societies in the world thanks to the strong promotion of the government. It is deeply satisfying to me to source my paper from the Chinese who invented paper so long ago and have now returned to their ancient roots, manufacturing a top-quality product with the best equipment and technology available.

Let me give you a sense of how far and fast China has come in recent years. Many economists now believe that the probability of improving your station in life in China today exceeds your chances in the United States, the legendary land of the "American Dream" that has until recently served as a beacon of opportunity to the world. Entrepreneurship in China has emerged as a highly appealing alternative for a generation disillusioned with the lack of opportunities to advance to leadership roles abroad or dead-end manufacturing jobs at home that once enticed their parents to abandon farming and head to the cities in droves. Premier Li Keqiang recently claimed that "mass entrepreneurship and innovation" are at the core of China's economic strategy. The country's startups are now flush with cash from both public and private sources. Venture capital investment in China reached over $40 billion in 2017—a 15 percent increase from the previous year, with 25 percent of global VC coming from its own wealthy citizens. Chinese entrepreneurs have taken the global lead in attracting venture capital, garnering 47 percent in the second quarter of 2018, while the U.S. and Canada combined raised only 35 percent. Much of this money is doled out through innovation-focused accelerators like those proliferating along Beijing's Zhongguancun Inno Way (which translates as "Entrepreneurship Street"). Even in Silicon Valley Beijing is providing much of the funding for China-focused accelerators that are moving rapidly to identify and acquire promising U.S. startup ventures—and their valuable technology and talent. The nation now leads the world in the number of researchers, patents, scientific and technical publications, and is a close second to the United States in R&D expenditures. China is clearly on a strong and dynamic trajectory to become the world's next great innovation society.[1]

China's heady burst of entrepreneurship and capitalism is a radical change from the nation's past economic woes. Following a century of subordination to foreign powers, three decades of isolation, starvation under Chairman Mao, and four decades of economic reform initiatives launched by Deng Xiaoping in 1978, the Middle Kingdom is now attempting to reclaim its historical position as the world's leader in technology and innovation. In a speech at the 19th Communist Party Congress in 2017, President Xi Jinping declared that "Innovation is the prime driving force behind development: it is the strategic underpinning for building a modernized economy." The most powerful ruler since Mao, Xi has focused his government firmly on innovation as the key to promoting sustained economic growth. The innovation leadership enjoyed by the United States since World War II is now under heavy siege as China seeks to take its place in such critical emerging fields as Artificial Intelligence and quantum computing. Of the top twenty technology firms in the world by market capitalization, nine are Chinese. The United States and China are locked in a heated, front-page battle for high-tech supremacy, one that is underscored by mounting political controversy. Yet the blueprints and strategies of these two nations for winning this high-tech war are written from polar opposite political ideologies and traditions.

China Forges its Own Path

While my own model and those of many leading experts support the argument that innovation flourishes best through a stable government that champions freedom of expression, free markets, and the protection of intellectual property rights, China has forged a somewhat different path. It is indeed difficult for Westerners to understand how China's meteoric economic rise and mounting achievements in science and technology can be reconciled with the heavy hand of an authoritarian state. Nobel prize-winning economist Milton Friedman was invited to China in 1988 to give his advice on how the Asian giant could reform its economy. To get rich, he said, China must be free. So, freedom, by this claim, is a precursor for innovation that translates into economic success. Or is it? China has remained resolute in its decision to keep the Communist party firmly in charge as it reforms its economy and opens to global commerce at its own pace. An exploration of the top-down, bottom-up and other forces that promoted—or impeded—innovation in China's past may provide insight into its modern-day quest to reclaim its former glory as the world's innovation leader. What are the roots of this modern-day tension between an authoritarian government and a free market economy that is encouraging a new form of "state capitalism"? And how does China's extraordinary track record of invention, particularly during its earlier imperial age, fit with our model of innovation?[2]

State-supported Innovation

Today, the Chinese people are convinced they are on the verge of a renaissance not witnessed since their nation's greatest eras in history, a period of inventiveness and openness that stretched from the first century to roughly 1600 CE. The Song dynasty (960-1279 CE) in particular was a period of remarkable socioeconomic change and innovation in China that ushered in the invention of printing, gun powder, the compass, civil service, paper money, tea cultivation, and restaurants. Some of these breakthroughs made their way to Muslim lands through the Silk Road or via the Indian Ocean, which served as the primary conduits for the transmission of new Chinese ideas across the continent to Europe. Today, Chinese leaders are reinventing the Silk Road through the Belt and Road initiative. President Xi launched this grand infrastructure plan in 2013 to expand China's economic and geopolitical muscle by building dams, industrial corridors, as well as roads, ports, and railways that will link the nation with Asia, Europe, the Middle East, and Africa. One of the most innovative aspects of the Belt and Road effort is that China is financing these developments within its own borders and in other nations to facilitate its entry into foreign markets. "The Chinese people are very proud of the Silk Road and its role as a global trade route when China was at its most powerful," explains Diane Wang, founder of DH.gate, which links buyers from around the world to Chinese businesses. "We think China again has a chance of regaining a similar glory." This link to the past recalls China's golden era when it awed the world with its vibrant culture, superior technology, bountiful harvests and a growing population, and openness to other nations. In fact, prior to 1400, China had no "dark ages" like Europe, and, as we have seen, was much in advance of that region in many ways.[3]

In the past as today, the state played a leading role in China's flourishing. In ancient and medieval China, artisans and engineers were under the direct control of the state bureaucracy, where they conducted experiments and devised naturalistic theories to understand the material world. They participated in the nationwide administrative network through elaborate imperial workshops and arsenals that were located at the capitals of each successive dynasty as well as in key provincial cities. During certain periods, activities with some of the most advanced technologies were nationalized, as occurred with the Salt and Iron Authority under the Han dynasty (202 BCE – 277 CE). Localities rich in valuable natural resources also served as major centers of specific types of production, like the lacquer makers of Fuchow, the ceramic artists of Ching-te-chen, and brine and natural gas drillers in Szechuan. Major civil engineering projects were conducted through imperial workshops or under the careful supervision of key government officials. Under imperial command, these workshops closely guarded their manufacturing secrets, which bears similarity to today's heated debates over ownership of intellectual property. The process for manufacturing porcelain with clay bodies rich in kaolin, for example, was a highly guarded state secret that no other country could duplicate for millennia. Manufacturing of porcelain in China started around 600 BCE, and it was heavily exported during the Song Dynasty. Dutch traders introduced this highly prized commodity to Europe in the seventeenth century, but it took quite a while before Europeans could replicate what the Chinese had invented some 2,300 years earlier![4]

Before 1400, the Chinese government oversaw the minting of coins and hydraulic projects crucial to agriculture. Government officials wrote and disseminated treatises explaining and elaborating on agricultural breakthroughs, like a superior new strain of drought-resistant and faster-ripening rice introduced from Southeast Asia during the eleventh century. Even as early as the third century BCE, government authorities provided peasants with funding for agricultural improvements and promoted the widespread use of better-quality plows. The state also played a key role in the development of transport technology, with huge investments in canals, roads, bridges, couriers and a postal system, as well as in the dissemination of medical knowledge. Top-down intervention in the economy included the stabilization of food supplies through the state granary system, the monopolization of the national trade in critical commodities, as well as international trade when it existed during certain dynasties.[5]

Some high government officials themselves achieved major scientific and technological feats. Chang Heng, President of the Imperial Chancellery, was an outstanding mathematician, the inventor of the first seismograph, and is believed to be the first to apply the power of motion to the rotation of astronomical instruments. Prefect of Nanyang in 31 CE, Tu Shih introduced the water-powered metallurgical blowing-engine. Chinese princes and other imperial relatives also formed networks of scientific investigation and dedicated time and resources to the pursuit of science, like Prince Li Kao of Tshao who studied physics and acoustics and invented paddle-wheel warships. The Prince of Huai-Nan, Liu An surrounded himself with an informal entourage of astronomers and naturalists, and alchemists. While the state bureaucracy helped drive the nation's technological momentum, innovation also arose through independent innovators like the alchemists who were not officially sanctioned by the state. Minor imperial officials in the Ministry of Works were the most numerous groups of technicians and were well-educated. Many of the artisans and master craftsmen, however, were illiterate, and never able to reach the higher levels of imperial administration.[6]

The Imperial Age of Invention

How well did this system work for China? Let's take a look at some of the most transformative Chinese innovations from the imperial age in such fields as horology, mining and metallurgy, agronomy, chemistry, warfare, medicine, textiles, ceramics, navigation, hydraulics, and architecture. As we have already seen, several great centers of innovation rose and fell in the world over the past two thousand years. But during much of that period, China remained an important source of technology, consumer goods, commodities, and scientific knowledge that travelled to the Middle East, Europe, and eventually even the New World. China's importance in innovation and the world only declined in the face of Western dominance in the nineteenth and twentieth centuries.

All Chinese schoolchildren learn of their nation's four great inventions: Papermaking, printing, the compass, and gunpowder. They also know about the pinnacle of Chinese architecture, the Great Wall that snakes majestically across the mountains north of Beijing, constructed from the seventh century

BCE through the Ming dynasty (1368-1644) to fend off attacking hordes of nomads. The invention of papermaking is attributed to Cai Lun in 105 CE, who was Director of the Imperial Workshops, though modern scholarship has shown that paper was used in China several centuries before. More evidence of the importance of bottom-up innovation, Buddhist monks developed woodblock printing in the late seventh to early eighth centuries for disseminating religious texts. Buddhism formed the conduit through which paper and printed books were first circulated during the first millennium CE. Many millions of copies of the 130-volume set of Confucian classics were published in 953 in the nation's enormous printing shops. During the eleventh century, a commoner named Bi Sheng invented movable type printing. He carved individual characters on pieces of porcelain clay, baked them in fire and then glued them to iron plates to print each page. While metal moveable type was used by the Koreans starting in the thirteenth century, the technique never really caught on in China and woodblock printing retained its popularity. Even so, it seems that Chinese printing and manuscript production was incredibly well organized and could keep up a rapid output to meet demand for the written word.[7]

Gunpowder is believed to have been developed by Taoist alchemists around 850 CE. Their search for longevity elixirs yielded this very volatile mixture of sulfur, charcoal, and saltpeter. While it was once thought that the Chinese merely used their amazing invention for firecrackers, in fact Song dynasty inventors deployed gunpowder in rockets and bombs during the tenth century.[8] Geomancers invented the magnetic compass during the fourth century BCE and during Feng Shui divination ceremonies they used it to advise families on the most propitious siting of houses and tombs. Chinese traders used navigational compasses as early as 1117 CE to find their way to the East Indies and the Persian Gulf. During the tenth and eleventh centuries, Chinese clockmakers constructed water-powered mechanical clocks that operated by dripping water on a wheel that completed one revolution in a 24-hour period. Clock technology utilizing waterpower reached its zenith when Su Sung erected a great clock tower measuring forty feet high at Khaifeng in 1086 CE. Prior to 1400, the government monopolized knowledge of the measurement of time and the calendar much like the caliphs did during the Golden Age of Islam. These time-telling innovations were crucial in support of agriculture, dictating the optimal dates for planting and harvesting major crops.[9]

The origin of silk production dates to sometime before the third millennium BCE when the Chinese discovered the lengthy thread of a typical silkworm cocoon could be reeled off, spun, and woven into the finest fabric then known to mankind. An important part of the rural economy, the silk industry dates to the fourteenth century BCE, becoming a chief export through the Silk Road during the Han dynasty (206 BCE – 220 CE). Han era silk has been discovered in Egypt and in graves in northern Mongolia. The Chinese built remarkable looms of 1,800 parts that spun dazzling silk fabrics in great demand among the upper classes throughout the civilized world. Here, too, the Chinese imperial government during the Yuan and early Ming periods played a key role in the textile industry, and actively promoted the use of certain textile crops such as cotton.[10]

The Chinese also contributed significantly to metallurgy and geology and began to cast iron and steel by the second century BCE with their invention of the double-acting piston-bellows that provided a continuous blast. Enormous state-owned iron foundries soon encouraged the widespread use of new iron tools and other implements. Europeans, by contrast, did not master the casting of iron until the late fourteenth century, unable to achieve the necessary temperatures to liquefy iron. With the ability to produce iron in quantity, the Chinese used wrought-iron chains to improve their suspension bridges around 600 CE, and the engineer Li Chhun is credited with the invention of the segmental arch bridge. Drilling for brine, a key source of salt, led to the discovery of natural gas resources. Engineers then constructed bamboo pipelines to carry the gas for many miles, sometimes overhead on trestles, and used it for fuel and light as early as the fourth century BCE. The technical skills of Chinese artisans and engineers were also well known throughout Europe. Chinese metallurgists and well-drillers were known in the second century in Parthia and Ferghana, and Russian diplomats requested Chinese bridge-builders come to their country in 1675.[11] Inventors were revered in China and were honored for the benefits they brought to the nation. The names of master-craftsmen and key artisans were carefully recorded, unlike their counterparts in Europe whose names are largely forgotten.[12]

The advancement of medicine in China was built upon a bedrock of systematic experimentation. Chinese medical innovations included the invention of acupuncture as well as the isolation of sex and pituitary hormones from human urine for medicinal purposes. While the exact date and origin of the procedure is unclear, smallpox inoculation is thought to have developed independently in China, India, and Europe. Some sources indicate it may have been practiced in China as early as 200 BCE. During the Middle Ages, Chinese cities were in advance of Europe in such key public health measures as sanitation and the provision of clean water.

When it came to many advanced technologies, Europe was on the receiving end of China's discoveries through the fourteenth century. Only in certain areas did Europe move well beyond China. For example, there were no basic conceptual medical breakthroughs in China to parallel those of Europe like William Harvey's discovery of the circulation of the blood (published in 1628). Chinese doctors and scientific thinkers lacked the kinds of institutional developments such as scientific societies and autonomous universities that promoted independent thinking in Europe, which as we have seen was one of Europe's great institutional innovations. So, while technology and engineering reigned supreme in China, Europeans were simultaneously developing a modern, mathematized science that would fuel the Scientific Revolution.[13]

Still, well before European science and technology burst forth to world leadership, the Chinese culture of the golden era gave birth not only to many critical inventions that profoundly affected the world, but also to an enormous expansion of commerce, culture, and government institutions. At the household level, rural citizens engaged in the production of goods by cultivating silkworms and growing tea. This rise in pre-modern industry was paralleled by urbanization and the growth of the largest, most sophisticated cities in the world. Population levels surged during the Song period, thanks to successful advances in agriculture and the control of water through advanced hydraulic engineering. The government oversaw the construction of grand canals supporting the more efficient transportation of agricultural products from the south to the north, helping to unify China's strong agrarian economy and further boost population levels. By the High Middle Ages (1200-1500), the population of China reached 100-115 million, roughly twice that of Europe.[14]

The Song emperors were also quite open to people from other cultures, such as Arab and Persian merchants who settled in China. Some of these foreigners even became part of the government bureaucracy. The openness of China during this era can be seen in the numerous peoples, cultures, and religions with which it had contact and exchange: Muslims, Buddhists, Daoists, Nestorian Christians from Persia, and Turks from Central Asia.[15] Looking outward, the Chinese built ocean going junks of great size, plying the trade between Java, Indonesia, India, and into the Red Sea. Navel advances for this trade included inventions such as the stern post rudder, moveable sails, the compass, start charts, and detailed knowledge of winds and currents. Such knowledge and technology moved around the world from China, contributing eventually to the European voyages five hundred years later. At home the Chinese empire was under pressure from Mongols from central Asia, who would eventually conquer the land and establish their own Yuan dynasty for a time. But in this conflict, the Chinese were able to rapidly and substantially ramp up iron production, to some 150,000 tons annually, a level that Europe would not match until 1700. In short, this was a vital, open society, with vibrant contributions being made in art, literature, design, and philosophy. This was a society at least as creative as Europe during the height of its Renaissance. [16]

One important thing to remember is that "China" was a vast, diverse landscape of different environments, peoples, cultures, and products. It was more akin to Europe as a whole than to one nation within Europe. So, with a large and growing population, interregional trade and specialization, there were many improvements, adaptions, and diffusions of innovations taking place just within China. North and South China were different places, in competition with each other and also looking to each other for new ideas they could adapt. Wheat, traditionally grown in the North, was adapted to the relatively dry and arid parts of upland and hilly areas in southern China, traditionally the rice growing area. When the Mongol invasion split China

North and South the remaining Southern Song dynasty established new contacts for trade with Southeast Asia, and also a sea going trade with Japan. Credit markets, futures markets, and partnerships all evolved to support this trading.[17]

Innovations occurred not only in technology and commerce but in governing too. Under Song dynasty Emperor Tai-tsu, who ruled from 960 to 976, the role of the state in society increased dramatically with the establishment of the foundations of modern government through a system of centralized, bureaucratic, and autocratic rule that, in many ways, endures today. The Emperor convinced military rulers to resign and surrender their commands across the entire country. He then transformed the government from one based on hereditary power to a semi-meritocratic system that selected government workers based on a new Civil Service Examination that tested applicants on neo-Confucian morality and ethics. Administered from the thirteenth century through the birth of the Republic in 1912, this exam enabled the Emperor to push aside the rich and powerful military families that had been in control for centuries.[18]

The Limits of Chinese Society

Although Chinese artisans and engineers produced considerable technical and natural knowledge until about 1400, merchants were the ones who had been transmitting their discoveries to the rest of the world. As we saw with the case of Islam, such critical breakthroughs as papermaking, the compass, and gunpowder made their way from China to the Middle East and then to Europe and North Africa through merchants along the Silk Road and through such highly cosmopolitan cities like Cha'ang-an where people from nearly every country in the known world visited. During the Golden Age of the Song and Ming period as well as after, merchants were granted more freedom and played a particularly important role in interregional trade and organizing the work in the production of silk and cotton textiles as well as pottery, important export products that linked China to the world.

Still, at a time when merchants and princes were leading Europe aggressively outward to discover and conquer new lands, Chinese merchants played a more limited role. Although they could acquire great wealth, they were never truly secure and were subjected to laws that allowed officials to seize their assets through inordinate taxation and many other kinds of governmental interference. They were more a tolerated or permitted class than a protected one.[19] As a result, they could never achieve the kind of status and positions of power like that of European merchants, and they failed to develop mercantile and industrial capitalism. Sons of the wealthiest Chinese merchants often aspired to enter the official bureaucracy rather than follow their fathers into trade, thus siphoning off the brightest into secure government careers rather than riskier entrepreneurial ventures.[20]

Throughout China's golden era, the dominant agrarian-based ideology reigned supreme, while mercantile interests stood in conflict with state ideology. Like many great agrarian empires, China looked inward, focused on securing adequate calories for the population, taxing peasant land cultivators, and securing its internal borders against barbarian invaders. This agrarian system continued to prosper for a time. During the Ming Dynasty from 1368 to 1644, a number of factors coalesced to promote the rise and importance of commerce, trade, and markets. These included a dramatic increase in population from some 75 million to 150 million, making China the greatest economic power on earth; a long period of peace and stability under the Ming; internal migrations to the southern regions; and successful new crops introduced from the New World. As a result, families grew larger, the newly introduced spinning wheel stimulated the opening of new markets for cloth, and incredible amounts of silver coins were introduced by foreign traders in exchange for Chinese goods. These coins helped bring about the monetization of the Chinese economy by the late sixteenth century. Commercial crops appeared across Chinese markets, including cotton, tea, and tobacco and sugarcane from the New World.[21] Chinese agricultural productivity was able to feed a growing population with these new crops as well as improved strains of rice that ripened quickly and permitted two harvests per year.

While China was certainly a hierarchical society with a high concentration of wealth, power, and education at the top and a large state active in economic and technological affairs, many of the important advances came about through the efforts of ordinary people. They cultivated land that they owned, grew cotton, raised silkworms, spun thread and fiber, engaged in the artisanal tasks of making iron or ceramics. They were oriented to the market and opportunity and had access to credit and trade networks that allowed them to sell what they produced and learn about opportunities elsewhere. These were classic examples of innovation from below as anonymous cultivators experimented with different strains of crops and new methods of growing, such as paddies in low lying areas and hillside terraces in elevated terrain. With good interconnected markets and canals for transport, practices and tools developed in one place were diffused elsewhere inside of China.[22]

The agrarian orientation of China, especially during the Ming era, tended to isolate the country from international events and opportunities. For a time, though, it seemed that China would use its wealth and power to push outward into the world, much as Europe was doing. The highlight to Ming global engagement occurred between 1405-1433. During these decades Chinese admiral Zeng He commanded an enormous flotilla of ships, some 300 strong with 27,000 sailors. He brought his armada to Indonesia, into the Indian Ocean to Calicut in India, to Hormuz in the Persian Gulf, and to Mogadishu and East Africa. It was actually only a small part of the navy that China had built, which would number almost 1,700 ships in total, using so much wood that the southeast coast of China was deforested. Zeng He's voyages were mostly diplomatic in nature, though he brought back an astounding array of goods from India, the Middle East, and Africa including leopards, rhinos, zebras, and giraffes. The goal was to establish trade relations with these distant places, for which the Chinese state would expect payment and tribute. Still, it was an enormous effort at inter-cultural connection. Zeng He himself was a complex figure, a Muslim from the East Coast of Africa who was taken as a slave back to China where he became a eunuch in the Ming emperor's court.[23]

For reasons still not fully understood, the end of Zeng He's voyages put an end to the Chinese navy and to its ambitious trade policies. Under subsequent Ming emperors the ideal society remained, and indeed was reemphasized as, a settled agrarian society with tax paying peasant farmers.[24] Merchants continued to be involved in regional trade with Southeast Asia and Japan. Many took a hand in the port city trade that came to China. These activities were still suspect, though entrepreneurial Chinese merchants nonetheless carried on quite a bit of officially illegal maritime commerce.[25] But too much trade, openness, and mercantile exchange, it was feared, would bring in foreign influences that would upset the ideal agrarian order. Indeed, after Zeng He's adventure, the Lung-chiang shipyards on the Yangtze River received no further orders for ships and the knowledge of how to build the great treasure ships, probably the largest and most impressive the world had seen to that point, was lost. Taking the inward turn still further, the maps, charts, logs, and handbooks Zeng He had compiled on his voyages were burned in the sixteenth century.[26]

China's agrarian ideal stood in contrast to the increasingly outward, trade focused, competitive states of Europe that were transitioning away from traditional agrarian society. But economically China continued to flourish, and all evidence indicates that it remained on par with the European world in the seventeenth and eighteenth centuries. The state allowed long-distance merchants to self-regulate through their own rules and guilds, and was content to extract taxes and command tribute from weaker states in Korea, Vietnam, and Southeast Asia. Eventually pressure by non-Chinese people at the borders, notably tribes from the North, led to the replacement of native Chinese rulers with a new Manchu ruling class taking the name Qing dynasty (1644-1912). Under Qing rule China again focused on its internal territory, doubling in size with the incorporation of Tibet, Mongolia, and the Muslim Uighurs.[27] While the entry of Europeans, starting with the Portuguese in the sixteenth century, had brought many foreign influences right to China's doorstep, these outsiders were regarded suspiciously and largely confined to trade ports such as Macau, Hong Kong, or Shanghai. Connections between Europeans and Chinese were closely regulated and watched.

None of this stopped China from being a highly successful commercial society. Any limits or failures did not stem from a lack of "western" style legal or market institutions, as was once claimed. China supported entrepreneurship and also promoted networking. The courts were receptive to the enforcement of commercial contracts. Increasingly sophisticated financial and commercial instruments served to bolster commerce, including new forms of profit-sharing and new corporate entities like lineage trusts. "These developments, when combined with the presence of an openly accessible market, allowed even those individuals who had little or no surplus capital to start small-scale, often family-run, business operations," says historian Wellington K.K. Chan. Most of the population continued to live on farms at or near subsistence level, but still made forays into small business ventures, allowing more people to become budding entrepreneurs. And with the rise of new practices in support of entrepreneurship, such as the enforcement of written contracts, many entered the business world.[28]

As historian Kenneth Pomeranz has noted, average incomes in China (as well as in Japan and other parts of Southeast Asia) were nearly the same as or even higher than those in Western Europe in the late eighteenth century. In some areas, China was doing even better. Chinese agriculture was significantly more productive than that of Europe, and its urban markets were larger. In fact, from the late sixteenth through the early nineteenth century, China produced roughly a third of the world's gross output. It manufactured some 4/5ths of the world's goods and contained 2/3rds of the world's population. But those halcyon days would not endure.

Before the middle of the nineteenth century, China's powerful, advanced agrarian economy was showing signs of strain, compounded by its tense trade relations with the outside world. Relentless population growth since 1700 caused numbers to skyrocket from 150 million to about 400 million by the early 1800s. Feeding that population required China to put more and more land under the plough, stretching into the frontier for food, fuel, and raw materials for metal and textile production. Even as the Chinese tried to keep up their robust cotton textile and metal industries, they began to devour available resources. Charcoal for smelting metals exhausted forests while growing cotton diverted labor and land from needed food production. In contrast, Europe, with its strong trading system and overseas empires, had access to the "ghost acres" of the New World for needed supplies, so could expand raw material production without sacrificing food production, or could procure food offshore. China, in short, was caught in a classic Malthusian trap, where success in agriculture leads to population growth but a growing population puts pressure on land until the need for calories and raw materials cannot be sustained.[29] So even though the Chinese empire had plenty of internal markets, good commercial institutions, strong and diverse financial instruments, canals for transport and interregional specialization, it did not have the world-wide connections that helped Europe make the leap to industrialization.

The Great Chinese Decline

Throughout its Golden Age, the Chinese economy was driven by a combination of state- sponsored education, infrastructure, and technological advances plus a strong undercurrent of rural and urban private entrepreneurship. This balance produced a great outpouring of innovations in science, engineering, manufacturing, agriculture, and the arts. But over the centuries that followed, the Chinese engine of growth and innovation sputtered and eventually stalled completely. Although the economy continued to expand and the population continued to grow, some technologies that were once widely known fell into disuse or were forgotten altogether. By the sixteenth century, for example, knowledge of Su Sung's water clock design was lost. When Jesuits visited China in the 1580s, they found that time measurement there was quite primitive compared to the mechanical clocks of Europe. A China that had seemed on the verge of world domination and industrialization experienced a pattern of regression somewhat like Europe after the end of the Roman Empire. The causes of this slow-down of creativity and innovation were many, and even today scholars are not sure what to pin the blame on. But a close examination of the institutional, scientific, and economic structures of China after its Golden Age points to a number of factors that my innovation model predicts can inhibit innovation.

During the eleventh century, the Chinese launched a universal education system that focused on literary and moral instruction derived from Confucian philosophy. All schools received sets of the officially sanctioned, block-printed Confucian classics that students were expected to memorize and recite. They also learned calligraphy and classic poetry, but the natural sciences and mathematics were excluded from the curriculum. Unlike the universities that emerged in Europe at this time, independent thinking was prohibited, leading to a uniformity of attitude and opinion reinforced by the Civil Service Examination. As we have seen, for the natural sciences, and more broadly for independent, creative, analytical thinking to flourish, official and public approval are essential, as are institutions that provide the foundation to nurture their evolution. These were all lacking in China from the Song dynasty to the twentieth century. The complete uniformity of thought, enforced by political indoctrination and the lack of institutions that supported the challenge to the status quo, culminated in the dearth of innovation in scientific, creative thought.

Similarly, the exam system offered a degree of expertise and competence in government, but also grew into one of the forces that tended to ossify Chinese society. Only the very well-off could afford to take it, and the exam system was notoriously rife with corruption and nepotism. As Europeans were decentralizing their administrative powers by separating religious and moral authority from the secular state and from autonomous guilds, universities, towns and cities, the Chinese launched an unprecedented program to do just the opposite. During the Ming Dynasty, the emperor and his enormous network of officials wielded complete control over all of China through an inflexible legal system that helped legitimize and promote this new power. An Office of Surveillance gave censors the power to watch over the nation's massive bureaucracy and enforce imperial law that allowed for absolutely no independent thinking or challenge to the emperor. This new system also inhibited the birth of the institutional basis for promoting intellectual freedom—including advanced scientific thought.

No great scientific thinkers emerged in China during this era that could rival Averroes in Islam, or Copernicus, Galileo, Harvey, Kepler, or Newton in Europe. Powerful cultural and institutional forces blocked the birth of modern science in China. Some scholars have maintained that the Confucian philosophy that reigned supreme, which was blended with Taoism since it was adopted as the state religion in 440 CE, was to blame for China's loss of leadership in technology and innovation. The philosophy was "this-worldly" in character and dedicated to social ethics to demonstrate the way for humanity to live harmoniously. While Confucianism dealt with social matters and Taoism focused on the search for meaning, the two philosophies shared common beliefs about man, society, and the universe and endured harmoniously in China until the end of the imperial age. Religious and cultural values have always played a key role in influencing—or retarding—the process of innovation. It was no different in Imperial China. Taoism supported the Order of Nature but did not embrace reason and logic. Followers of Taoism leaned towards the mystical-experimental, rather than the rational-systematic. The Taoist-Confucian world view emphasized that there was no compulsion to investigate the external world. Subjectivity, introspection, and intuition were highly valued, as was the harmonious cooperation of all human beings as part of a hierarchy that formed a cosmic pattern, one that was not based on the architecture imparted by a supreme deity. Other scholars, however, have dismissed this argument since Confucianism dominated Chinese philosophy during its golden age of invention as well. Regardless, China's great advances in technology did not generate a broad-based theoretical or metaphysical literature, or a more abstract investigation into the science and mechanics of motion.

China may also have suffered from a lack of governmental and institutional support for certain fields of inquiry, even though we have seen that the state was heavily involved in many industries and endeavors. Astronomy and mathematics did have the support of some emperors, but no formal schools for the study of these subjects or medicine existed. No work on optics was conducted; Emperor Kangxi even imported teams of European lens experts and grinders due to the lack of great craftsmen in optics. And the study of anatomy through post-mortem dissection was strictly forbidden. In fact, the officially sanctioned manual guiding forensics on human anatomy remained the same from the thirteenth to the nineteenth centuries because it was embedded in imperial law. After 1430 the imperial court decided to halt all geographical exploration while the Europeans were on the verge of colonizing the New World. Information was tightly controlled by central government bureaucrats, much like today. Even the name for library in Chinese (*Zungjing Pe*) translates as "Pavilion for Revering the Classics." Daily newspapers were not introduced until the early to mid-nineteenth century and the literacy gap between China and the West was not closed until the end of the twentieth century.[30] How much the limits on science and abstract inquiry into nature mattered for technological and economic innovation is unclear, since Europe's industrial revolution also depended on the efforts of craftsmen, engineers, and skilled fitters and fabricators more than high-level scientists. But over time, the importance of university level education, scientific research, and deep knowledge of the natural world grew more and more important in the economy, in technology, in the military, and in medicine, leaving China further behind the West.

While government had aided Chinese innovation during the Golden Age, it also showed itself capable of limiting or even quashing further change and advance. In Europe, advances in innovation were essentially private initiatives and the role of rulers was typically secondary or passive. In China, however, as we have seen, the role of the government through the enormously powerful imperial workshops was critical to building momentum in technology, but at some point, that support withered away. As economic historian Joel Mokyr notes about government support of innovation, "As long as the regime supports progress, progress can proceed. But the government can flip the switch off, so to speak, and private enterprise is unlikely to step in. Innovation that is run largely by bureaucrats is thus not impossible, but it depends on their goodwill .... The Chinese miracle is that it lasted so long. It ended when the state lost interest in supporting technological change." The absolutist rule of all-powerful monarchs who chose to enhance their power and maintain control over promoting innovation and technological progress sounded the death knell to the once dynamic forces that had shaped China's society for more than a thousand years. Those forces were beginning to surge through Europe because invention and innovation were private pursuits there that flourished in a decentralized, politically competitive environment that could—and did—sustain that energy, at least until the mantle passed to the United States in the twentieth century.[31]

Surging Western Influence

By the nineteenth century, China began to face significant pressure from Western societies that had advanced to the stage of industrialization. Many scholars have argued that labor in China was cheap and more than abundant, so the labor-saving inventions pioneered in the European Industrial Revolution did not need to be invented in China. This, no doubt, inhibited the drive for further technological innovation. If China did not focus on labor-saving technology, it did, nonetheless, produce innovations, particularly those that saved on fuel. China led the way in the use of coal fuel in producing iron, glass, beer, and other products. Although China's economy was still rural-based and agrarian, it was highly commercialized through the support of town and city governments. The guilds provided networking opportunities between merchants and officials. So, based on past patterns and history, it seemed that China would continue to be a major economy, not so much lacking in innovation but innovating differently than it had done historically.

Soon, though, China was facing exactly the situation that nations face when they cannot match the innovation going on in other parts of the world. Despite a long and illustrious history of technology, commerce, trade, and agricultural productivity, China fell behind in the sort of rapidly advancing systems of technology and the new business ventures the industrialized world created in Europe and its offspring colonies. This was a pattern that would be seen in many of what we might call "traditional" empires that emphasized agrarianism as the basis for their societies. China, Ottoman Turkey, and Iran were all once mighty empires that were not able to match the vast increase in productivity and power associated with the industrial revolution. For all the success in technology, trade, and agriculture, China was out of step with the new direction innovation had taken, toward machinery, manufacturing, labor saving technologies, and new mineral sources of energy. China could be quite innovative and creative when it came to traditional agrarian activities, with its vast population of cultivators, artisans, and rural manufacturers making incremental improvements in technology and productive processes. But industrialization was a radical break with the past, one that in Europe and America worked in tandem with trade, immigration, population diversity, educational freedom, private intellectual life, and continual competition among cities, states, and empires.[32] China's very imperial dominance of its vast territory thus worked against it in this regard.

With an emphasis on stability over change and a repudiation of outward-focused ventures starting in the Ming Period, China lacked the innovative capacity to keep up or even to adopt many of the new technologies originating elsewhere. Indeed, sensing these deficits, China's leaders after 1860 tried to embark on a policy of "self-strengthening." Their goal was to imitate and learn from the West, particularly its advances in armaments such as canon, iron ships, and other crucial implements of military defense, as well as engineering and machinery production. It was a step too far. In part the effort failed because the needed intellectual and educational infrastructure had not been built, making Chinese industry dependent on expensive western workers and managers. China's strong intellectual and educational institutions were not oriented to the deep discoveries of nature that helped to promote the further industrialization of the late nineteenth century in chemicals, medicine and pharmaceuticals, petroleum, metals and electronics that pushed the United States to the top rank of innovators. Families were still suspicious of Western influences, and smart children could still aspire for careers as civil servants if they could master the knowledge needed for the intense examinations, as opposed to Western science and mathematics. Conservative elites agreed, fearing an education that emphasized mere technical knowledge would undermine spiritual and moral values.[33] Losing its technological and economic edge, China fell prey to imperialist incursions and control by the great Western powers. Western powers instituted a treaty system that forbade the Chinese from conducting trade and foreign affairs on an equal footing. Military defeats exacerbated the growing economic crisis. Beginning in the late eighteenth century, the import of opium drained the nation's precious silver resources. Realizing that opium imports were one way to pay for the export of tea and other valuable commodities out of China, the British in the nineteenth century forced the Chinese to accept the drug, which was cultivated and manufactured in British held India. Indian profits from opium in turn were used to buy British exports, such as manufactured goods. Despite high numbers of addicted opium users disrupting social life, China was unable to resist the pressures of the mandated opium trade. It had suffered a humiliating loss of sovereignty at the hand of the Western powers.

China was at a low point by the end of the nineteenth century, under the thumb of Western imperialism. Even so, its economy had not completely stagnated. There were still signs of the vibrant commercial culture and inventiveness that had been part of Chinese history for many centuries. In the mid-eighteenth century, the government had allowed a group of licensed merchants to trade with a chartered group of European traders. From these trade relationships Chinese merchants gained new skills, new ideas for starting businesses, new ways of organizing their businesses, new sources of capital through Western banks, and a new understanding of Western legal and administrative systems. Some of these merchants began to travel abroad and enter business in the West. They brought their new ways of entrepreneurship back home where they founded the first Western-style businesses in the 1870s. The social status of merchants and their relations with government were also improving. "Throughout Chinese history, political control over all aspects of business activities has always been a given," notes Pomeranz, but "merchants had significant autonomy so long as they did not infringe upon the power of the state."[34] These shoots of future economic growth were still young, and before they could flower, political and military events overtook the Chinese economy.

The Turmoil of the Twentieth Century

With the nation subjugated to foreign powers, overrun by warlordism, and consumed by civil war, the Xinhai Revolution of 1911 toppled the last emperor and gave birth to the Republic of China. In 1937 Japan invaded China and held control until the end of World War II. During this period China's domestic trade and industry were decimated. The country, now so far removed from its past glories, was riven with internal political divisions, with conservative nationalists and left-wing communists vying for control. Ultimately, the communists won the conflict, but the nation fared even worse under the subsequent rise of Chairman Mao Zedong's communist state in 1949 than it had during the Japanese occupation. Mao's "Great Leap Forward" (1958 to 1962) turned China from an agrarian economy to an industrial one through a rapid but brutal socialist transformation. The collectivization of agriculture prohibited farm ownership and drove the peasantry from their individual small holdings. Working communally, they were forced to give up nearly all of their harvest to a state that tragically increased exports while letting the people starve to death. An estimated 36 million people died during the Great Chinese Famine. "History will record the role you and I played in the starvation of so many people," China's president, Liu Shaoqi, wrote to Mao in the summer of 1962, "and the cannibalism will also be memorialized." Liu had personally visited his home province of Hunan where a million died from starvation and some of the survivors had eaten the dead or killed and consumed their comrades.[35]

By the late 1970s, the Communist Party was in shambles and the nation mired in chaos. During this era, much of the world felt rudderless in the face of stagnant economic growth and high inflation, and many grew open to the idea of radical change and pioneering market reforms. As is commonly the case during periods of great crisis, many embraced new leaders: Margaret Thatcher in Britain, Ronald Reagan in the United States, and Deng Xiaoping in shell-shocked China. Widely considered the maker of modern China, Paramount Leader Deng rose to power in 1978 and began to reengineer the economy through a series of gradual reforms readily accepted by a people mired in poverty.

Deng's tumultuous path to leadership began under Mao when he was twice purged during the Cultural Revolution. For many others purge meant a grim death, but Deng survived, served as a guerrilla in the People's Liberation Army and was appointed by Mao secretary of the Communist Party in 1954. Once Deng became Paramount Leader, he rejected Mao's preaching that "communes are good," believing rather that *markets* are good. "I am a layman in the field of economics," he said in 1984. "I proposed China's economic policy of opening to the outside world, but as for the details or specifics of how to implement it, I know very little indeed."[36]

Through Deng Xiaoping's charismatic leadership over the course of a quarter century, the Chinese Communist Party maintained power and control while gently and gradually encouraging capitalism—a remarkable juggling act that allowed the continued embrace of socialism without inhibiting entrepreneurship or innovation. While Deng and his government had no clear blueprint on how to build a modern economy, they had learned from the successes of Japan, Taiwan, and South Korea, as well as from the disastrous missteps of their old allies in Russia that triggered the collapse of the Soviet Union, decline in Russian life expectancy, a rise in infant mortality, and plunging incomes. They also learned from that collapse that economic reform and growth must precede military spending. They wanted to reform the economy and support the growth of new businesses *without* allowing democracy to flourish. "Taking precedence over all China's problems is stability," Deng told President George H.W. Bush in 1989.[37] A strong state can tax effectively, maintain national unity, ensure political stability, and place national interests above those of powerful vested interest groups.

"We will give you a policy that allows you to charge ahead and cut through your own difficult road," said Deng of his trial and error economic reform process he likened to "crossing the river by feeling the stones." Accordingly, local governments started granting licenses quite liberally for people to start household businesses. Party leaders who once decided where everyone worked and dictated what every manufacturer made and how much everything cost very gradually loosened their stranglehold on the economy. Factories that met their government-mandated quotas were allowed to sell anything extra they produced at whatever price they decided. The government set up special economic zones in cities like Shanghai without the investment restrictions that they continued to impose in the rest of the country. They wooed foreign investment. They began to dismantle collective farms owned by the state, though "decollectivization" was not followed by private ownership of land. They had also observed the rise of Japan and South Korea through a centralized, top-down approach to innovation fueled by a strong dedication to science and technology, which they slowly began to adopt as essential ingredients in the country's experimental plan for modernization. "Gradualism instead of a rapid and radical overhaul of the system," argues Douglas Fuller, "avoided massive destabilizing shortfalls in demand over the short term that in turn could have become much larger systemic problems." China's leaders reengineered the economy and society through a potent combination of gradualism and control.[38]

During the early 1980s, Party leaders began to allow multinational firms to move production units to China. And indigenous, private companies like the appliance manufacturer Haier grew internationally and began to compete globally without government interference. In 1986 Deng launched a government-funded high-tech R&D program focusing on IT, robotics, space, lasers, and biotechnology. Two years later the government passed the first constitutional amendment to give legal status to private enterprises. But such state actions were not promoting the public ownership economy. They were merely providing legitimacy to a growing wave that was bringing its people out of devastating poverty.[39]

The Power of Networks

By the early 1990s China emerged as the world's fastest growing economy. It opened its markets more rapidly and with greater success than any other country in history. Deng's famous "Southern Visit" during the early 1990s inspired some government officials to quit their "iron rice bowl" posts and "jump into the sea" by making highly speculative leaps into uncharted new businesses. This took a tremendous amount of courage, given the history of persecution and murder of capitalists under Mao. Though it was not possible to go back to their protected and coveted jobs if they failed, these entrepreneurs borrowed money from family and friends to establish small manufacturing firms. Most lacked any formal business education, and Chinese law did not support them with strong intellectual property rights and enforceable contracts. Nonetheless they persevered in an insecure environment and began to develop strong social networks based on trusted relationships to build support for their fragile enterprises. Through cooperation they helped one another and developed strategic interfirm alliances that facilitated the flow of information across market interfaces that gave entrepreneurs access to innovative ideas and technologies from the global economy.

As was true in the transformations that drove innovation in other societies in the past, an important part of the Chinese story involved the work of many, often anonymous (or certainly not well known) entrepreneurs and innovators who learned from experience and informal means as much as through formal education. These networks of many individuals fueled bottom-up capitalist economic development in the private enterprise economy. Called the "Gang of 1992," they were surprisingly successful. They forged political connections and sought favor from officials to navigate around oppressive regulations and gain access to the scarce resources that the government lavished on state-owned enterprises (SOEs). They sought good treatment from local governments, which were key to the emergence of the market-economy. Similar industries clustered together which further facilitated the growth of networks that shared technical support and operational know-how. Although these smaller firms had little or no financial capacity to build research and development programs, interfirm networks within the clusters shared information that facilitated innovation throughout them. By the time of Deng's death in 1997, annual economic growth was surging to double digits, a testament to his crucial role in transforming an impoverished, brutalized China into a stable, controlled, economic juggernaut.[40]

The Rise of Technology in the 21st Century

China's comeback activated just the sort of learning and cross-cultural connections that we have seen again and again in places where innovation is flourishing. Beginning in the late 1990s, China's first successful group of private internet entrepreneurs drew upon the model of Silicon Valley to forge companies particularly well-suited to the needs of their country's consumers. In 1998 Pony Ma founded Tencent, China's answer to Yahoo, Jack Ma launched Alibaba in 1999 based on Amazon's business model, and in 2000 Robin Li built Baidu following Google's approach. These younger, more dynamic entrepreneurs were better educated (most studied in the U.S. or gained experience there) and possessed greater international business acumen than their earlier counterparts. As we have seen throughout history, innovators draw on multiple, external cultural and business models and influences as they start to bring change to their own society, an important part of the innovation process.[41]

The new class of Chinese entrepreneurs also knew enough to stay away from industries dominated by the SOEs, preferring to work in an environment with less government oversight. They were savvy enough to express complete party loyalty and hired staff to remove anti-government messaging from their systems, which has grown into an enormous industry today with thousands of low-wage workers in "censorship factories" scouring the Chinese Internet for forbidden content. Once again, we see how the government suppresses freedom of expression to maintain stability over economic growth, and once again the question arises: How important is freedom for innovation and how far should it go in society as a whole? When freedom means unrestricted access to government by citizens it can be a force for democracy and the social good, but it can also allow insiders and existing, powerful interests too much influence. Gun control lobbyists have been largely unsuccessful in stemming the tidal wave of gun violence that plagues the United States, taking the lives of hundreds of school children and other innocent victims each year.

Right now, it does not look like acceding to government control and limits on expression are impeding Chinese innovation in the technology sector. One reason may be that the private sector has remained strongly committed to research, development, and broad-based global learning. The private tech giants are investing heavily in R&D, especially in AI. In fact, today 78 percent of R&D spending in China comes from the private sector. The Internet entrepreneurs, who learned from the mindset, culture, and organizational principles of Silicon Valley, are working to reverse the cautious inward-looking culture that stifled the nation for centuries after its Golden Age. Today, China conducts 42 percent of global e-commerce, up from 1 percent only ten years ago. It has nearly become a cashless society, leapfrogging over credit card transactions, with nearly the entire society relying on mobile payments. So deep and fast is this transformation that today beggars on the street hold signs displaying their mobile financial data so anyone can send them money through their phones.[42]

At the national level as well, China combined a commitment to socialist principals and state control at home with a new openness to the larger world. An important turning point in its coming of age in the global economy was 2001, when it joined the World Trade Organization with the support of the United States. President Clinton believed that political reform in the form of Western-style democracy would naturally follow economic liberalization, stating that "if you believe in a future of greater openness and freedom for people in China, you ought to be for this agreement."[43] Other American leaders shared his conviction, but they were wrong. China continued to reform its economy under solid Communist Party Rule. New enterprises continued to emerge in many fields, including energy, healthcare, financial services, education technology—businesses that were fueled by the growth of science and technology. While much of this trade, investment, and innovation reflect the success of its entrepreneurs and networks of innovators, China also made heavy use of government actors and capital. During the early 2000s, state-owned-enterprises dipped into China's $4 trillion in foreign exchange reserves and were making billion-dollar deals, gobbling up companies around the world, satisfying China's insatiable thirst for growth and for innovative technologies. Along the way, the nation gained access to foreign resources in energy, land, and raw materials through the Belt and Road initiative. State-owned construction firms began to build infrastructure in the nations where China was doing business to support development and provide the transportation to bring their goods back home and sent around the world. SOEs expanded their edge in such industries as insurance, banking, telecom, energy, airlines, autos, steel, and construction, and were criticized both internally and externally for receiving unfair advantage.

The result is that China now has a dual system, two major endogenous engines pushing its growth: Government and private industry. The new class of Chinese entrepreneurs that emerged at home does business with less direct government influence or support than their counterparts in SOEs. In 2006

China formally adopted an industrial policy that allowed "indigenous innovation" by private firms. By 2009, private firms accounted for 40 percent of industrial profit, while only 20 percent came from SOEs. A 2010 ranking of the fifty most innovative companies in the world included four Chinese companies—three of which were private enterprises (Lenovo, Haier, and BYD).

An exogenous engine has also been producing growth in China since the mid-1990s, one that many consider the next wave of globalization: Multinational companies are increasingly offshoring R&D to China (and India) in growing numbers. Initially, the first foreign-run R&D centers in China were set up to support their local manufacturing efforts and were motivated by cost-savings. By the late 1990s, however, Chinese competitors "had quickly become masters at serving local needs." Multinationals could no longer transfer technology; they needed to adapt to local demand, which ushered in a market-driven effort rather than a simple cost-cutting endeavor. By the mid to late 2000s, a third phase of innovation led by multinationals was a knowledge-based effort to "integrate their R&D with the latest research coming out of Chinese institutions." This also means that the challenge to compete for top Ph.D. local talent is surging, forcing foreign companies to forge strong ties with the best Chinese universities and research institutions to tap into the best graduates.[44]

Today, multinational companies headquartered in the United States with R&D budgets of over $100 million are offshoring innovation in China and India across a broad spectrum of business, spanning from semiconductors, software, technology and telecom to gambling, chemical manufacturing, oil and gas, and instruments. They consider global engineering to be a strategic advantage far beyond mere cost-cutting measures. They embrace powerful global innovation leadership in their home countries and abroad by both bringing in strong managers and hiring top professionals in China and India. They then empower these local teams to make their own decisions and partner with local educational and research institutions to promote greater synergies in the innovation process.[45]

The Xi Era

When Xi Jinping took office in 2013, his new government moved quickly to liberalize the economy even further by starting to move beyond state-driven investment, allowing the market to play an important role, and calling for a freer hand for the private sector. New government policies began to give private enterprises greater access to financing, ease regulations for establishing new businesses, and promote the creation of venture capital and private equity firms. By 2014, ninety-two Chinese companies had earned a spot-on *Fortune's* Global 500 list that ranks top firms in the world according to revenue, and ten of these were privately held. Since 2004, the number of SOEs has been reduced by about half. Today, the private sector employs more than 80 percent of workers, provides 90 percent of new jobs, and generates more than 60 percent of the nation's economic output. By some accounts, China has outflanked the United States with the largest number of billionaires in the world.[46]

China's transformative journey into a high-tech, innovation economy is drawing on substantial investments in education made over the past forty years. Although the Cultural Revolution had left the education system in disarray (particularly at the universities and research institutions), Deng and the Chinese Communist Party leaders understood that China had to step up its commitment to education to catch up with the West and the Asian Tiger economies (South Korea, Taiwan, Hong Kong, and Singapore) in science and technology. They sought to build synergies between academia and industry to tackle social and economic development. By the 1990s, they increased R&D funding dramatically for the leading universities and research institutions, with an eye towards elevating a select group of them into the top tier globally.

In line with my own model of innovation that places education at the core of any national plan for sustained innovation, these reform initiatives were important, both because they provided potential innovators with valuable skills and techniques, but for a related reason as well. As we have seen, innovation societies flourish when they can borrow and mix ideas and practices from many cultures, something that had been impossible in China during the dark Maoist days. After assuming leadership, Deng began to send young party officials to the United States and other nations to gain an understanding of how modern, successful societies worked. Many attended foreign universities, others found jobs abroad or went on study tours. "When our thousands of Chinese students abroad return home, you will see how China will transform itself," Deng said. Party leaders promoted the careers of these so-called "sea turtles" when they came back and encouraged them to share their new knowledge with others. In addition, the state invested in formal education and improved access to schools and universities. The nation's university-educated population rose from 3.8 percent of 18-22-year olds in 1991 to 27 percent by 2012, while higher education enrollment skyrocketed from one million in 1991 to 19 million in 2007.[47]

Today, mainland China generates more graduates in science and engineering annually than the United States, South Korea, Japan, and Taiwan combined. Universities in the United States remain a critical training ground for some 300,000 Chinese students annually who then return home in greater and greater numbers to assume tech leadership positions. In 2017 eight in ten Chinese students educated in American universities returned home. Many, like Kai-Fu Lee of Sinovation Ventures, gained valuable experience in American companies before returning to China to start a key AI company as well as a tech venture capital firm. Companies like Microsoft have had research laboratories in China for two decades that also serve as important centers of training.[48]

A Chorus of Criticism

The question for the future is how effective China's educational system will be in producing graduates with the broad perspective, critical skills and creative mindsets necessary for innovation, as opposed to adopting things other have invented. A lack of encouragement of creativity and fundamental, scientific thought has precedents deep in China's past, as we have seen. And we know that education alone does not guarantee innovative leadership. China's terribly stressful national exam system, with roots stretching back

1,300 years, punishes those who do not score well by forbidding them from attending college. Even elementary school students are heavily focused on their one chance to do well on the dreaded national exams, which have been known to cause breakdowns and even suicides.

President Xi and other party leaders have begun to reform the system, moving it away from its historic Confucian roots. They have expressed concern that the national tests are prohibiting the growth of creativity that could generate China's own Steve Jobs. The Chinese government has been on a crusade to promote childhood creativity and reduce academic stress and has prohibited courses considered too advanced for younger school children. It also wants to prevent wealthier families from gaining advantages for their children through expensive private tutoring, which has grown into an enormous industry. Many families now pay for their children to attend weekend art classes to boost creative thinking, an essential ingredient for innovation. However, in spite of the government voicing concern over student stress, the exams remain in place to determine which schools students can attend and whether or not they can go to college or vocational schools (a policy similar to that of many European nations).

To link education and commercial innovation more closely in this vast nation of 1.3 billion inhabitants, China has started some 115 university science parks and more than 1,600 technology business incubators to provide mentoring, office space, and legal advice to the growing numbers of entrepreneurs. The Chinese online education system is also growing by leaps and bounds, with some 90 million educating themselves on government-sanctioned sites in 2016. That number is predicted to soar to 240 million by 2021 in an industry valued at $64 billion. Leading Chinese Internet giants Tencent, Alibaba, and Baidu are all investing heavily in online education startups. And while China only has a few world-class universities, the government aims to establish 42 such learning centers by 2050. But will China reduce bureaucratic control and promote the autonomy of these institutions so that they can experiment more freely and better prepare graduates, allowing them to compete more effectively in the global innovation market for science and technology? As in the past, the question of how well a strong, central state committed to producing the best administrative system for its people can work with a vibrant, innovative culture of entrepreneurship is central to China's economic future.[49]

Despite its decades of economic growth, China continues to be the subject of criticism for what Western observers believe are limits on its ability to thrive and innovate. A 2014 *Harvard Business Review* article entitled "Why China Can't Innovate" claimed that "China is largely a land of rule-bound rote learners—a place where R&D is diligently pursued but breakthroughs are rare." Then Vice President Joe Biden echoed that same sentiment during a speech: "I challenge you," he said to his audience, "name one innovative project, one innovative change, one innovative product that has come out of China." One prominent Cornell University professor claimed that China must shift away from a culture of suppression of dissent toward freedom of expression and the encouragement of critical modes of thinking if it wants to get to the cutting edge. Other culprits stunting innovation in China, critics argue, include failure to protect intellectual property rights, theft of technology and forced technology transfer, and an authoritarian government that overregulates the economy and provides unfair support to its nearly monopolistic state-owned enterprises.

These criticisms ignored the amazing bursts of creativity Chinese culture has had in the past. And today China *is* innovating—perhaps not yet through breakthrough inventions like those of its earlier imperial age—but through smaller, piecemeal advances gained through trial and error and imitation, especially those that drive stunningly rapid improvements and efficiencies in manufacturing processes and meet the unmet needs of its vast army of online consumers. As we have seen, imitation of the best global technologies seems to be a natural progression of a nation's path towards indigenous innovation. Patents were of little consequence in the industrialization of Britain, and the United States brazenly and successfully appropriated British technology and innovations (as did other follower nations). Networks of entrepreneurs, inventors, engineers, technologists, and artisans were responsible for innovations ranging from ocean-going sailing ships, to ploughs, to cathedrals, to spinning and weaving machines earlier in history. Many of the ways that China has emerged (or re-emerged) as an innovation leader follow the examples of other nations.[50]

A New Innovation Ecosystem

Even government policy plays a different, more complex and varied role in innovation in China than in purely market-based economies. First, China has made strategic use of government resources, policies, and capital, while at the same time shifting away from earlier policies that had stifled innovation by protecting state-owned-enterprises at the expense of those privately held. This shift began in 2006 when officials announced their decision to transform China into an innovative society by 2020 and become a global leader in science and technology by 2050. In 2013, Beijing announced a multibillion-dollar investment into ten transformative technologies highlighted in its controversial "Made in China 2025" plan, forming a critical component of its path towards fulfilling that vision, one that draws together state and private expertise, money, and institutions. In this regard, China is little different than the United States, which in the twentieth century leveraged both private and government funding and initiative to promote breakthroughs in the medical sciences, computing and information technology, aerospace and "big science" projects. Today, in Europe and around the capitalist world, government remains a major player in the innovation race, so in this the Chinese model of executing innovation is both following common patterns but the nation's leaders are carving a unique path.

For example, China is starting to shed much of the older style bureaucracy while empowering its entrepreneurial class. In recent years, the Chinese government has introduced further initiatives geared towards increasing both entrepreneurship and homegrown innovation. In addition to building a substantial number of new schools to train tomorrow's workforce, Beijing is radically abbreviating the process for forming a new business and allowing existing firms to enter new industries more freely. "The more companies an industry has thinking about a problem," says Nobel laureate economist Edmund S. Phelps, "the more likely a solution is to be found." And the Chinese now claim to fully grasp the value of this approach in building a more competitive landscape to stimulate indigenous innovation. Thus, Beijing is removing protections on redundant firms—even SOEs—to facilitate their exit from the market in true Schumpeterian fashion. It also claims to be opening its markets to foreign experts who wish to work on new Chinese business projects. Officially at least, this is what Beijing is telling the world, that it will continue the process of opening up and becoming more market oriented. There is some concrete evidence that the policy is making a difference. China's entrepreneurs have shed their earlier pariah status and developed into a potent economic force. Whole neighborhoods of startups are popping up in Beijing, Shanghai, and the Shenzhen-Hong Kong hub. This bottom-up development of a socialist market economy (as Deng Xiaoping called the process) continues to be empowered by social networks that support interfirm cooperation through fluid exchanges, both formal and informal, national and global, that connect businesses, universities, research laboratories, funders, government, suppliers, and customers.[51]

While many in the West remain highly skeptical of this improvisational process of "crossing the river by feeling the stones," China's gradual, controlled, incremental approach to economic reform has paid off. This year, 2021, marks the fortieth anniversary of China's radical experiment in "reform and opening up" that has engendered an economic expansion without precedent in modern history, one that has lifted some 800 million people out of crushing poverty. According to the World Bank, in 1981 the poverty rate in China was 88 percent; today it is less than 1 percent. Economic output per capita in the world's second largest economy is $12,000 today, up from $3,500 a mere ten years ago. Life expectancy has also skyrocketed. The economy surged from $395 billion GDP in 1990 to $12 trillion today. And China now has more homeowners, internet users, and college graduates than any other country in the world. In 2014, 14 percent of global unicorns (private tech start-ups with a market capitalization of $1 billion or more) were Chinese. Today, that number has grown to 35 percent.[52]

Despite the negative chorus of voices from the West, this spectacular forty-year boom suggests that Chinese authoritarian capitalism may very well be a model for developing countries to emulate. It certainly presents a challenge and a conundrum to those who assumed innovation and democracy must go together. "Autocrats sometimes do succeed," says economist Ruchir

Sharma. "Authoritarian rulers can often ignore or overrun opposition from the legislature, the courts, or private lobbies, and that power allows visionary leaders to accomplish a lot more than democratic rivals." In fact, at a time when the vast inequality of wealth and opportunity is creating social upheaval and destabilization in democratic societies in the West, many Asian economies are following a path closer to China's than America's. Just think of the lasting economic miracles wrought by President Park Chung-hee in South Korea during the 1960s and 70s and President Chiang Kai-shek and his son who reigned in Taiwan from 1949 to 1978.[53] Innovation seems to benefit from political and social stability, so long as it does not impose stultifying conformity. Which political system can best produce that ideal level of stability?

So far, the evidence is mixed. It appears that in the high stakes race to generate strong, sustained economic growth, both democratic and authoritarian systems have advantages and disadvantages—neither seems to have decisively buried the other. Out of 124 cases where a country had GDP growth of better than 5 percent for ten years, 64 occurred under democratic rule, while 60 came under an authoritarian regime. One weakness of autocratic regimes is that they are subject to an "authoritarian roller-coaster effect" characterized by radical swings between times of very high and very low growth, as well as very long economic downturns. Stable and enduring growth has, over the past century, been better sustained in democratic societies.[54] But with many democratic regimes under severe stress in places ranging from Italy to Hungary to Britain, the United States and Brazil, it is not yet clear how well they will perform.

Beijing seems aware of the plusses and minuses of different political regimes. So, while it has substantially opened its economy to market forces and private entrepreneurship, it is now showing signs of simultaneously expanding central control of the economy on many other fronts, a mixture that is uncommon in the West. Private companies take on high levels of debt from government banks, and when the companies lose money the government buys some of their shares to bail them out. "Regulators have determined that they, not corporate executives, know best how Chinese companies should invest overseas," says one journalist. "Capital controls remain as tight as ever; the currency is still under the thumb of the central bank. The opening of China's market to foreign business is going nowhere fast. Nor does the state allow the market alone to choose winners and losers. It dominates the financial industry and doles out large subsidies to favored industries and companies. Even censoring of the internet has intensified, constraining the free exchange of information supposedly indispensable to innovation."[55] While Xi Jinping's powers have increased exponentially with the recent abolition of presidential term limits, he remains hugely popular in very stark contrast to President Trump who has one of the lowest approval ratings of any American president in history.

This combining of innovation with central control is perhaps most evident in China's plan, unveiled in 2017, to dominate artificial intelligence. Many experts believe that AI holds the key to China's future economic growth and will seal its bid to become the dominant global economic force in the next two decades. Yet critics argue that China is using this innovation for Orwellian surveillance of its citizens as never before. This, to many outsiders, seems a distinctive and troubling feature of Chinese society, though at the same time, video and other forms of surveillance on the street in cities from London to Dubai have also increased enormously over the past decade. In this latest phase of the nation's economic transformation, China is embracing the sort of big scale, scientific and technological breakthroughs it had produced during its golden era (and for which the United States was famed after World War II). The country is advancing aggressively in a whole range of critical areas at the forefront of science and technology research, making serious inroads into autonomous vehicles, educational technology, virtual reality, robotics, and advanced manufacturing. Its scientists successfully cloned the first primates (identical monkeys) and created the world's first genetically edited babies, a move that sparked widespread international and Chinese condemnation. China has also taken the lead in the race to develop the first quantum computers, one with broad national security ramifications that would provide the tools to break digital encryption information.[56]

Rising Expectations

Supremacy in technological innovation will undoubtedly determine which country surfaces as the world's dominant economic power in the long run. For China's economic miracle to continue, its businesses must become even more competitive and innovative. The government is doing its part through controlled stimulus to innovation in a fashion difficult for Western nations to replicate. It is increasing R&D spending, financing start-ups, giving low-cost loans to Chinese companies, and providing private sector initiatives. It is also singling out tech companies and nurturing individual efforts in particular areas, like Ofo for dockless shared bikes. Some argue that this level of granular control achieved by an autocratic state could, in the long run, do more harm than good, preventing innovation from flourishing by making markets less competitive. It has happened in the past: From the Roman Empire to Islam, to China itself in the Middle Ages, once powerful states and highly creative societies let their desire for control and stability undercut their creative potential. For all of China's investments in education and targeting of cutting-edge areas of science and technology, original inventions and engineering breakthroughs are still much less common than meeting consumer demands through internet juggernauts like Alibaba, or driving efficiencies in manufacturing in such industries as appliances where China has been quite successful.

So, there are clearly challenges to China's dream of leading the world in innovation as it did during its imperial age. The nation's economy is showing serious signs of strain as the trade war with the United States continues. Its volatile stock market has tumbled more than 20 percent in 2018 (though Western markets have fared poorly as well). Mounting government debt, which is at 25 percent of GDP, and surging corporate debt at 170 percent of GDP, are just some of the problems China faces in the global economic slowdown. The greying of its population and projected lack of workers in the years ahead is another serious concern, as it is for the United States, the EU, Japan, and most major economies of the world.[57]

In spite of such challenges, visitors describe the startup atmosphere in China as electric, and as fierce as any other place in the world. China's young entrepreneurs are creating their own Silicon Valley, replicating another of the staple institutions of innovation that we have seen appearing throughout history. Huddling together inside the cafes along "Inno Way" in Beijing, many of which cater to these twenty-somethings by helping newbies get acclimated and organizing meetings with potential investors. They provide a critical networking vibe. Studies have shown that these new entrepreneurs share such characteristics as acceptance of risk and a strong work ethic, (reportedly working much longer hours each day than their Silicon Valley counterparts). They are tremendously ambitious, optimistic, and driven by an insatiable curiosity. As we have shown, nations have copied one another throughout history as part of an evolutionary process of becoming more organically creative. During the Middle Ages, Islam and Europe freely copied from China's extraordinary advances, as did America with Great Britain during the Industrial Revolution. Today, China's meteoric evolution along the innovation spectrum shows a dynamic trajectory that has placed it in the top 25 of the world's most innovative nations since 2016. More and more Chinese entrepreneurs are realizing that home-grown innovations form the engine that will drive their competitiveness in the years ahead. Networks link entrepreneurs both nationally and internationally with businesses, government officials, venture capital companies, universities, and government research centers.[58]

At this point, observes the President of MIT, L. Rafael Reif, China is no longer "an innovation also-ran that prospers mainly by copying other people's ideas and producing them quickly at low cost." China has now followed the well-worn path of other "catching up" nations we have seen, from South Korea, to Japan, to the United States, imitating the existing leader until it is able to become an innovator in its own right. The transformation is nowhere more evident than in Yabuli, a frigid, rugged region in northeastern China that is now home to the Chinese Entrepreneur Forum. Since 2017 this annual summit celebrates and fosters innovation among the nation's business leaders and the leading lights of its entrepreneurial community. The Yabuli conference center, a remarkably progressive structure that blends into the stark landscape and mimics the snow-capped mountains on the horizon, stands as a metaphor for China's rebirth as a formidable center of innovation. Can the Western world afford to continue to ignore the possibility that China is rewriting the playbook on fostering innovation and entrepreneurship? The nation's dynamic experiment blending authoritarianism with capitalism seems to be working.[59]

CHAPTER 7:

The Global Innovator in an Anti-Global Age

The landscape of innovation has been shifting for millennia. Our journey through history has traced the rise and decline of many great innovation societies, from Islam in its golden age, through Europe in its industrial age, followed by the rise of the United States and the resurgence of China. History shows us that while some societies have mastered the art of innovation and have grown and flourished, others failed to or lost their innovative edge, and fell behind. Innovation has been a key factor in determining which nations have held the foremost economic and geopolitical power in each period as leadership passed from one society to another. Let's take a look at how well our model has helped us understand why certain places rose to become innovation leaders and how that leadership waned.

A nation's innovation ecosystem is comprised of many different interactive parts consisting of entrepreneurs, researchers, and other workers; local, state, and federal governments; private and public enterprises of a variety of sizes; public and private universities and research centers; and individual lenders, banks, and venture capital firms. Looked at over the broad sweep of time, we see a fairly consistent story. Innovation societies shared some policies and practices that fostered the germination, development, and execution of seminal ideas. These policies included openness to ideas, technologies, products, and practices from other cultures; strong immigration policies that served as a magnet for top talent; supportive governments whose policies promoted innovation; a regulatory environment that protected intellectual property; an advanced educational system that engendered critical, independent thinking; good financial practices and institutions to back entrepreneurial ventures; the rule of law; freedom of religion and thought; and a government that is accountable and responsive to its citizens. Conversely, those that became closed, fearful of foreigners, orthodox, repressive, incurious, intolerant, unwilling to learn and borrow from others, and grew highly stratified have, over time, lost the innovation edge. Open societies provide opportunity for as many potential innovators as possible, to assure that the maximum of available human talent could be brought into play. Opportunity must include the chance to gain an education, particularly today when so much innovation requires a combination of technical, commercial, and "soft" skills of critical analysis, communication, and collaboration. Societies that position themselves at the confluence of many different cultures are best set to learn, borrow, and make new combinations of ideas. Immigration has served as a powerful force for generating and disseminating fresh ideas from new people. Finally, all of these factors will not be enough if the society is unwilling to take risks with new ideas, which means giving entrepreneurs who are not part of the existing business elite access to capital and markets to try out their new ideas.

Much like a healthy human body whose organs and systems are functioning properly and harmoniously, innovation can reach dizzying heights when all of these elements work in concert. It is true that some great societies became innovative *without all* of the elements in our model. But they have leveraged several of them to success, and over the course of history societies have achieved higher levels of innovation by putting a substantial number of these policies into practice, and lost ground when they failed to maintain them. So, for example, the Golden Age of Islam was ruled by a powerful caliphate that supported education as a religious pursuit and was welcoming to scholars and intellectuals of many different cultures. Yet because the caliphate never institutionalized education as a separate, independent system that supported free and critical thinking, innovation eventually ground to a halt. Europe in the Middle Ages had fallen significantly behind the Middle East when it came to science, education, trade, and commerce, but it began to develop a strong innovation culture as it borrowed significantly from Islamic advances and picked up the baton of leadership, and created independent educational institutions—a critical factor in any innovation ecosystem. Great Britain and other European nations also developed representative, accountable governments, the rule of law, and practically every other aspect of our model, which allowed them to attain global economic and geopolitical dominance for nearly six centuries.

The United States took from Europe many of these institutions and borrowed (and stole) much of its technology and industrial practices. But over time the U.S. began to master innovation through strong and enforceable patent laws, a brilliant financial system, an expansive, open educational system, and bankruptcy laws that gave people a second chance, which all coalesced to support inventors and entrepreneurs as never before. In a nation built by immigrants determined to improve their station in life, Americans have risk-taking in their DNA and a tolerance for failure—qualities that helped forge the country's unique innovation ecosystem. During World War II, the federal government began to forge unprecedented innovation networks linking government, universities, and the private sector, leading to extraordinary advances in such fields as pharmaceuticals and vaccines that transformed global health, developed the most powerful and lethal weapons ever known to mankind, and a space program that landed the first man on the moon. And just after the war, under the leadership of top engineer Vannevar Bush (one of the organizers of the Manhattan Project), the U.S. government supported R&D through clear, long-term policies that provided strong and sustained investment in the sciences. Today more than ever, such networks are playing a critical role in pressing national innovation agendas forward around the world. Germany's High-Tech Strategy 2020 and Made in China 2025 are just two examples of such long-term strategic innovation plans brokered through public-private partnerships. The case of China also shows that different forms of government may well be compatible with innovation, as long as those governments are stable and supportive.

Assumptions that innovation requires a form of liberalism found in the West are no longer acceptable given how far and how fast China has risen.

As in the past, though, innovative societies can stumble, lose their way by forgetting about the policies that made them great innovators. In the United States, there is troubling evidence that commitment to innovation may be fading. No longer is the nation, perhaps the strongest example of the innovation model at work, cultivating all the elements of a healthy innovation ecology that it once did. No longer does it have clear, government-supported, long-range plans to support innovation nationally. As a percentage of GDP, U.S. federal spending on R&D has fallen sharply from about 1.2 percent in 1976 to about 0.8 percent in 2016. During the 1960s, some 70 percent of total R&D was federally funded, with the private sector providing the remaining 30 percent. Today that scenario is reversed: Nearly 70 percent of R&D funding derives from the private sector with 29 percent from the federal government. While private support for research is important, it is almost totally applied research geared towards short-term horizons. And yet since the Cold War, basic R&D funded by the federal government has been at the core of America's innovation ecosystem. Research institutions are underperforming because of government cuts to critical basic research funding. Once the world leader in government-funded R&D, the U.S. now ranks 12th (as a percentage of GDP). By contrast, China's enormous R&D machine and industry-focused efforts in AI and robotics are leading to significant gains in the military and commercial arenas.[1]

Strong educational systems are also critical to any nation's innovation ecosystem, and the U.S. has eight out of ten of the top universities in the world. Such universities conduct basic STEM research, employ thousands of scientists, engineers, and mathematicians, and educate and train students in STEM disciplines. They drive commercial invention and form the backbone for vibrant tech hubs where innovation flourishes in public-private networks. Yet since the 1980s, state governments in the U.S. have been reducing support for state universities and forcing students to pay for this public good. The current state of federal R&D policies and spending, combined with diminishing state support for higher education and an ongoing deficit in

STEM graduates, paints a grim picture for the important educational pillar of the innovation ecosystem.

Another traditional American strength, immigration and openness to foreign talent, is also under threat. After World War II, the United States was the free world leader in openness and free trade and benefited immensely from programs that reached out to the world and brought in first-rate talent from abroad in fields ranging from physics to electrical engineering to medicine to literature and the arts. At the height of immigration in the 1910s, the foreign-born constituted some 16 percent of the American population. Today that figure has again reached almost the same level, a bit over 14 percent. But as in the past, xenophobia is threatening to shut down this great immigration pipeline.[2]

Newly implemented U.S. immigration policies are now impeding top foreign talent from bringing fresh ideas and energy to businesses and research institutions. The United States has long served as a magnet for, and has greatly benefitted from, the creativity and dynamism stemming from the enormous numbers of skilled immigrants that have graced its shores. Only two members of the Manhattan Project were U.S.-born, and the nation's space science and rocket technology programs were launched by immigrants like Wernher von Braun. Foreign-born students earn nearly half of all STEM doctoral degrees in the United States, and foreign-born entrepreneurs have founded more than a half of all U.S. unicorns (businesses valued at $1 billion or more). But now tens of thousands of American-educated workers are returning to their homelands (particularly China and India) as never before, where they will lead the charge to compete with the U.S. and the rest of the world. Losing its global draw as a nation brimming with entrepreneurial immigrants will surely hurt the U.S. in the long run. Taking advantage of America's dysfunctional immigration system, Canada launched a Startup Visa program in 2013 to offer permanent visas to entrepreneurs.[3]

In fact, right now the global movement of people is a driving force of innovation and economic success in many of the world's most advanced industrial nations other than the U.S. On average those nations have about 13 percent foreign born, very close to the U. S. figure. It is probably surprising for Americans to learn that supposedly "homogenous" places such as Germany and Sweden, which place very highly in global innovation indices, exceed the United States in foreign born population, at 14.9 percent and 18 percent respectively. Tiny, neutral Switzerland clocks in at 29 Percent. Some nations rely on immigration even more, as with Australia, where the non-native constitutes 30 percent of the population. The European Union's Schengen Agreement allows for free movement of people among the member nations and has generated high levels of mobility within Europe as well. A cross fertilization of people and their ways has brought talented financiers from all over Europe to London, as well as small-scale entrepreneurs who transformed that city from something of a culinary backwater to one of the great gastronomic centers of the world. That is just the sort of innovation the movement of people can bring.[4] Fast-growing, advanced countries attract workers as well as middle-class professionals, students, and would-be entrepreneurs. The big immigrant nations are actually found in the oil states of the Middle East, which rely on foreign workers at both the blue collar and professional levels, and in small trading nations such as Singapore and Hong Kong, as well as my home of Dubai in the United Arab Emirates where almost 84 percent of inhabitants were born elsewhere!

But unfortunately, as in America, anti-globalism is spreading across other parts of the world as well, most notably in England, with its exit from the EU driven in good part by a rejection of the foreign-born. Growing nativist movements can be found among the far-right parties in France, Hungary, Italy, Germany, even in my old home of Austria. Although immigration has grown across the world, it remains at levels consistent with that seen since the industrial era, so much of the backlash against immigrants is based less on facts and more on fears and misapprehensions. Polls show people consistently overestimate the number of immigrants in their midst, often double the real figure. In the United States, people think three times as many of their neighbors are foreign born as actually are.[5]

It is not just anti-immigrant sentiment that is the problem though. The broader threat is in a rejection of the foreign made ideas, practices, and cultural forms. Immigration of people is just one (admittedly important) way for nations to thrive. Many innovative places are relatively closed to outsiders or are homogenous in population. The key lesson is that the ones that stay on top connect to the larger world in multiple ways. Take for example Japan, a famously insular and homogenous culture. Yet after the Meiji Restoration of the late nineteenth century it opened up to industrialization and foreign ways, to great success. Japan sent thousands of its people out into the world to learn, observe, and educate themselves in the knowledge and best practices found among more advanced nations. It renounced the formerly closed ways of the past, the long-standing rejection of foreign practices, ideas, and religions that had marked the Edo period. We can see the same pattern in China as well. China too has gone through inwardly focused periods of restriction, as in the later Ming dynasty, followed by a new openness after the humiliating imperial conquest of the nineteenth century, back to a closed Maoist period, to openness once again in recent decades. China and another ancient civilization, India, now connect to the world by sending their best young people out to be educated and start their careers in the United States and other nations, much as I started my own career by leaving Egypt for Austria decades ago.

The divergent paths that Japan and China are taking today may also serve as a warning to the United States and other nations that close themselves off to talent and ideas from outside. While China has embarked on its Belt and Road initiative reaching out to the world, providing new capital to new business partners, and sending its young people to be educated at the world's top universities, Japan has grown more insular in the past several decades. Less than 2 percent of Japan's population is foreign-born, and it places severe restrictions on immigration visas.[6] Japan innovates largely from within, by corporate intrapreneurship. This has historically been one of the nation's strengths, but today it threatens to become a debilitating weakness. Technology has moved away from stable and closed systems controlled by large corporations to platforms, open operating systems, continual software innovation, independently produced smartphone apps, all benefitting from the presence of swarms of start-ups funded by venture or angel investors. With its homogenous culture and rigid corporate sector, Japan is poorly positioned to innovate in a world of rapidly changing technology and global interconnections.[7]

Today, innovation has become a global pursuit as both developed and developing nations have created and implemented plans to shore up their innovation engines to compete more effectively in the interconnected world economy. Many multinational corporations are locating their research and development facilities around the world, no longer following the earlier pattern of only offshoring manufacturing or assembling and keeping design and research at home. More and more multinationals are also tapping into a vast online pool of global talent.[8] Today, governments around the world are deeply engaged in long-range strategic planning to develop their innovation capacity as the driving force to fuel their strategies for building modern, competitive economies. All of this suggests that, in order to compete effectively globally, innovative firms will have to accelerate their operations across physical boundaries, to find and recruit talent anywhere in the world, to bridge private and public sectors to build inventive networks, and intensify their work with key centers of knowledge. Global innovation will put pressure on nations, and to keep up they will have to be even more connected and networked across the globe and more open to working in and with multiple cultures and people if they do not want to be left behind in the race for knowledge and technology.

Connecting to these global networks can be a challenge for nations that lack political stability or are being rent by polarizing political and social divisions, conditions that often produce the "anti-global" backlash that undermines the global innovator. Some places that have strong and deep traditions of innovative excellence have made the transition to the emerging global innovation system while retaining the necessary stability. Sweden, for example, a small nation of less than ten million people, is well respected for its social cohesion, strong social welfare programs, and good, efficient government. Yet it also has one of the greatest innovation ecosystems in the world, one that is frequently underestimated. Like Japan, Sweden played a rapid catchup game at the end of the nineteenth century and did so with an outward focus. Because of the small size of the domestic market, Swedish firms have always had to think about exports and external markets. The strongest of them, venerable corporations like Ericsson, were multinationals early on and proved effective at innovating in response to different market conditions so they could manufacture products at sufficient scale. Sweden today continues to maintain an open and outward orientation. In 1900, when the United States was attracting huge numbers of immigrants, less than 1 percent of Sweden's people were foreign-born. But that has changed dramatically. Today 18 percent of Sweden's population is born elsewhere, a figure above that of the United States.

In contrast to Japan, Sweden has exhibited all the signs of a vibrant start-up culture. It has been among the most successful nations for breeding "unicorns" that reach over 1 billion dollars in value. Silicon Valley is, of course, a famous breeding ground for unicorns, but on a per capita basis, Sweden is the second largest unicorn incubator.[9] The Scandinavian nation has added to its historic strengths in manufacturing, electronics, heavy industry, and natural resources to make itself a world player in fintech, gaming, digital commerce, and health technology. With its vigorous outward orientation, Sweden also has no problem attracting funding for innovation from elsewhere, garnering some $4.4 billion in investment capital over the past five years, a vast amount of money in a small economy. Sweden's generous social safety net allows talented young people to get an education without incurring heavy debt and to try new ventures without fear that if they fail they will starve, lowering the risk of entrepreneurship. Likewise, the nation's strong traditions of transparency in government encourage bonds of trust. This allows for private-public partnerships and the easy transfer of information, and resources, across private, public, and nonprofit sectors.[10]

Although at first glance not many people would compare Israel to Sweden, when it comes to innovation they share a number of similarities. Israel, though much smaller in size than Sweden, is similar to the northern nation in having a small population, 8.2 million people to Sweden's 9.9 million. It has in the past decade transformed itself into an innovation powerhouse, and like Sweden it has leveraged its social, intellectual, and cultural strengths to make this transition. Israel has been successful in new technology areas ranging from artificial intelligence to drones, greentech, fintech, and medtech. Like Sweden it has nurtured numerous startups and attracted billions in finance capital, some 60 percent of the funding for its technology sectors coming from outside the country. Multinationals have invested heavily in research in Israel, which actually leads the world in percentage of GDP going to R&D. As others have noted, both Sweden and Israel have small and compact populations, with strong social welfare systems, producing high levels of cohesion and trust. And as small nations both have long looked abroad for markets and opportunity, while attracting immigrant talent. As with other successful examples of innovative societies in the global age, government in Israel has been an important partner, along with universities. The state has supported research, helped to set up research centers at universities and technology incubators, and provided early venture capital for startups, stimulating the growth of private venture capital.[11]

As these examples reveal, successful places are following policies that are missing or in retreat in the United States today. Take for example the role of government. Sweden, Israel, and one could add South Korea, Japan, and of course China, are all able to overcome the dichotomy between big and small government to focus on how government can provide incentives, stimulate research and learning, and facilitate private sector investments into new technology sectors. Unfortunately, the United States continues to frame the debate only in terms of big versus small government. Likewise, all the above examples show the value of social capital and cohesion that encourages trust and sharing, and permits risk taking by providing a variety of public and social services, ranging from low-cost education to widely available heath care, to unemployment insurance. This social infrastructure provides young entrepreneurs with a safety net to try and fail, and then try again.

The virtues of this sort of public-private partnership can be seen in the case of another nation that is often missed when people talk about innovation—Germany. Like Sweden, Germany has high levels of social cohesion, strong labor unions, and a substantial welfare system. It is also a nation that attracts and employs immigrant talent. In fact, it has a higher percentage of the foreign-born than the United States does, taking advantage of the free movement of people across the EU. Germany's strength is less in making breakthroughs and more in adapting technologies (its own and others) and facilitating their spread. In a way, the diffusion of technology, which itself often involves changes to hardware, software, and most importantly, organizational routines, practices, and behavior, is as innovative as the initial invention of a product or technology. The spread of good ideas and technologies has the biggest impact on overall productivity—for what value does a new product or machine deliver if it is not being as widely used as it can be? Here too the United States shows signs of falling behind. Productivity growth has stagnated in the United States over the past decade, a surprising result given how long the United States was a productivity leader in the world. In part, this decline reflects low net capital formation—capital being the way that technology and other innovations are embodied in the economy. The low level of capital formation in turn reflects low net business investment.[12] American firms are extremely good at increasing share prices, engaging in financial engineering, and minimizing costs, including taxation, but they have not been investors in their own future.

Germany's success with the diffusion of innovation stems from its strong connections between government, research, education, and social institutions. Its network of high-quality research and technical universities, its string of some eighty-four institutes doing basic science and engineering research, and its emphasis on worker apprenticeships and continual training and education among a broad sector of the population help to make the wide diffusion of new technology and practices easier and more self-sustaining—a commitment to continual innovation.[13] Government, from the federal to the state level, assists in these efforts in a coordinated fashion. Germany has also drawn talent and created institutions that span other nations, taking advantage of the size and diversity of the vast European Union. The Fraunhofer Society consists of seventy-two applied research organizations in Germany and more than half a dozen other countries, doing contract work for industry and government that is especially helpful to Germany's vibrant and entrepreneurial *mittelstand* or small to medium-sized firms that are often key parts of the supplier infrastructure of the large corporate sector. The education-social welfare-labor organization system also minimizes the friction of change, by making sure that new technology benefits labor as well as capital and providing insurance and retraining for those affected by technology, reducing the potential for conflict and resentment.[14]

The United States has never had a labor and social welfare system to the extent of many European and Asian nations. But it has, historically, been a place of individual opportunity for those coming up from below. Unfortunately, just as its historic commitment to openness and immigration is faltering, so too is its long-standing reputation as a place of opportunity. Today, only about 50 percent of young people stand a chance of doing better economically than their parents, a stark contrast to the 90 percent a generation or so ago. Likewise, the United States now ranks lower than some supposedly rigid European and Asian societies in terms of social mobility. Those born poor (or even middle class) stay in their station, something that would have been shocking to Americans in the day of Abraham Lincoln, or for that matter John F. Kennedy. At the same time those born well off pass on these advantages, and financial assets, to their children.[15]

This sort of "class homogeneity" has detrimental consequences for innovation, notes economist Raj Chetty. His argument that class, racial, gender, and ethnic barriers are causing us to lose out on potential Einsteins reflects his research that shows entrepreneurship and innovation are stimulated when children and young people are exposed to other innovators, something that the poor rarely have the opportunity to experience.[16] Any social division that isolates children from successful role models and mentors will tend to undermine the potential of those children to move up the socioeconomic scale and especially to become inventors themselves. This exposure, far more than inherent ability, educational attainment, or even access to capital and finance, is what makes an innovative generation.[17] Similarly, investments in human capital make a big difference for innovation by tapping into latent talent and encouraging would-be entrepreneurs and inventors to take risks. By many measures human capital, like physical capital, is deteriorating in the United States, a perilous situation in a world that depends more and more on the skills, knowledge, and abilities of humans.[18] Many basic measures of wellbeing are falling in the United States. Health, education levels, and life expectancy lag the world leaders such as Japan and Finland. The minimal American childcare system places greater stress on American mothers compared to those elsewhere, limiting the opportunities of would-be female innovators. The United States also lags well behind its peers in key educational indicators in science, math, and reading.[19]

Today, the global age of innovation has essentially shifted away from the United States. The fastest growing innovators and spenders on research and development are nations like China, South Korea, Israel, Germany, and Sweden. And India is gaining a growing percentage of software patents. The need for talent is moving people to these fast-growing economies, or in the case of China and India, moving them back home after they have been educated in the United States.[20] Silicon Valley and all the other U.S. tech hubs must compete all the harder for this sort of talent, given the growth of innovation and new technology in other countries. At the same time, the U.S. still only issues 150,000 H1B visas that allow employers to hire foreign workers, compared to the 500,000 foreign students who graduate each year.[21]

Over time, innovative businesses tend to migrate to where there is fast growth, abundant human capital, and cities that provide a good quality of life. Many technologies, as mundane as an iPhone or as cutting edge as satellites or electric automobiles, require a complex ecology of knowledge and skill and manufacturing capabilities. Batteries, visual displays, semiconductors, expertise in metallurgy, manufacturing, and software all come together in technologically complex products today.[22] By shutting itself off from the global migration of talent and implementing policies that make it harder for students to come to America and harder still for them to stay after they have been educated, the United States is working against its own long-term interests in innovation. [23]

There are some indications that this reduction in both immigrant and native-born entrepreneurial opportunities is starting to take a toll. The United States has dropped out of the top ten innovation nations as measured by Bloomberg, with South Korea, Singapore, and Sweden among the new leaders. Measured as a percentage of population, new business startups have been on a long-term decline in the United States since the 1970s. Although the United States still has one of the highest entrepreneurship rates among twenty-five industrial nations, it is not clear it can maintain its position if current conditions continue. The United States has historically been a great place to execute good ideas, from whatever source, but the combination of underinvestment in human and physical capital, threats to immigrant entrepreneurs, and decline of new business startups may be reversing this historic strength.[24]

History tells us what countries can do to reverse decline or stagnation, and what not to do as well. One thing history demonstrates is that a totalitarian state committed to total central planning is NOT the answer to the social tensions of innovation. The failure of the Soviet Union is the most obvious example here, and China's successful escape from that trap in the 1970s is a clear example of how the innovative state embraces the tendency to replace control and ideological purity with pragmatic flexibility and openness to private initiative. Today in fact, there is some growing concern about a return to authoritarianism and illiberal values in nations such as Hungary, Brazil, Venezuela, and, the rise of xenophobic and racist parties even in the otherwise democratic West. China itself is now faced with question of how much it will open its markets and society in a liberal fashion, and how much it wishes to (and successfully can) retain strong state control. The laudable political value of stability can become harmful to innovation when it turns to a narrow conformity, as we have seen. Throughout history, government acceptance and/or support for private experimentation and the competitive testing of new ideas have been crucial to innovation—the free universities, artisanal guilds, and scientific societies that arose in Europe, the towns and city-states of the early modern Mediterranean, the private networks of merchants that marked the great commercial innovations in the Golden Age of Islam. I believe it will grow increasingly important for governments to allow and promote experimentation, knowledge exchange, and risk-taking new ventures.

The future is going to belong to those places that strengthen their connections to the new global ecology of innovation. As in the past, so in the future, connections to cultures and peoples beyond one's own nation will be crucial, along with investments in education, training, and critical thought to promote an attitude of inquiry, investigation, and openness to new things and new values. The winning nations will find, attract, and cultivate the largest, broadest pool of talent regardless of where it is from—whether that talent is online or physically present—and seize on sources of capital to make it possible to execute new ideas. The race is now on across the globe to build the institutions that can accelerate training and promote startups and entrepreneurial incubators. Typically funded by a single venture capital group that provides seed money in exchange for a percentage of equity in the start-up, incubators offer training, office space, investment capital, mentoring, peer collaboration, networking opportunities with potential investors, and assistance with marketing. They compress years' worth of training into just a few months. Vocational and apprenticeship programs at community colleges are also key to training millions of everyday workers in the knowledge economy. Germany is one of the leading nations in apprenticeship training, which has served its advanced manufacturing industry exceedingly well, as well as its banking and IT sectors. The European powerhouse offers students a blend of classroom education in vocational schools with apprenticeship training on the job, reflecting a growing collaboration between its educational system, the private sector, and business and civic organizations.[25]

New tech hubs of innovation are also going well beyond some of the older historic sites such as Silicon Valley. According to a recent KPMG survey of tech industry leaders, Silicon Valley will lose its top slot to Beijing as the world's leading tech innovation hub by 2023. The reason? A massive, global movement towards decentralizing innovation is underway, stimulated by investment in other cities and regions around the world. What had once been simply a global economy built on trade or the offshoring of some production stages has now become a giant global supply and production network with every function, from the highest level research to the skilled design and management work, to the sophisticated and the basic manufacturing jobs located across many different places on the world map.[26] Dramatic increases in cost-of-living, compounded by increasingly politicized issues surrounding corporate culture and technology regulation are making Silicon Valley less attractive to entrepreneurs and investors. Although California along with New York, Boston, and Austin, Texas will remain world class tech centers for the near future, Beijing, Shanghai, Taipei, Singapore, and Seoul are among the top ten and rising fast.[27]

It will be difficult for any hub, even a historically successful one, to remain competitive given the growing accessibility of knowledge across borders and the increasing availability of training to would-be challengers. Vast armies of consultants from KPMG, PwC, the Boston Consulting Group, and others, advise governments and companies around the world on how to develop their innovation strategies. Many efforts are underway to teach executives how to make their companies more innovative. Harvard's Innovation Labs supports both students and a global network of alumni entrepreneurs in pursuing and accelerating innovation ventures. *The Economist* lists 221 innovation courses located around the world for business executives. In addition, there are global organizations like The Startup Genome which is dedicated to increasing the success rate of startups through collaborations with hundreds of public and private organizations in more than thirty countries. Similarly, the Global Entrepreneurship Network (GEN) operates in 170 countries with a mission of making it easier for anyone, anywhere, to start and scale a business. Companies like Microsoft also have accelerator programs for startups. Citibank runs one in Tel Aviv. "Many enterprise companies realize they need to engage with startups if they want to be exposed to advances in technologies and new methodologies, and ultimately be able to secure their future," explains Zack Weisfeld of Microsoft.[28]

In this brave new world of innovation the global innovator will flourish. Those who remain too fearful of change, wedded to the old ways and comfortable only with the familiar, unable to work across multiple languages, cultures, and social and political systems, will be at a grave disadvantage. As has happened throughout history, they will be superseded by the new innovation leader, wherever that leadership comes from.

ENDNOTES

Introduction

1 After World War II, economists began to gain better data on overall macroeconomic performance. Through national income accounting they began to realize that growth, particularly in modern industrial economies, was due far less to traditional inputs like land, labor, and capital, and far more to improvements in productivity. These improvements, it was believed, resulted from changes and improvements in technology. Changes in technology we call innovations, and they were a crucial part of economic growth. But innovations could only be counted as a "residual," or that part of economic growth that was not explained by the traditional factors of production. The residual was a black box. Something caused technology to change, improve, and contribute to productivity, but what, and how? Moses Abramovitz, "Resource and Output Trends in the United States since 1870," *American Economic Review* 46, no. 2 (May 1956): 5-23; Joseph Schumpeter, *Capitalism, Socialism, and Democracy* (Harper & Brothers, 1942). Robert Solow developed the growth model that revealed the crucial role of productivity in economic growth. See Robert Solow, "Technical Change and the Aggregate Production Function," *Review of Economics and Statistics* 39, no. 3 (August 1957): 312-20; and Benton Massell, "Capital Formation and Technological Change in U. S. Manufacturing," *Review of Economics and Statistics* 42, no. 2 (May 1960):182-88.

2 There are many ways to define innovation. A good place to start thinking about it is Benoit Godin, *Innovation: The History of Category, Working Paper No. 1, Project on the Intellectual History of Innovation* (Montréal, 2008).

3 Peter F. Drucker, *Innovation and Entrepreneurship: Practice and Principles* (Harper, 1985), 249-54.

4 Carl Benedikt Frey, *The Technology Trap: Capital, Labor and Power in the Age of Automation* (Princeton University Press, 2019), 33-59.

5 The classic statement of this is W. F. Ogburn, *Social Change with Respect to Culture and Original Nature* (B.W. Huebsch, 1922). For a look at the vast changes in technology and life in the twentieth century, see Robert J. Gordon, *The Rise and Fall of American Growth:*

The U.S. Standard of Living since the Civil War (Princeton University Press, 2016). Some economists and historians also think in terms of broad "general purpose technologies" that stimulate many smaller innovations and improvements and provide a platform for productivity enhancing innovations of many sorts. See Boyan Jovanovic and Peter L. Rousseau, "General Purpose Technologies," *in Handbook of Economic Growth, Volume 1*, eds. Philippe Aghion and Steven N. Durlauf (Elsevier B.V., 2005), 1181-1221.

6 Lisa Eadiccio, Matt Peckham, John Patrick Pullen, and Alex Fitzpatrick, "The 20 Most Successful Failures of All Time," *Time*, April 5, 2017.

7 Mark J. Perry, "Fortune 500 firms 1955 v. 2017," AEIdeas, October 20, 2017 at http://www.aei.org/publication/fortune-500-firms-1955-v-2017 -only-12-remain-thanks-to-the-creative-destruction-that-fuels-economic-prosperity/.

8 Mark Kurlansky, *Paper: Paging Through History* (W.W. Norton., 2016), xviii; Holland Cotter, "Shelf Life: The Story of Islam's Gift of Paper to the West," *New York Times*, December 29, 2001, p. 15.

9 Some authors will speak of radical versus incremental innovation. The revolutionary and evolutionary work together, one picking up where the other leaves off, though there can also be a tradeoff between the two. The most famous discussion of this potential tradeoff is Clayton Christensen, *The Innovator's Dilemma: When New Technologies Cause Great Firms to Fail* (Harvard Business Review Press, 2013).

10 Henry Petroski, *The Evolution of Useful Things: How Everyday Artifacts-From Forks and Pins to Paper Clips and Zippers-Came to be as They Are* (Alfred A. Knopf, 1992).

11 Mark Zachary Taylor, *The Politics of Innovation: Why Some Countries Are Better Than Others at Science and Technology* (Oxford University Press, 2016).

12 https://www.wipo.int/edocs/pubdocs/en/wipo_pub_gii_2019_keyfindings.pdf.

13 Alfred D. Chandler, Jr. *Scale and Scope: The Dynamics of Industrial Capitalism* (Belknap Press of Harvard University, 1990); Martin Wiener, *English Culture and the Decline of the Industrial Spirit, 1850-1980* (Cambridge University Press, 2004).

14 Mariana Mazzucato, *The Entrepreneurial State: Debunking Public vs. Private Sector Myths* (Public Affairs, 2015).

15 George Gilder, *Wealth and Poverty* (Basic Books, 1981) and *Telecosm: The World after Bandwidth Abundance* (Simon and Schuster, 2000).

16 Christensen, *Innovator's Dilemma.*

17 Quinn Slobodian, *Globalists: The End of Empire and the Birth of Neoliberalism* (Harvard University Press, 2018); Angus Burgin, *The Great Persuasion: Reinventing Free Markets since the Depression* (Harvard University Press, 2012).

18 Malcolm S. Salter, "Crony Capitalism, American Style: What Are We Talking about Here?" HBS Working Paper No. 15-025 (Harvard, 2014), online at SSRN: http:// ssrn.com/abstract=2513490. Luigi Zingales, *A Capitalism for the People: Recapturing the Lost Genius of American Prosperity* (Basic Books, 2012); Anders Aslund, *Russia's Crony Capitalism: The Path from Market Economy to Kleptocracy* (Yale University Press, 2019).

19 Daron Acemoglu and James Robinson, *Why Nations Fail: The Origins of Power, Prosperity, and Poverty* (Crown, 2012).

20 Thomas Piketty, *Capital in the Twenty-First Century* (Belknap Press of Harvard University, 2014); and Lant Pritchett, "Divergence, Big Time," *Journal of Economic Perspectives* 11, no. 3 (Summer 1997): 3-17.

21 Clay Chandler, "Why China is Emerging as a Tech Superpower to Rival the U.S.," *Fortune*, November 21, 2017.

22 James McGregor, "China's Drive for 'Indigenous Innovation:' A Web of Industrial Policies," U.S. Chamber of Commerce, 2010, p. 4; Bob Davis, "China's Authoritarian State Has an Edge in Artificial Intelligence Development," *Wall Street Journal*, February 25, 2018; "China Keeps A Close Eye on Muslims," *Bloomberg Businessweek*, January 22, 2018; Jonathan Woetzel, et al., "The China Effect on Global Innovation," *McKinsey Global Institute Research Bulletin* (July 2015).

23 Thomas L. Friedman, "China Deserves Donald Trump: It took a human wrecking ball to get China's attention," *New York Times*, May 21, 2019; Samm Sacks, "Beijing Wants to Rewrite the Rules of the Internet," *The Atlantic*, June 18, 2019.

24 Quoted in Davis, "China's Authoritarian State Has an Edge in Artificial Intelligence."

25 Taylor, *Politics of Innovation*.

26 As the economist Ester Boserup noted, the larger the population and higher its density the more innovation it produced. But we do not have to stop with just overall population size. Mobilization of the population potential is even more crucial. Ester Boserup, *Population and Technological Change: A Study of Long-Term Trends* (University of Chicago Press, 1981).

27 In the United States, the recent emphasis on narrow training and testing may be having a similar negative effect on innovation, something we discuss in a later chapter.

28 Samuel Beckett, *Worstward Ho* (Grove Press, 1983).

29 Openness does not necessarily mean from outside of political borders. It can come from within, from the otherwise marginal, immigrant, or excluded subgroups who are allowed to bring their talents and ideas forward.

30 "How Much Money did Jonas Salk Potentially Forfeit by not Patenting the Polio Vaccine?" *Forbes*, August 9, 2012.

31 Russell King, *Atlas of Human Migration* (Struik Publishers, 2008); Patrick Manning, *Migration in World History* (Routledge, 2005).

32 Peter Frankopan, *The Silk Roads: A New History of the World* (Vintage Books, 2017).

33 Victor Hugo, *The Hunchback of Notre Dame*, 87.

34 Andrew Ross Sorkin, "What Trump's Huawei Reversal Means for the Future of 5G," *New York Times*, July 1, 2019.

35 Some would argue that, correctly measured, China is already the world's largest economy. See https://www.bbc.com/news/magazine-30483762; and https://www.imf.org/external/datamapper/PPPSH@WEO/OEMDC/WEOWORLD/ADVEC/CHN/USA.

36 Richard Florida, *The New Urban Crisis: How Our Cities Are Increasing Inequality, Deepening Segregation, and Failing the Middle Class-and What We Can Do About It* (Basic Books, 2017); Paul Krugman, "Increasing Returns and Economic Geography," *Journal of Political Economy* 99, no. 2 (June 1991): 483-99; Jane Jacobs, *The Economy of Cities* (New York, 1969).

37 Ronald Findlay and Kevin O'Rourke, *Power and Plenty: Trade, War and the World Economy in the Second Millennium* (Princeton, 2007), 49; Maurice Lombard, *The Golden Age of Islam* (Amsterdam, 1975).

38 See https://ourworldindata.org/urbanization. One thing this statistic tells us is that with the world now more than 50 percent urban, cities have grown much more important to innovation.

39 This idea shares much with the evolutionary theory of economic change. See Richard Nelson, et al. *Modern Evolutionary Economics: An Overview* (Cambridge University Press, 2018).

40 Jeff Muskus, "Out From Under the 'Bamboo Ceiling,'" *Bloomberg Businessweek*, January 22, 2018.

Chapter 1

1 Cyril Stanley Smith, *From Art to Science: Seventy-Two Objects Illustrating the Nature of Discovery* (MIT Press, 1980).

2 J. R. McNeill and William McNeill, *The Human Web: A Birds-Eye View of History* (W. W. Norton, 2003).

3 Graeme Barker *The Agricultural Revolution in Prehistory: Why Did Foragers Become Farmers?* (Oxford University Press, 2006); Heather Pringle, "The Slow Birth of Agriculture," *Science* 20 (November 1998) vol. 282, issue 5393, p. 1446; David Harris, ed., *The Origins and Spread Of Agriculture And Pastoralism In Eurasia: Crops, Fields, Flocks And Herds* (Routledge, 1996).

4 John Humphrey *Ancient Technology* (Greenwood Press, 2006), 1-35; J. G. Manning, *The Open Sea: The Economic Life of the Ancient Mediterranean World from the Iron Age to the Rise of Rome* (Princeton University Press, 2018), 39-72.

5 Michael Jursa, "Babylonia in the First Millennium BCE: Economic Growth in Times of Empire," in *The Cambridge History of Capitalism, Vol. 1, The Rise Of Capitalism: From Ancient Origins to 1848,* eds. Larry Neal and Jeffrey G. Williamson (Cambridge University Press, 2014), 24-42.

6 Benoît Godin, "How Innovation Evolved from a Heretical Act to a Heroic Imperative," in *Does America Need More Innovators?* eds. Matthew Wisnioski, Eric S. Hintz, and Marie Stettler Kleine (MIT Press, 2019), 141-64.

7 Andrew Russell and Lee Vinsel, "Make Maintainers: Engineering Education and an Ethics of Care," in Wisnioski et al., *Does America Need More Innovators?*, 249-69.

8 Mark Lehner, *The Complete Pyramids: Solving the Ancient Mysteries* (Thames and Hudson, 1997).

9 J. G. Manning, "Hellenistic Egypt," in *The Cambridge Economic History of the Greco-Roman World*, eds. W. Scheidel, I. Morris, and R.P. Saller (Cambridge University Press, 2007), 434-59.

10 Manning, *Open Sea*, 231-37.

11 Alain Bresson, "Capitalism and the Ancient Greek Economy," in Neal and Williamson, *Cambridge History of Capitalism*, 43-74; Clementina Panella and André Tchernia, "Agricultural Products Transported in Amphorae: Oil and Wine," in *The Ancient Economy*, eds. Walter Scheidel and Sitta von Reden (Routledge, 2002), 173-87.

12 Manning, *Open Sea*, 264-66.

13 Helmuth Schneider, "Technology," in Scheidel, Morris, and Saller, *Cambridge Economic History of the Greco-Roman World*, 145-47. Manning, *Open Sea*, 231-37.

14 Manning, *Open Sea*, 73, 220-25.

15 Manning, *Open Sea*, 3-5.

16 Humphrey *Ancient Technology*, 114-15; K. D. White, *Greek and Roman Technology* (Thames & Hudson, 1984), 37; Desmond Lee, "Science Technology and Philosophy in the Ancient World," *Greece & Rome* 20, no. 2 (October 1973):180-93.

17 David S. Landes, Joel Mokyr, and William Baumol, eds., *The Invention of Enterprise: Entrepreneurship from Ancient Mesopotamia to Modern Times* (Princeton University Press, 2010); William V. Harris, "The Late Republic," in Scheidel, Morris, and Saller, *Cambridge Economic History of the Greco-Roman World*, 521-23.

18 Willem M. Jongman, "Re-constructing the Roman Economy," in Neal and Williamson, *Cambridge History of Capitalism*, 75-100; Elio lo Cascio, "The Early Roman Empire: The State and the Economy," in Scheidel, Morris, and Saller, *Cambridge Economic History of the Greco-Roman World*, 626-28.

19 Peter Temin, "The Economy of the Early Roman Empire," *Journal of Economic Perspectives* 20, no. 1 (Winter 2006): 133-51: M. I. Findley, "Technical Innovation and Economic Progress in the Ancient World," *Economic History Review* 18, no. 1 (1965): 9-45.

20 White, *Greek and Roman Technology*, 91-100.

21 By comparison the manumission rate in the U.S. south was a mere .2% in five years. Temin, "The Economy of the Early Roman Empire," 142.

22 Dominic Rathbone, "The Ancient Economy and Graeco-Roman Egypt," in Scheidel and von Reden, *Ancient Economy*, 158-62.

23 Temin, "The Economy of the Early Roman Empire"; Harris, "The Late Republic," 527-28.

24 Dominic W. Rathbone, "Roman Egypt," in Scheidel, Morris, and Saller, *Cambridge Economic History of the Greco-Roman World*, 710-11.

25 Robert Hitchner, "Olive Production and the Roman Economy: The Case for Intensive Growth in the Roman Empire," in Scheidel and von Reden, *Ancient Economy*, 73-74, 77; Helmuth Schneider, "Technology," in Scheidel, Morris, and Saller, *Cambridge Economic History of the Greco-Roman World*, 157-58.

26 Willem Jongman, "The Early Roman Empire: Consumption," in Scheidel, Morris, and Saller, *Cambridge Economic History of the Greco-Roman World*, 592–618; Dennis P. Kehoe, "The Early Roman Empire: Production," in Scheidel, Morris, and Saller, *Cambridge Economic History of the Greco-Roman World*, 543-69.

27 Schneider, "Technology," 154-55.

28 White, *Greek and Roman Technology*, 42.

29 Harris, "The Late Republic," 531, 535-536.

30 Humphrey, *Ancient Technology*.

31 Adapted from the model used by Humphrey in *Ancient Technology*.

32 David Edgerton, *The Shock of the Old: Technology and Global History since 1900* (Oxford University Press, 2007).

33 Henry Petroski, *The Evolution of Useful Things: How Everyday Artifacts-From Forks and Pins to Paper Clips and Zippers-Came to be as They Are* (Alfred A. Knopf, 1992).

34 Even papyrus continued to thrive in the Mediterranean world long after paper was introduced; printing did not cause penmanship to die out, and television did not kill radio, nor did the Internet kill television. Cindi May, "A Learning Secret: Don't Take Notes with a Laptop," *Scientific American*, June 3, 2014 at https://www.scientificamerican.com/article/a-learning-secret-don-t-take-notes-with-a-laptop/; Michael Schaub, "92% of College Students Prefer Print Books to e-books, Study Finds," *Los Angeles Times*, February 8, 2016, at http://www.latimes.com/books/jacketcopy/la-et-jc-92-percent-college-students-prefer-paper-over-pixels-20160208-story.html.

35 Robert K. Merton, "Singletons and Multiples in Science," in *The Sociology of Science: Theoretical and Empirical Investigations*, ed. Norman W. Storer (University of Chicago Press, 1973).

Chapter 2

1 J.L. Berggren, "Islamic Mathematics," in *The Cambridge History of Science, Vol. 2: Medieval Science*, eds. David C. Lindberg and Michael H. Shank (Cambridge University Press, 2013), 62-83.

2 Martin Luther King, Jr., "The Purpose of Education," *Maroon Tiger*, February, 1947, at https://kinginstitute.stanford.edu/king-papers/documents/purpose-education.

3 This is not to say it was the only innovation society. In fact, there were also important advances in knowledge, science, and technology taking place in India and China as well. Islam had a strong presence in India and learned much from this culture, as well as from China in more indirect ways. We will hear more about the flourishing of learning and innovation in Tang and Song China later.

4 Tamim Ansary, *Destiny Disrupted: A History of the World Through Islamic Eyes* (Public Affairs, 2009), 51; Y. Tzvi Langermann, "Science in the Jewish Communities," in Lindberg and Shank, *Cambridge History of Science*, 170, 191; María Rosa Menocal, *The Ornament of the World: How Muslims, Jews, and Christians Created a Culture of Tolerance in Medieval Spain* (Little, Brown and Company, 2002), 61; Mark Kurlansky, *Paper: Paging Through History* (W.W. Norton, 2016), 57; Toby E. Huff, *The Rise of Early Modern Science: Islam, China, and the West* (Cambridge University Press, 1993), 73-74.

5 Jonathan Lyons, *House of Wisdom: How the Arabs Transformed Western Civilization* (Bloomsbury Press, 2009), 56-57, 32-33; Maurice Lombard, *The Golden Age of Islam* (Marcus Wiener Publishers, 2009), 98.

6 Kurlansky, *Paper*, 50; Clifford D. Conner, *A People's History of Science: Miners, Midwives, and "Low Mechanicks"* (Nation Books, 2005), 161-62; Menocal, *Ornament of the World*, 54-56; Jim Al-Khalili, *The House of Wisdom: How Arabic Science Saved Ancient Knowledge and Gave Us the Renaissance* (Penguin Press, 2010), 43-68.

7 Jonathan M. Bloom, *Paper Before Print: The History and Impact of Paper in the Islamic World* (Yale University Press, 2001), 1-11, 45- 53, 89, 117, 136; Lombard, *Golden Age of Islam*, 190.

8 Bloom, *Paper Before Print*, 11.

9 Lombard, *Golden Age of Islam*, 118. Some have estimated Baghdad's population at 360,000 and others at 2,000,000. See Jacob Lassner and Michael Bonner, *Islam in the Middle Ages: The Origins and Shaping of Classical Islamic Civilization* (Praeger, 2009), 158-59. Some authors think China's Chang'an (Xi'an) may have been slightly larger. By contrast the largest city in Christendom, Constantinople, had perhaps 200,000 inhabitants, while London had about 10,000.

10 Lyons, *House of Wisdom*, 56-57, 32-33; Kurlansky, *Paper*, xv, 49-54; Ansary, *Destiny Disrupted*, 1-3, 87-89; Huff, *Rise of Early Modern Science*, 80; Bloom, *Paper Before Print*, 2, 48-50, 91.

11 Lyons, *House of Wisdom*, 58; Kurlansky, *Paper*, 69; Michael Shank, "School and Universities in Medieval Latin Science," in Lindberg and Shank, *Cambridge History of Science*, 207-39; Huff, *Rise of Early Modern Science*, 75-77; Bloom, *Paper Before Print*, 113-14.

12 Ansary, *Destiny Disrupted*, 100.

13 F. Jamil Ragep, "Islamic Culture and the Natural Sciences," in Lindberg and Shank, *Cambridge History of Science*, 37.

14 Kurlansky, *Paper*, xv, 49-54, 69; Lyons, *House of Wisdom*, 32-33, 56-57; Ansary, *Destiny Disrupted*, 1-3.

15 While tolerant of some religions, Muslims were not indifferent to all faiths either. They treated pagans, for example, quite mercilessly and forced them to convert to Islam. Menocal, *Ornament of the World*, 123-26.

16 Huff, *Rise of Early Modern Science*, 65, 85; Conner, *People's History of Science*, 162; Bloom, *Paper Before Print*, 136.

17 Charles Burnett, "Translation and Transmission of Greek and Islamic Science to Latin Christendom," in Lindberg and Shank, *Cambridge History of Science*, 360; Huff, *Rise of Early Modern Science*, 51-53, 65. On Copernicus's reliance upon the Maragha astronomers, Huff quotes Noel Swerdlow and Otto Neugebauer, *Mathematical Astronomy in Copernicus's "De revolutionibus"* (Springer Verlag, 1984), 46.

18 Bruce S. Eastwood, "Early-Medieval Cosmology, Astronomy, and Mathematics," in Lindberg and Shank, *Cambridge History of Science*, 304-15; Lyons, *House of Wisdom*, 32-33; Huff, *Rise of Early Modern Science*, 51-55.

19 Al-Khalili, *House of Wisdom*, 43-68; Goldziher, "The Attitude of Orthodox Islam Toward the Ancient Sciences," in *Studies on Islam*, ed. Merlin L. Swartz (Oxford University Press, 1981), 195.

20 Ansary, *Destiny Disrupted*, 103; Goldziher, "Attitude of Orthodox Islam," 196.

21 Berggren, "Islamic Mathematics," 77-85; Goldziher, "Attitude of Orthodox Islam," 185-86.

22 Eastwood, "Early-Medieval Cosmology, Astronomy, and Mathematics," 313; Ansary, *Destiny Disrupted*, 110-118; Goldziher, "Attitude of Orthodox Islam," 186.

23 Conner, *People's History of Science*, 161-62; Lombard, *Golden Age of Islam*, 25-26, 181-87.

24 Emilie Savage-Smith, "Medicine in Medieval Islam," in Lindberg and Shank, *Cambridge History of Science*, 143-44.

25 Savage-Smith "Medicine in Medieval Islam,"167; David C. Lindberg, "Science and the Medieval Church," in Lindberg and Shank, *Cambridge History of Science*, 282; Lombard, *Golden Age of Islam*, 238-39.

26 Conner, *People's History of Science*, 161-62; Savage-Smith, "Medicine in Medieval Islam," 139-67.

27 Ansary, *Destiny Disrupted*, 101; Kurlansky, *Paper*, 58-59; Bloom, *Paper Before Print*, 129; Huff, *Rise of Early Modern Science*, 50.

28 Conner, *People's History*, 72-74, 171; Al-Khalili, *House of Wisdom*, 62; Lombard, *Golden Age of Islam*, 129-35, 146-47, 161; Bloom, *Paper Before Print*, 136. Joseph Needham has also argued that slaves from China were also an important conduit for the transmission of that empire's knowledge of science and technology.

29 Sevket Pamuk, "Institutional Change and Economic Development in the Middle East, 700-1800," in *The Cambridge History of Capitalism, Vol. 1, The Rise Of Capitalism: From Ancient Origins to 1848*, eds. Larry Neal and Jeffrey G. Williamson (Cambridge University Press, 2014), 203. The same sort of flexibility would be found later in Medieval Europe, where religious prohibitions against usury did not stand in the way of commerce. Maya Shatzmiller, "The Economic History of the Medieval Middle East: Strengths, Weaknesses, and the Challenge Ahead," International *Journal of Middle East Studies* 44 (August 2012): 529-31.

30 William J. Bernstein, *A Splendid Exchange: How Trade Shaped the World* (Grove Press, 2008), 58-62.

31 Bernstein, *Splendid Exchange*, 75; Maya Shatzmiller, "Transcontinental Trade and Economic Growth in the Early Islamic Empire: The Red Sea Corridor in the 8th-10th Centuries," in *Connected Hinterlands: Proceedings of Red Sea Project IV*, eds. Lucy Blue et al. (British Archaeological Reports, 2010); Lyons, *House of Wisdom*, 39.

32 Robert S. Lopez, *The Commercial Revolution of the Middle Ages, 950-1350* (Cambridge University Press, 1976). Lopez notes that while at the height of the Roman Empire, agricultural productivity could produce yields of four to ten times the seed planted in Sicily or Tuscany, after in Western Europe it fell to at best two times.

33 Lopez, *Commercial Revolution.*

34 Huff, *Rise of Early Modern Science*, 77-83.

35 Huff, *Rise of Early Modern Science*, 34-35, 71-87, 232; Ansary, *Destiny Disrupted,* 110-15.

36 Pamuk, "Institutional Change," 201-11.

Chapter 3

1 Toby Huff, *The Rise of Early Modern Science* (Cambridge University Press, 1993), 111-22; Tamim Ansary, *Destiny Disrupted: A History of the World Through Islamic Eyes* (Public Affairs, 2009), 132-36.

2 P. J. Kpolovie, S. Ewansiha, and M. Esara, "Continental Comparison of Human Development Index (HDI)," *International Journal of Humanities Social Sciences and Education* 4, no. 1 (January 2017), 9; World University Rankings 2018, Times Higher Education.com; Soumitra Dutta, Bruno Lanvin, Sacha Wunsch-Vincent, eds., *Global Innovation Index Report 2018* (Cornell University, INSEAD, World Intellectual Property Organization, 2018), 45-46; World Intellectual Property Organization, "Global Innovation Index 2018," Press Release/2018/819.

3 In no culture did learning and education operate completely free from political or religious authorities, including Europe, as Galileo found out when he challenged the Catholic Church approved Earth centered model of the universe by putting the sun at the center. See Huff, *Rise of Early Modern Science*, 138, 181.

4 4 Universities were not completely autonomous of course. Their members would still be subject to the rules and scrutiny of the church and corporate status was granted by the sovereign. Corporate charters, in these early days, were limited, setting clear and well-defined terms on what universities could do, and which areas it was permitted to operate in.

5 Frances and Joseph Gies, *Cathedral, Forge and Waterwheel: Technology and Invention in the Middle Ages* (Harper Collins, 1994), 48; Terry Reynolds, *Stronger than a Hundred Men: A History of the Vertical Waterwheel* (Johns Hopkins University Press, 1988); Clifford D. Connor, *A People's History of Science: Miners, Midwives, and "Low Mechanicks"* (Nation Books, 2005), 162-82; Lissa Roberts, et al., *The Mindful Hand: Inquiry and Invention from the late Renaissance to Early Industrialisation* (Edita Publishing House, 2007), xxi.

6 Gies and Gies, *Cathedral, Forge and Waterwheel*, 48, 112-14; Huff, *Rise of Early Modern Science*, 111-22.

7 It cut both ways though. So, when Galileo proposed a model of the universe that contradicted interpretations of the religious texts by placing the sun and not the earth at the center, he was condemned by the church for his error. Clearly any scientific proposition that contradicted the bible must be wrong.

8 Harold J. Berman, *Law and Revolution: The Formation of the Western Legal Tradition* (Harvard University Press, 1983).

9 Berman, *Law and Revolution*, 141-42.

10 Huff, *Rise of Early Modern Science*, 100, 115-18, 128, 150-57, 179-89; Pamela Smith and Benjamin Schmidt, eds., *Making Knowledge in Early Modern Europe: Practices, Objects, and Texts*, 1400-1800 (University of Chicago Press, 2008), 2.

11 Vincent Ilardi, *Renaissance Vision from Spectacles to Telescopes* (American Philosophical Society, 2007), 118-25; Huff, *Rise of Modern Science*, 295; Lutfallah Gari, "The Invention of Spectacles between the East and the West," at muslimheritage.com. There is some controversy over whether the West or the East developed spectacles, and it is known that the Chinese also used magnifying lenses placed in frames for reading. But the first spectacles are generally believed to have been developed in Italy.

12 Joseph Needham, *Science in Traditional China* (Harvard University Press, 1981), 9; Joseph Needham, *The Grand Titration: Science and Society In East and West* (University of Toronto Press, reprint, 1979), 11.

13 Jonathan M. Bloom, *Paper Before Print: The History and Impact of Paper in the Islamic World* (Yale University Press, 2001), 215; Gies and Gies, *Cathedral, Forge, and Waterwheel*, 243-47; Huff, *Rise of Modern Science*, 293-94; https://courses.lumenlearning.com/suny-musicapp-medieval-modern/chapter/the-printing-press-e/.

14 Herman Pleij, "Novel Knowledge: Innovation in Dutch Literature and Society in the Fifteenth and Sixteenth Centuries," in Smith and Schmidt, *Making Knowledge in Early Modern Europe*, 109-26; Conner, *People's History of Science*, 171-72; Bloom, *Paper Before Print*, 215-16.

15 See Smith and Schmidt, *Making Knowledge in Early Modern Europe*, 2-3 on the criticisms of book printed knowledge by the cleric Adrien Ballet and the proposed "book wheel" solution to information overload by the Italian inventor Agostino Ramelli.

16 Huff, *Rise of Modern Science*, 330, 294.

17 Gies and Gies, *Cathedral, Forge and Waterwheel*, 238; Mark Kurlansky, *Paper: Paging Through History* (W.W. Norton, 2016), 93; Bloom, *Paper Before Print*, 225; Huff, *Rise of Early Modern Science*, 330, 293-94.

18 Janet Abu-Lughod, *Before European Hegemony: The World System A.D. 1250-1350* (Oxford University Press, 1991), 44.

19 Access to the Persian Gulf was through Baghdad and the Red Sea via Egypt. While European crusaders had established a beachhead in the Levant, they were pushed back by the Seljuk Turks led by Saladin in 1187, and the establishment of the Ayyubid Dynasty there.

20 Abu Lughod, *Before European Hegemony*, 154-58, 177.

21 Steven A. Epstein, *An Economic and Social History of Later Medieval Europe* (Cambridge University Press, 2009), 95.

22 Abu-Lughod, *Before European Hegemony*, 123 and see map, 213-15; William J. Bernstein, *A Splendid Exchange: How Trade Shaped the World* (Grove Press, 2008), 121-29. Many of those sold as slaves came from the Crimean Black Sea region. They were Slavic peoples, which is how the word "slave" entered the English language.

23 Thomas Madden, *Venice: A New History* (Penguin, 2012). Over time this openness became more exclusive and closed, note Daron Acemoglu and James A. Robinson in *Why Nations Fail: The Origins of Power, Prosperity, and Poverty* (Crown, 2012).

24 Edwin S. Hunt and James M. Murray, *A History of Business in Medieval Europe, 1200-1550* (Cambridge University Press, 1999); Ansary, *Destiny Disrupted*, 202-03.

25 Epstein, *Economic and Social History*, 85; Robert S. Lopez, *The Commercial Revolution of the Middle Ages, 950-1350* (Cambridge University Press, 1976), 76-77; Abu-Lughod, *Before European Hegemony*, 119.

26 Compagni, from which we get company, is from the Italian, *com pane*, or one with whom one shares bread.

27 Hunt and Murray, *History of Business in Medieval Europe*, 59; Lopez, *Commercial Revolution*, 93.

28 Lopez, *Commercial Revolution.*

29 Madden, *Venice*, 266.

30 Ansary, *Destiny Disrupted*, 199; Abu-Lughod, *Before European Hegemony*, 16, 67-69 on various ways Italians took from the East.

31 Abu-Lughod, *Before European Hegemony*, 216-24; Epstein, *Economic and Social History*, 87-88.

32 Lopez, *Commercial Revolution*, 109-11. Later Italian colonies would be established on the coast of India at Goa, in Canton and Malacca. See Gies and Gies, *Cathedral, Forge and Waterwheel*, 167.

33 Gies and Gies, *Cathedral, Forge and Waterwheel*, 181; Needham, *Grand Titration*, 99-100; Conner, *People's History of Science*, 174. On the fascinating story of indigo, see Catherine E. McKinley, *Indigo: In Search of the Color that Seduced the World* (Bloomsbury, 2011); Jean Gimpel, *Medieval Machine: The Industrial Revolution of the Middle Ages* (Holt, Rinehart and Winston, 1976), 102.

34 Epstein, *Economic and Social History*, 282-83.

35 Abu-Lughod, *Before European Hegemony*, 79-88.

36 Eventually Amsterdam replaced Bruges. We know about the importance of Amsterdam's drapers from the famous Rembrandt painting, often misnamed the Dutch Masters because it was used on the packaging of that cigar brand. But it is actually a portrait of the syndics of the draper's guild of Amsterdam. The syndics were responsible for testing and assuring the quality of the cloth.

37 Lopez, *Commercial Revolution*, 121.

38 Lopez, *Commercial Revolution*, 111.

39 Hunt and Murray, *History of Business in Medieval Europe*, 213-27.

40 Hunt and Murray, *History of Business in Medieval Europe*, 127. For the full story of these plagues and famines, see William Chester Jordan, *The Great Famine: Northern Europe in the Early Fourteenth Century* (Princeton University Press, 1996).

41 Epstein, *Economic and Social History*, 162.

42 Epstein, *Economic and Social History*, 168; Hunt and Murray, *History of Business in Medieval Europe*, 127, 174-75; Peter Tyson, "A Short History of Quarantine," PBS.org, posted October 12, 2004.

43 Epstein, *Economic and Social History*, 163-65, 239. There were also examples of lashing out in irrational ways. The old, sick, and young were often victimized during these unstable times and anti-Semitism rose to a deadly level, with murders against Jews carried out across Europe despite the intervention of Pope Clement. In other parts of the world hit hard by plague, such as the Muslim regions, antisemitism did not rise.

44 While Venice, with support from the Pope in Rome and other parts of the Christian world, turned back the Ottoman threat in western Europe with the victory at the Battle of Lepanto in 1571, the fact is the powerful Ottoman empire pressed hard on the borders of western Europe, making it as far as the gates of Vienna.

45 Madden, *Venice*, 324-25. Despite their victory at Lepanto, the Venetian empire was in decline as the Ottomans under Suleiman the Magnificent and his successor Selim had expanded the Muslim empire across Africa and provided a unifying force not seen in Islam since the days of the caliphates centuries before.

46 Gies and Gies, *Cathedral, Forge and Waterwheel*, 214-16; Stephan R. Epstein, "Transferring Technical Knowledge and Innovating in Europe, c.1200-1800," Working Papers on The Nature of Evidence: How Well Do 'Facts' Travel? no. 01/05 (May 2005), 14.

47 Gies and Gies, *Cathedral, Forge and Waterwheel*, 71.

48 Abu-Lughod, *Before European Hegemony*, 111-12; Hunt and Murray, *History of Business in Medieval Europe*, 59; Richard Unger, "The Technology and Teaching of Shipbuilding, 1300-1800," in *Technology, Skills and the Pre-Modern Economy in the East and the West*, eds. Maarten Prak and Jan Luiten van Zanden (Brill, 2013), 161-204.

49 Wolfgang Schivelbusch, *Tastes of Paradise: A Social History of Spices, Stimulants, and Intoxicants* (Vintage, 1993).

50 Hunt and Murray, *History of Business in Medieval Europe*, 176.

51 Kenneth Pomeranz, *The Great Divergence: China, Europe, and the Making of the Modern World Economy* (Princeton University Press, 2001), 75. As Pomeranz notes, China was quite equal to Europe economically at this point, the seventeenth century, and showed the signs of early industrialization but failed in part because of these resource constraints, lacking the New World acreage. Stephen Ezell and Philipp Marxgut, *Comparing American and European Innovation Cultures* (The Information Technology and Innovation Foundation, 2015), 157 at www2.itif.org.

52 Ansary, *Destiny Disrupted*, 203; Joseph A. Schumpeter, *Capitalism, Socialism, and Democracy* (Harper and Brothers, 1942), 75.

Chapter 4

1 More recent competitors might also include electrification. In the future we may see comparable macro inventions from artificial intelligence and advances in medicine. On this first industrial revolution in Europe, see Jean Gimpel, *Medieval Machine: The Industrial Revolution of the Middle Ages* (Holt, Rinehart and Winston, 1976); Clifford D. Conner, *A People's History of Science: Miners, Midwives, and "Low Mechanicks"* (Nation Books, 2005), 180-82.

2 Of course, the fact that everyone *can* does not mean everyone will. Today's great unevenness of wealth and income between advanced and less advanced societies means that adapting a breakthrough, both large and small ones, is not easy. We will discuss the case of China, which has aggressively been adapting innovations from elsewhere to transform itself into an economic powerhouse, as well as the possibility of a global innovation system in later chapters. Stephen Ezell and Philipp Marxgut, *Comparing American and European Innovation Cultures* (The Information Technology and Innovation Foundation, 2015).

3 L. Hilaire-Pérez, "Technology as a Public Culture in the Eighteenth Century: The Artisans' Legacy," *History of Science* 45 (June 2007): 137-39; Carlo Belfanti, "Guilds, Patents, and the Circulation of Technical Knowledge: Northern Italy during the Early Modern Age," *Technology and Culture* 45, no. 3 (2004): 569-89.

4 Stephan R. Epstein, "Transferring Technical Knowledge and Innovating in Europe, c.1200-1800," Working Papers on The Nature of Evidence: How Well Do 'Facts' Travel?, no. 01/05 (May 2005).

5 Paul Bairoch, "Agriculture and the Industrial Revolution, 1790-1914," in *The Fontana Economic History of Europe, Vol. 3*, ed. Carlo M. Cipolla (Collins/Fontana, 1973); B. A. Slicher van Bath, *The Agrarian History of Western Europe from 500 to 1850 A.D.* (Edward Arnold, 1963); Gregory Clark, "Too Much Revolution: Agriculture in the Industrial Revolution, 1700-1860," in *The British Industrial Revolution: An Economic Perspective*, ed. Joel Mokyr (Westview Press, 1999), 206-240.

6 Bairoch, "Agriculture and the Industrial Revolution," 462; W. O. Henderson, *The Industrialization of Europe, 1780–1914* (Harcourt, Brace and World, 1969).

7 Morgan Kelly, Cormac Ó Gráda, and Joel Mokyr, "Precocious Albion: A New Interpretation of the British Industrial Revolution," UCD Centre for Economic Research Working Paper Series, 2013; Duan Biggs and John W. Wilson, "The Unexpected Factor Holding Back Research and Innovation," World Economic Forum, October 11, 2016, at Weforum.org; UNESCO, "International science collaboration has become a must, says report," UNESCO Science Report: Towards 2030, at https://en.unesco.org/unescosciencereport; Ezell and Marxgut, "Comparing American and European Innovation Cultures," 185-89.

8 Bairoch, "Agriculture and the Industrial Revolution," 477. Even as it industrialized, England continued to export food until as late as 1850.

9 Ellen Meiksins Wood, *The Origins of Capitalism: A Longer View* (Verso, 2017), 132; Nicholas Crafts, "The British Industrial Revolution in an International Context," *Journal of Interdisciplinary History* 19, no. 3 (Winter 1989): 415-28; Nuala Zahedieh, *The Capital and the Colonies: London and the Atlantic Economy, 1660-1700* (Cambridge University Press, 2010), 3-5; Patrick K. O'Brien, "European Economic Development: The Contribution of the Periphery," *Economic History Review* 35 (February 1982): 1-18.

10 Kenneth Pomeranz and Steven Topik, *The World that Trade Created: Society, Culture, and the World Economy, 1400 to the Present* (Routledge, 2005), 258-91; Peter F. Drucker, *Innovation and Entrepreneurship* (Harper Collins, 1985), 133-34.

11 Steven Epstein, *An Economic and Social History of Later Medieval Europe, 1000-1500* (Cambridge University Press, 2009), 168.

12 Robert C. Allen, *The British Industrial Revolution in Global Perspective* (Cambridge University Press, 2009); Nicholas Crafts, "Explaining the First Industrial Revolution: Two Views," *European Review of Economic History* 15 (April 2011): 153–68.

13 Joel Mokyr, *The Lever of Riches: Technological Creativity and Economic Progress* (Oxford University Press, 1990), 85-91.

14 Mokyr, *Lever of Riches*, 95-96, 116-19.

15 Peter Temin, "Two Views of the British Industrial Revolution," *Journal of Economic History* 57 (March 1997): 63-82; Nathan Rosenberg, "Technological Change in the Machine Tool Industry, 1840-1910," *Journal of Economic History* 23, no. 4 (1963): 414-43.

16 Arnold Pacey, *The Maze of Ingenuity: Ideas and Idealism in the Development of Technology* (MIT Press, 1992).

17 Dan Wadhwani and Christina Lubinski, "Reinventing Entrepreneurial History," *Business History Review* 91, no. 4 (2017): 767-99.

18 One of the big obstacles to effective ship navigation, for example, was an accurate navel chronometer, to measure time and hence calculate longitude. With its evolving navel strength, the British were especially interested in accurate navigation, so the government set out a prize of £20,000 for a successful device (almost $5,000,000 today). A Yorkshire carpenter named John Harrison claimed the prize after working through and improving four designs.

19 Temin, "Two Views of the Industrial Revolution" and Joel Mokyr, *The Enlightened Economy: An Economic History of Britain 1700-1859* (Yale University Press, 2009).

20 Cormac O'Grada, "Did Science Cause the Industrial Revolution?" *Journal of Economic Literature* 5, no. 1 (2016): 224-39; Robert Allen, "The Industrial Revolution in Miniature: The Spinning Jenny in Britain, France, and India," *Journal of Economic History* 69, no. 4 (December 2009): 901-27.

21 Peter Drucker, *Innovation and Entrepreneurship: Practice and Principles* (Harper, 1985), 134-35.

22 O'Grada, "Did Science Cause the Industrial Revolution?"

23 Ralf Meisenzahl and Joel Mokyr, "The Rate and Direction of Invention in the British Industrial Revolution: Incentives and Institutions," in *The Rate and Direction of Inventive Activity Revisited*, ed. Josh Lerner and Scott Stern (University of Chicago Press, 2012), 443-79; John Gapper, "Europe's Innovation Comeback: Continent Gains a Second Chance," FT Series on Europe's innovation comeback, *Financial Times,* December 12, 2017.

24 Peter Mathias, *The Transformation of England: Essays in the Economic and Social History of England in the Eighteenth Century* (Methuen, 1979).

25 Maxine Berg, "The Genesis of 'Useful Knowledge,'" *History of Science* 45 (June 2007), 128.

26 Michael D. Stephens and Gordon W. Roderick, "The Role of Scientific and Technical Education in Early Industrialisation in America and England," *The Vocational Aspect of Education* 35, no. 90 (1983): 17-22.

27 Stephens and Roderick, "Role of Scientific and Technical Education."

28 See Steven Johnson, *Where Good Ideas Come From: The Natural History of Innovation* (Riverhead, 2010), 238-40.

29 Johnson, in *Where Good Ideas Come From,* notes that this fluidity can be stifled if property rights are set too strongly. He also reminds us that while individual firms may seek to protect their intellectual property—Apple is famous for this—they are innovative because they breakdown walls and allow knowledge to move fluidly *inside* the boundaries of their firms.

30 Kelly, Ó Gráda, and Mokyr, "Precocious Albion."

31 Mathias, *Transformation of England*, 1-50.

32 Mathias, *Transformation of England*, 23, 31-36.; Meisenzahl and Mokyr, "Rate and Direction of Invention," 4; Patrick O'Brien and Roland Quinalt, eds., *The Industrial Revolution and British Society* (Cambridge University Press, 1993), 3-5.

33 Hilaire-Pérez, "Technology as a Public Culture," 143.

34 Berg, "Genesis of 'Useful Knowledge,'" 129.

35 Maxine Berg, "From Imitation to Invention: Creating Commodities in Eighteenth-Century Britain," *Economic History Review* 55 (February 2002), 6, 23.

36 David Landes, *The Unbound Prometheus: Technological Change and Industrial Development in Western Europe from 1750 to the Present* (Cambridge University Press, 1969), 124.

37 Berg, "Genesis of 'Useful Knowledge,'" 125.

38 Berg, "Genesis of 'Useful Knowledge,'" 124.

39 Maxine Berg and Kristine Bruland, eds., *Technological Revolutions in Europe: Historical Perspectives* (Edward Elgar Publishing, 1998), 12-13.

40 Jean-Laurent Rosenthal and Roy Bin Wong, *Before and Beyond Divergence: The Politics of Economic Change in China and Europe* (Harvard University Press, 2011); J. R. McNeill and William McNeill, *The Human Web: A Bird's-Eye View of World History* (W. W. Norton, 2003), 137-47.

41 Mathias, *Transformation of England*, 31.

42 Mathias, *Transformation of England*, 31. For a time England tried to prohibit this movement of skilled workers to rival nations, but simply gave up as the law was so ineffective

43 David Mitch, "The Role of Human Capital in the First Industrial Revolution" in Mokyr, *British Industrial Revolution*, 267-307.

44 Sascha O. Becker, Erik Hornung, and Ludger Woessmann "Catch Me If You Can: Education and Catch-up in the Industrial Revolution," IZA Discussion Paper No. 4556 (November 2009), available at https://ssrn.com/abstract=1506308. Sweden seems to have followed a similar pattern. See Kevin O'Rourke and Jeffrey G. Williamson, "Education, Globalization and Catch-Up: Scandinavia in the Swedish Mirror," *Scandinavian Economic History Review* 43, no. 3 (1996): 287-309; Lars Sandberg, "The Case of the Impoverished Sophisticate: Human Capital and Swedish Economic Growth before World War I," *Journal of Economic History* 39, no. 1 (1979): 225-41; Fernando Belinchon, "These are the 20 most innovative countries in Europe," *Business Insider Espana*, at Washingtonpost.com, July 3, 2018.

45 Mathias, *Transformation of England*, 26-31.

46 Mokyr, *Lever of Riches*, 119-26; Mathias, *Transformation of England*, 63-65.

47 Mathias, *Transformation of England*, 88-109.

48 Alexander Gerschenkron, *Economic Backwardness in Historical Perspective* (Harvard University Press, 1962); Caroline Fohlin, *Finance Capitalism and Germany's Rise to Industrial Power* (Cambridge University Press, 2007); Moses Abramovitz, "Catching Up, Forging Ahead and Falling Behind," *Journal of Economic History* 46 (June 1986): 385-406.

49 Louis Galambos and Franco Amatori, "The Entrepreneurial Multiplier Effect," *Enterprise & Society* 17, no. 4 (2016): 763–808.

50 Forbes, "World's Most Innovative Companies," 2018, at www.forbes.com; Michelle Jamrisko and Wei Lu, "The U.S. Drops Out of the Top 10 in Innovation Ranking," Bloomberg, January 22, 2018 at https://www.bloomberg.com/news/articles/2018-01-22/south-korea-tops-global-innovation-ranking-again-as-u-s-falls; Hugo Hollanders and Nordine Es-Sadaki, "European Innovation Scoreboard 2018," (European Union, 2018.)

51 "The Future of Innovation in Europe: A Conversation with Marc Lhermitte," at Steelcase.com, 2018; Ezell and Marxgut, "Comparing American and European Innovation Cultures," 157-59.

52 Ruchir Sharma, *The Rise and Fall of Nations: Forces of Change in the Post-Crisis World* (W. W. Norton, 2016), 16-17, 23; Ezell and Marxgut, "Comparing American and European Innovation Cultures," 194.

Chapter 5

1 Bloomberg ranked the U.S. out of the top ten innovation ranking for 2018, and others warn that the U.S. may continue to lose ground. Other indices still place the U.S. among the top five nations for innovation. See Michelle Jamrisko and Wei Lu, "The U.S. Drops Out of the Top 10 in Innovation Ranking," Bloomberg, January 22, 2018 at https://www.bloomberg.com/news/articles/2018-01-22/south-korea-tops-global-innovation-ranking-again-as-u-s-falls; Cornell University, INSEAD, and WIPO, *The Global Innovation Index 2017: Innovation Feeding the World* (Ithaca, Fontainebleau, and Geneva: 2017).

2 Peter Lindert and Jeffrey Williamson, "Unequal Gains: American Growth and Inequality since 1700," (June 16, 2016) at https://voxeu.org/article/american-growth-and-inequality-1700.

3 There was of course one glaring exception, African Americans, as well as a number of not so glaring exceptions for certain other ethnic groups, and of course for a long time, women.

4 Wesley Frank Craven, *The Virginia Company of London*, 1606-1624 (Williamsburg, VA: 350th Anniversary Celebration Corporation, 1957).

5 John Frederick Martin, *Profits in the Wilderness: Entrepreneurship and the Founding of New England Towns in the Seventeenth Century* (University of North Carolina Press, 1991); Richard S. and Mary Maples Dunn, eds., *The World of William Penn* (University of Pennsylvania Press, 1986); Gary B. Nash, *Quakers and Politics: Pennsylvania, 1681–1726* (Princeton University Press,1968).

6 Trevor Burnard, *Planters, Merchants, and Slaves: Plantation Societies in British America, 1650-1820* (University of Chicago Press, 2015); Sidney Mintz, *Sweetness and Power: The Place of Sugar in Modern History* (Penguin, 1985).

7 Peter H. Lindert and Jeffrey G. Williamson, "American Incomes Before and After the Revolution," *Journal of Economic History* 73 (September 2013): 725-65; Trevor Burnard and John Garrigus, *The Plantation Machine: Atlantic Capitalism in French Saint-Domingue and British Jamaica* (University of Pennsylvania Press, 2016).

8 Peter Coclanis, *The Shadow of a Dream: Economic Life and Death in the South Carolina Low Country, 1670-1920* (Oxford University Press, 1989); Allan Kulikoff, *Tobacco and Slaves: The Development of Southern Cultures in the Chesapeake*, 1680-1800 (University of North Carolina Press, 1986).

9 The effects were telling over time. By 1900 in the rural sections of the United States 74 percent of households owned land, whereas in Mexico it was 2.4 percent and in Argentina 18.8 percent. Stanley Engerman and Kenneth Sokoloff, *Economic Development in the Americas: Endowments and Institutions* (Cambridge University Press, 2011), 66.

10 David W. Galenson, *White Servitude in Colonial America* (Cambridge University Press, 1981); John J. McCusker and Russell R. Menard, *The Economy of British America: 1607-1789* (University of North Carolina Press, 1985).

11 Edmund Morgan, "Headrights and Head Counts: A Review Article," *The Virginia Magazine of History and Biography* 80, no. 3 (July 1972): 361–71; Bernard Bailyn, *The Barbarous Years: The Peopling of British North America: The Conflict of Civilizations, 1600-1675* (Knopf, 2012).

12 Daron Acemoglu and James Robinson, *Why Nations Fail: The Origins of Power, Prosperity, and Poverty* (Crown, 2012); Christopher Niggle, "Equality, Democracy, Institutions, and Growth," *Journal of Economic Issues* 32, no. 2 (June 1998): 523-30; John Gerring, Philip Bond, William T. Barndt, and Carola Moreno, "Democracy and Economic Growth: A Historical Perspective," *World Politics* 57, no. 3 (April 2005): 323-64; Dimitri Landa and Ethan Kapstein, "Inequality, Growth and Democracy," *World Politics* 53, no. 2 (January 2001): 264-96.

13 Lindert and Williamson, "Unequal Gains." It would rise after 1776, though still be more equal than Britain or other European and New World societies. Peter Lindert and Jeffrey Williamson, *Unequal Gains: American Growth and Inequality since 1700* (Princeton University Press, 2016); Peter Lindert and Jeffrey Williamson, *American Inequality: A Macroeconomic History* (Academic Press, 2001).

14 Engerman and Sokoloff, *Economic Development in the Americas*, 111; Alexander Keyssar, *The Right to Vote: The Contested History of Democracy in America* (Basic Books, 2000). Eligible population meant, of course, free white men, not women, not the enslaved and often not even free African Americans.

15 Edward Pessen, "The Egalitarian Myth and the American Social Reality: Wealth, Mobility, and Equality in the 'Era of the Common Man,'" *American Historical Review* 76, no. 4 (October 1971): 989-1034: Pessen, "Social Mobility in American History: Some Brief Reflections," *Journal of Southern History* 45, no. 2 (May 1979): 165-84; Stuart Blumin, *The Emergence of the Middle Class: Social Experience in the American City*, 1760-1900 (Cambridge University Press, 1989).

16 Charles Sellers, *The Market Revolution: Jacksonian America, 1815-1846* (Oxford University Press, 1991); Peter Temin, *The Jacksonian Economy* (W.W. Norton, 1969).

17 Daniel Walker Howe, *What Hath God Wrought: The Transformation of America, 1815-1848* (Oxford University Press, 2007).

18 Engerman and Sokoloff, *Economic Development in the Americas*, 245-95; Rowena Olegario, *A Culture of Credit: Embedding Trust and Transparency in American Business* (Harvard University Press, 2006); Howard Bodenhorn, "Private Banking in Antebellum Virginia: Thomas Branch & Sons of Petersburg," *Business History Review* 71, no. 4 (Winter 1997): 513–42, esp. p. 514. Richard Sylla estimates that in the 1850s private banks may have accounted for one-third of all commercial banks, and over one-quarter of all bank capital. Richard Sylla, "Forgotten Men of Money: Private Bankers in Early U.S. History," *Journal of Economic History* 36, no. 1 (March 1976): 173–88. States applied same open and free process to businesses that wanted to incorporate as well.

19 Richard Sylla, "The Political Economy of Early U.S. Financial Development," in *Political Institutions and Financial Development,* eds. Stephen Haber, Douglass C. North, and Barry R. Weingast (Stanford University Press, 2007), 60-91; Howard Bodenhorn, "Antebellum Banking in the United States," (March 26, 2008) at http://eh.net/encyclopedia/antebellum-banking-in-the-united-states/.

20 Engerman and Sokoloff, *Economic Development in the Americas*, 288, 272.

21 Naomi R. Lamoreaux, *Insider Lending: Banks, Personal Connections, and Economic Development in Industrial New England* (Cambridge University Press, 1994).

22 This is probably a bigger consideration today, when information technology allows one bank to handle transactions in far greater bulk than a century and a half ago.

23 Christopher Grandy, "New Jersey Corporate Charter Mongering, 1875-1929," *Journal of Economic History* 49, no. 3 (September 1989): 677-92; Harwell Wells, "A Long View of Shareholder Power: From the Antebellum Corporation to the Twenty-First Century," *Florida Law Review* 67, no. 3 (January 2016): 1033-98; Naomi R. Lamoreaux and William J. Novak, "Corporations and American Democracy: An Introduction," at http://tobinproject.org/sites/tobinproject.org/files/assets/Lamoreaux%20%26%20Novak%20-%20Introduction.pdf.

24 Stephen Mihm, *A Nation of Counterfeiters: Capitalists, Con Men, and the Making of the United States* (Harvard University Press, 2009); Edward Balleisen, *Fraud: An American History from Barnum to Madoff* (Princeton University Press, 2017).

25 Engerman and Sokoloff, *Economic Development in the Americas*, 259-60.

26 Sascha O. Becker, Erik Hornung, Ludger Woessmann, "Catch Me If You Can: Education and Catch-up in the Industrial Revolution," IZA Discussion Paper No. 4556 (November 2009), available at https://ssrn.com/abstract=1506308, esp. pp. 3-5 for discussion of literature on following nations and catching up.

27 Percentages at https://ourworldindata.org/literacy.

28 Percentages at https://ourworldindata.org/primary-and-secondary-education.

29 Engerman and Sokoloff, *Economic Development in the Americas*, 126-36; Ellwood Hubberley, *The History of Education* (Houghton Mifflin, 1920).

30 Engerman and Sokoloff, *Economic Development in the Americas*, 187-92.

31 Transportation revolution, internal improvements; America had far more post offices per capita than its European peers. Towns wanted post offices so they would have fast access to the latest news. See Richard John, *Spreading the News: The American Postal System from Franklin to Morse* (Harvard University Press, 1995).

32 Carter Goodrich, *Government Promotion of American Canals and Railroads*, 1800-1890 (Columbia University Press, 1960); John Stover, *History of the Baltimore and Ohio Railroad* (Purdue University Press, 1987).

33 Mira Wilkins, *The History of Foreign Investments in the United States to 1914* (Harvard University Press, 1989); Michael Clemens and Jeffrey Williamson, "Where did British Foreign Capital Go?: Fundamentals, Failures and the Lucas Paradox, 1870-1913," NBER Working Paper 8028 at https://core.ac.uk/download/pdf/6606273.pdf.

34 Robert Dalzell, *Enterprising Elite: The Boston Associates and the World They Made* (Harvard University Press, 1987); Barbara Tucker, *Samuel Slater and the Origins of the American Textile Industry, 1790-1860* (Cornell University Press, 1984); Barbara Tucker, and Kenneth H. Tucker, *Industrializing Antebellum America: The Rise of Manufacturing Entrepreneurs in the Early Republic* (Palgrave Macmillan, 2008).

35 Lance Davis and H. Louis Stettler III, "The New England Textile Industry, 1825–60: Trends and Fluctuations," in *Output, Employment, and Productivity in the United States after 1800,* ed. Dorothy Brady (National Bureau of Economic Research, 1966), 221 at https://www.nber.org/chapters/c1569.pdf.

36 David Hounshell, *From the American System to Mass Production, 1800-1932: The Development of Manufacturing Technology in the United States* (Johns Hopkins University Press, 1984); Merritt Roe Smith, *Harpers Ferry Armory and the New Technology: The Challenge of Change* (Cornell University Press, 1977); Nathan Rosenberg, "Technological Change in the Machine Tool Industry, 1840-1910," *Journal of Economic History* 23, no. 4 (December 1963): 414-43.

37 Duncan McDougall, "Machine Tool Output, 1861-1910," in Brady, *Output, Employment and Productivity*, Table A-3 at https://www.nber.org/chapters/c1576.pdf; Nathan Rosenberg, "Economic Development and the Transfer of Technology: Some Historical Perspectives," *Technology and Culture* 11, no. 4 (October 1970): 550-75.

38 Bo Carlsson, "The Development and Use of Machine Tools in Historical Perspective," *Journal of Economic Behavior and Organization* 5, no. 1 (March 1984): 91-114; Carroll Pursell, "Machines and Machine Tools, 1830-1880," in *Technology in Western Civilization Vol. I*, eds. Melvin Kranzberg and Carroll Pursell (Oxford University Press, 1967), 392-408.

39 James P. Womack, Daniel T. Jones, and Daniel Roos, *The Machine that Changed the World* (Free Press, 1990).

40 Ran Abramitzky, and Leah Boustan, "Immigration in American Economic History" *Journal of Economic Literature* 55, no. 4 (December 2017): 1311-45 at https://www.ncbi.nlm.nih.gov/pmc/articles/PMC5794227/. Today the foreign born are approaching these nineteenth-century levels.

41 Emery Roth II, *Brass Valley: The Fall of an American Industry* (Schiffer Publishing, 2015); Wayne Broehl, *Precision Valley: The Machine Tool Companies of Springfield, Vermont* (Prentice Hall, 1959).

42 David Meyer, "The Roots of American Industrialization, 1790-1860," at https://eh.net/encyclopedia/the-roots-of-american-industrialization- 1790-1860; David Meyer, "Midwestern Industrialization and the American Manufacturing Belt in the Nineteenth Century," *Journal of Economic History* 49, no. 4 (December 1989): 921-37.

43 Eric Hintz, "Failed Inventor Initiatives, from the Franklin Institute to Quirky," in *Does America Need More Innovators?*, eds. Matthew Wisnioski, Eric S. Hintz, and Marie Stettler Kleine (MIT Press, 2019), 165-90.

44 It is not clear that patents are necessary or even that useful to innovation, but the United States did have a strong patent system and many innovators made use of it. Still, many innovations in the United States and elsewhere occurred outside of the patent system. Petra Moser, "Patents and Innovation: Evidence from Economic History," *Journal of Economic Perspectives* 27, no. 1 (Winter 2013): 23-44.

45 Naomi Lamoreaux, and Kenneth L. Sokoloff, "Inventors, Firms, and the Market for Technology in the Late Nineteenth and Early Twentieth Centuries," in *Learning by Doing in Markets, Firms, and Countries*, eds. Naomi R. Lamoreaux, Daniel M. G. Raff, and Peter Temin (University of Chicago Press, 1999); B. Zorina Khan and Kenneth L. Sokoloff, "History Lessons: The Early Development of Intellectual Property Institutions in the United States," *Journal of Economic Perspectives* 15, no. 3 (Summer 2001): 233-46; B. Zorina Khan, *The Democratization of Invention: Patents and Copyrights in American Economic Development*, 1790-1920 (Cambridge University Press, 2005); B. Zorina Khan and Kenneth L. Sokoloff, "Schemes of Practical Utility: Entrepreneurship and Innovation among 'Great Inventors' in the United States, 1790-1865," *Journal of Economic History* 53, no. 2 (June 1993): 289-307.

46 Eric Hintz, "The Post-Heroic Generation: American Independent Inventors, 1900–1950," *Enterprise & Society* 12, no. 4 (December 2011): 732–48; National Science Board: Science and Engineering Indicators 2018 at https://www.nsf.gov/statistics/2018/nsb20181/report/sections/invention-knowledge-transfer-and-innovation/invention-united-states-and-comparative-global-trends.

47 Gavin Wright, "The Origins of American Industrial Success," *American Economic Review* 80, no. 4 (September 1990): 651-68.

48 Manual Castells, *The Rise of the Network Society* (Blackwell, 1996).

49 Wright, "American Industrial Success," 663-65.

50 Gavin Wright, *The Political Economy of the Cotton South: Households, Markets, and Wealth in the Nineteenth Century* (W. W. Norton, 1978); Sven Beckert, *Empire of Cotton: A Global History* (Knopf, 2014); Edward Baptist, *The Half Has Never Been Told: Slavery and the Making of American Capitalism* (Basic Books, 2014).

51 Lindert and Williamson, "American Incomes Before and After the Revolution," 725-65.

52 Gavin Wright, *Old South, New South: Revolutions in the Southern Economy since the Civil War* (Basic Books, 1986); Gavin Wright, *Slavery and American Economic Development* (Louisiana State University Press, 2006); John Majewski, *A House Dividing: Economic Development in Pennsylvania and Virginia before the Civil War* (Cambridge University Press, 2000); Fred Bateman and Thomas Weiss, *A Deplorable Scarcity: The Failure of Industrialization in the Slave Economy* (University of North Carolina, 1981); William H. Phillips, "The Democratization of Invention in the American South: Antebellum and Postbellum Technology Markets in the United States," (2010) at https://thebhc.org/democratization-invention-american-south-antebellum-and-postbellum-technology-markets-united-0. Phillips shows that patenting improved markedly in the South after the end of slavery, though mainly in the border states, not so much in the deep South where slavery and cotton reigned.

53 Judith Carney, *Black Rice: The African Origins of Rice Cultivation in the Americas* (Harvard University Press, 2001); Etta Fields-Black, *Deep Roots: Rice Farmers in West Africa and the African Diaspora* (Indiana University Press, 2014).

54 Juliet Walker, *The History of Black Business in America: Capitalism, Race, Entrepreneurship: Volume 1, To 1865* (University of North Carolina Press, 2009).

55 Juliet Walker, *Free Frank: A Black Pioneer on the Antebellum Frontier* (University Press of Kentucky, 1995).

56 Beginning with Johns Hopkins in 1876, top American public and private universities adopted the "German" model emphasizing research and graduate education. Roger L Geiger, *The History of American Higher Education: Learning and Culture from the Founding to World War II* (Princeton University Press, 2014); Roger L. Geiger, *Research and Relevant Knowledge: American Research Universities Since World War II* (Oxford University Press, 2001); Lawrence R. Veysey, *The Emergence of the American University* (University of Chicago Press, 1965).

57 Paul Conkin, *A Revolution Down on the Farm: The Transformation of American Agriculture since 1929* (University Press of Kentucky, 2008); William Brown, "H. A. Wallace and the Development of Hybrid Corn," *Annals of Iowa* 47, no. 2 (Fall 1983): 167-79.

58 Alfred D. Chandler, Jr., *The Visible Hand: The Managerial Revolution in American Business* (Harvard University Press, 1977); Douglas Brinkley, *Wheels for the World: Henry Ford, His Company, and a Century of Progress, 1903-2003* (Penguin Publishing, 2003); Ford production figures at http://www.mtfca.com/encyclo/fdprod.htm.

59 Philip Scranton, *Endless Novelty: Specialty Production and American Industrialization, 1865-1925* (Princeton University Press, 1997).

60 Appropriately enough Maytag named it "The Pastime."

61 John D. Anderson, *Inventing Flight: The Wright Brothers and Their Predecessors* (Johns Hopkins University Press, 2004); David McCullough, *The Wright Brothers* (Simon & Schuster, 2015); Rosenberg, "Technological Change in the Machine Tool Industry," 436-38.

62 Reese Jenkins, *Images and Enterprise: Technology and the American Photographic Industry*, 1839-1925 (Johns Hopkins University Press, 1987); Elizabeth Brayer, *George Eastman: A Biography* (Johns Hopkins University Press, 1996).

63 Neil Baldwin, *Edison: Inventing the Century* (University of Chicago Press, 2001); Paul Israel, *Edison: A Life of Invention* (Wiley, 1998); W. Bernard Carlson, *Tesla: Inventor of the Electric Age* (Princeton University Press, 2013).

64 Jill Jonnes, *Empires of Light: Edison, Tesla, Westinghouse, and the Race to Electrify the World* (Random House, 2003); W. Bernard Carlson, *Innovation as a Social Process: Elihu Thomson and the Rise of General Electric, 1870-1900* (Cambridge University Press, 1991).

65 David A. Hounshell and John Kenly Smith, Jr., *Science and Corporate Strategy: Du Pont R and D, 1902–1980* (Cambridge University Press, 1988); Alfred D. Chandler, Jr. and Stephen Salsbury, *Pierre S. Du Pont and the Making of the Modern Corporation* (Harper and Rowe, 1971).

66 Kenneth Lipartito, "Rethinking the Invention Factory: Bell Laboratories in Perspective," in *The Challenge of Remaining Innovative: Insights from Twentieth-Century American Business*, eds. Sally Clarke, Naomi R. Lamoreaux, and Steven Usselman (Stanford University Press, 2009), 150.

67 In a similar manner, the growing petroleum industry of America went far beyond its origins in exploiting the abundant natural supply of oil in America. Firms such as Exxon performed the research that led to catalytic cracking, a process for more efficiently refining or distilling out the various products that could be taken from crude oil---kerosene, gasoline, benzene, and the feedstocks of petrochemical, which would lead to a whole new petrochemical industry in America as well. See John Enos, *Petroleum Progress And Profits: A History Of Process Innovation* (MIT Press, 1962); and John Enos, "Invention and Innovation in the Petroleum Refining Industry," National Bureau of Economic Research, *The Rate and Direction of Inventive Activity: Economic and Social Factors* (Princeton University Press, 1962) at https://www.nber.org/chapters/c2124.pdf.

68 Charles Hyde, *Arsenal of Democracy: The American Automobile Industry in World War II* (Wayne State University Press, 2013); Arthur Herman, *Freedom's Forge: How American Business Produced Victory in World War II* (Random House, 2013); Mark Wilson, *Destructive Creation: American Business and the Winning of World War II* (University of Pennsylvania Press, 2016); Louis Galambos, *Values and Visions: A Merck Century* (Merck & Co., Inc., 1991), 76-77.

69 Richard Rhodes, *The Making of the Atomic Bomb* (Simon & Schuster, 1986).

70 Productivity figures at https://ourworldindata.org/economic-growth.

71 Peter Galison, *Big Science: The Growth of Large-Scale Research* (Stanford University Press, 1994); Naomi Oreskes and John Krige, *Science and Technology in the Global Cold War* (MIT Press, 2014).

72 David Hart, *Forged Consensus: Science, Technology, and Economic Policy in the United States, 1921-1953* (Princeton University Press, 1998); Lewis M. Branscomb and James H. Keller, *Investing in Innovation: Creating a Research and Innovation Policy that Works* (MIT Press, 1998).

73 Kenneth Flamm, *Creating the Computer: Government, Industry and High Technology* (Brookings Institution Press, 1988); Kenneth Flamm, *Targeting the Computer: Government Support and International Competition* (Brookings Institution Press, 1987). See also Linda Weiss, *America Inc.?: Innovation and Enterprise in the National Security State* (Cornell University Press, 2014), for more examples of how the national security state promoted technology and innovation.

74 Janet Abbate, *Inventing the Internet* (MIT Press, 1999).

75 Margaret Graham, "When the Corporation Almost Displaced the Entrepreneur: Rethinking the Political Economy of Research and Development," *Enterprise & Society* 18, no. 2 (June 2017): 245–81.

76 U.S. Bureau of Labor Statistics at https://www.bls.gov/; St. Louis FED (FRED) at https://fred.stlouisfed.org/; Martin Neil Baily and Barry Bosworth, "US Manufacturing: Understanding Its Past and Its Potential Future," *Journal of Economic Perspectives* 28, no. 1 (Winter 2014): 3–26.

77 Robert Gordon, *The Rise and Fall of American Growth: The U.S. Standard of Living since the Civil War* (Princeton University Press, 2016); Shawn Sprague, "Below Trend: The U.S. Productivity Slowdown since the Great Recession," (January 2017) at https://www.bls.gov/opub/btn/volume-6/below-trend-the-us-productivity-slowdown-since-the-great-recession.htm.

78 OECD, Gross Domestic Spending on R&D (2019) at https://data.oecd.org/rd/gross-domestic-spending-on-r-d.htm; AAAS, Historical Trends in Federal R&D at https://www.aaas.org/programs/r-d-budget-and- policy/historical-trends-federal-rd.

79 John Wu, "Why U.S. Business R &D is Not as Strong as it Appears," (June 2018) at http://www2.itif.org/2018-us-business-rd.pdf.

80 See William Lazonick, "The Curse of Stock Buybacks," (June 25, 2018) at https://prospect.org/article/curse-stock-buybacks-0.

81 https://www.oecd.org/pisa/PISA-2015-United-States.pdf; Linda Darling-Hammond, "What Can PISA Tell Us about U.S. Education Policy?," *New England Journal of Public Policy* 26, no. 1 (September 22, 2014) at https://edpolicy.stanford.edu/sites/default/files/publications/what-can-pisa-tell-us-about-us-education-policy.pdf.

82 Alex Bell, et al., "Who Becomes an Inventor in America?: The Importance of Exposure to Innovation," (November 2018) at http://www.equality-of-opportunity.org/assets/documents/inventors_paper.pdf; Alex Bell, et al., "Who Becomes an Inventor in America?: The Importance of Exposure to Innovation: Executive Summary" at http://www.equality-of-opportunity.org/assets/documents/inventors_summary.pdf.

83 Richard V. Reeves and Eleanor Krause, Raj Chetty in 14 Charts: Big Findings on Opportunity and Mobility We Should All Know," (January 11, 2018) at https://www.brookings.edu/blog/social-mobility-memos/ 2018/01/11/raj-chetty-in-14-charts-big-findings-on-opportunity-and-mobility-we-should-know/.

84 *Kauffman Compilation: Research on Immigration and Entrepreneurship* (October 2016) at https://www.kauffman.org/-/media/kauffman_org/resources/2016/kauffman_compilation_immigration_entrepreneurship.pdf; Peter Vandor and Nikolaus Franke, "Why Are Immigrants More Entrepreneurial?," (October 27, 2016) at https://hbr.org/2016/10/why-are-immigrants-more-entrepreneurial.

Chapter 6

1 Hannah Beech, "If China is Anti-Islam, Why Are These Chinese Muslims Enjoying a Faith Revival?" *TIME*, August 12, 2014; Javier C. Hernandez and Quoctrung Bui, "The American Dream is Alive. In China," *New York Times*, November 19, 2018; Edward Tse, "The Rise of Entrepreneurship in China," *Forbes*, April 5, 2016; Jeff Muskus, "Out From Under the 'Bamboo Ceiling,'" *Bloomberg Businessweek*, January 22, 2018; Koh Gui Qing, "In Silicon Valley, Chinese 'accelerators' aim to bring startups home," *Reuters*, May 17, 2018; Sintia Radu, "Too Much Money Hurts China's Startups," *US News and World Report*, July 27, 2018; Cornell University, INSEAD, and WIPO, *The Global Innovation Index 2018: Energizing the World with Innovation* (2018).

2 Shaun Rein, *The End of Copycat China: The Rise of Creativity, Innovation, and Individualism in Asia* (Wiley, 2014), 17, 35-36; Robert A. Manning and Peter Engelke, *The Global Innovation Sweepstakes: A Quest to Win the Future* (Atlantic Council, Scowcroft Center for Strategy and Security, 2018), 1-4, 17-18; Victor Nee and Sonja Opper, *Capitalism from Below: Markets and Institutional Change in China* (Cambridge University Press, 2012), 200-25; Clay Chandler, "Why China is Emerging as a Tech Superpower to Rival the U.S.," *Fortune*, November 21, 2017; Michael Schuman, "What If China Really is Exempt From the Laws of Economics?," *Bloomberg Businessweek*, January 29, 2018.

3 Rein, *End of Copycat China*, 14, 228-29; Edward Tse, *China's Disruptors: How Alibaba, Xiaomi, Tencent, and Other Companies are Changing the Rules of Business* (Penguin, 2015), 57; Joseph Needham, *The Grand Titration: Science and Society in East and West* (University of Toronto Press, 1969), 11, 26-27.

4 Needham, *Grand Titration*, 24-25.

5 Joel Mokyr, *The Lever of Riches: Technological Creativity and Economic Progress* (Oxford University Press, 1990), 208-38; Timothy Brook, "Communications and Commerce," in *The Cambridge History of China, vol. 8,* ed. Frederick Mote and Denis Twitchett (Cambridge University Press, 1997), 579-707.

6 Needham, *Grand Titration*, 26-27.

7 Robert Hymes, "Sung Society and Social Change," in Mote and Twitchett, *Cambridge History of China*, 543-46.

8 However, the Chinese never attained the superiority in weaponry achieved by the Europeans, particularly artillery. When a group of Jesuits arrived in China in the seventeenth century, Ming emperors asked them for assistance in purchasing cannons from Macao to fight against the Manchu Mongolians. Although Chinese officials wanted to adopt the European cannon for their army, the military continued to use inferior weapons of a sixteenth-century design until the Taiping Rebellion (1851-64). Jonathan M. Bloom, *Paper Before Print: The History and Impact of Paper in the Islamic World* (Yale University, 2001), 36, 38; Clifford D. Conner, *A People's History of Science: Miners, Midwives, and "Low Mechanicks"* (Nation Books, 2005), 127-78; Needham, *Grand Titration*, 11, 26-27.

9 Needham, *Grand Titration*, 22, 74-76; Conner, *People's History of Science*, 174-80.

10 Needham, *Grand Titration*, 99, 174.

11 Needham, *Grand Titration*, 25, 101-05; Conner, *People's History of Science*, 175-77; Mokyr, *Lever of Riches*, 234.

12 Needham, *Grand Titration*, 177-79, 267-69. The *I-Ching* (Book of Changes) listed many of their achievements, although it is considered to have had a stultifying effect on the development of the natural sciences because it may have precluded the need for further observation and experiment.

13 Conner, *People's History of Science*, 178; Arthur Boylston, "The Origins of Inoculation," *Journal of the Royal Society of Medicine* 105, no. 7 (July 2012): 309-13; Kenneth Pomeranz, *The Great Divergence: China, Europe, and the Making of the Modern World Economy* (Princeton University Press, 2000), 46-48.

14 Toby E. Huff, *The Rise of Early Modern Science: Islam, China, and the West* (Cambridge University Press, 2017), 245; "Asia for Educators," Columbia University, 2009, at http://afe.easia.columbia.edu; Ronald Findlay and Kevin O'Rourke, *Power and Plenty: Trade, War, and the World Economy in the Second Millennium* (Princeton University Press, 2009), 61-69.

15 Patricia Russo, *Merchants and Faith: Muslim Commerce and Culture in the Indian Ocean* (Westview Press, 1995); as well as Janet Abu Lughod, *Before European Hegemony: The World System A.D. 1250-1350* (Oxford University Press, 1991), 322-47.

16 Findlay and O'Rourke, *Power and Plenty*, 63-69; Hymes, "Sung Society and Social Change," 661-64.

17 Joseph P. McDermott and Shiba Yoshinobu, "Economic Change in China, 960-1279," in Mote and Twitchett, *Cambridge History of China*, 321-426.

18 Huff, *Rise of Early Modern Science*, 203-54; Mokyr, *Lever of Riches*, 236.

19 Brook, "Communications and Commerce," 579-707.

20 Huff, *Rise of Early Modern Science*, 171; Needham, *Grand Titration*, 39-41. This turning away from trade could also be found in parts of Europe, where successful merchants often sought to enter the landholding elite. Likewise, such seeking of social status may have also undercut the engine of growth and capitalism in Europe. David Hancock, *Citizens of the World: London Merchants and the Integration of the British Atlantic Community, 1735-1785* (Cambridge University Press, 1977).

21 Wellington K.K. Chan, "Chinese Entrepreneurship since Its Late Imperial Phase," in *The Invention of Enterprise: Entrepreneurship From Ancient Mesopotamia to Modern Times*, eds. David S. Landes, Joel Mokyr, and William J. Baumol (Princeton University Press, 2010), 471-72.

22 See for example the extensive interest in commerce in Hymes, "Sung Society and Social Change,"526-35.

23 Robert Marks, *The Origins of the Modern World* (Rowman and Littlefield, 2020), 44-47; Brook, "Communications and Commerce," 615-19.

24 Brook, "Communications and Commerce," 579-707.

25 John Wills, Jr., "Relations with Maritime Europeans, 1514–1662," in Mote and Twitchett, *Cambridge History of China*, 333-75.

26 Brook, "Communications and Commerce," 617.

27 Marks, *Origins of the Modern World,* 72.

28 Chan, "Chinese Entrepreneurship," 472-73; R. B. Wong, "China Before Capitalism" in *The Cambridge History of Capitalism, Vol. 1, The Rise Of Capitalism: From Ancient Origins to 1848,* eds. Larry Neal and Jeffrey G. Williamson (Cambridge University Press, 2014), 136-43.

29 Pomeranz, *Great Divergence*; Marks, *Origins of the Modern World*, 84-105; Ramon H. Myers and Yeh-chien Wang, "Economic Developments, 1644-1800," in Mote and Twitchett, *Cambridge History of China*, 563-645.

30 Huff, *Rise of Early Modern Science*, 253-95, 330; Needham, *Grand Titration*, 34-37, 328; Chan, "Chinese Entrepreneurship," 474.

31 Chan, "Chinese Entrepreneurship," 474; Mokyr, *Lever of Riches*, 236-38.

32 Justin Yifu Lin, "The Needham Puzzle, the Weber Question and China's Miracle: Long Term Performance since the Sung Dynasty" in *World Economic Performance: Past, Present and Future*, ed. D. S. Prasada Rao and Bart Van Ark (Edward Elgar Publishing, 2013), 43-51.

33 Ting-yee Kuo, "Self-Strengthening: The Pursuit of Western Technology," in Mote and Twitchett, *Cambridge History of China*, 491-542.

34 Pomeranz, *Great Divergence*, 49-52, 173; Chan, "Chinese Entrepreneurship," 469-80.

35 Chan, "Chinese Entrepreneurship," 469; Manning and Engelke, *Global Innovation Sweepstakes*, 18; Jonathan Mirsky, "Unnatural Disaster: 'Tombstone: The Great Chinese Famine, 1958-1962,"*New York Times*, December 7, 2012. See also Yang Jisheng, *Tombstone: The Great Chinese Famine, 1958-1962* (Farrar, Straus & Giroux, 2012); Tse, *China's Disruptors*, 3-9

36 Patrick E. Tyler, "Deng Xiaoping: A Political Wizard Who Put China on the Capitalist Road," *New York Times*, February 20, 1997.

37 Tyler, "Deng Xiaoping: A Political Wizard."

38 Tyler, "Deng Xiaoping: A Political Wizard;" Martin Ravaillion and Shaohua Chan, "China's (Uneven) Progress Against Poverty," World Bank, 2016; Philip K. Pan, "The Land that Failed to Fail," *New York Times*, November 18, 2018; Javier C. Hernandez and Quoctrung Bui, "The American Dream is Alive. In China," *New York Times*, November 19, 2018; Austin Ramzy, "China's Cultural Revolution Explained," *New York Times*, May 14, 2016; Ruchir Sharma, *The Rise and Fall of Nations: Forces of Change in the Post-World Crisis* (W.W. Norton, 2016), 71; "The Great Stabiliser," *The Economist*, October 22, 2011. See also Ezra Vogel, *Deng Xiaoping and the Transformation of China* (Belknap Press of Harvard University, 2011); Tse, *China's Disruptors*, 17; Douglas B. Fuller, "China's Political Economy," in *China's Innovation Challenge: Overcoming the Middle-Income Trap*, eds. Arie Y. Lewin, Martin Kenney, and Johann Peter Murmann (Cambridge University Press, 2016), 122-23.

39 Nee and Opper, *Capitalism from Below*, 5-7; Sharma, *Rise and Fall of Nations*, 64-65; Tse, *China's Disruptors*, 8-26.

40 Tse, "Rise of Entrepreneurship in China"; Nee and Opper, *Capitalism from Below*, 225-60; Manning and Engelke, *Global Innovation Sweepstakes*, 5, 18; Tse, *China's Disruptors*, 3-13, 55-57; "The Great Stabiliser," *The Economist*, October 22, 2011.

41 Dan Breznitz and Michael Murphree, *Run of the Red Queen: Government, Innovation, Globalization and Economic Growth in China* (Yale University Press, 2011). While this imitative learning is not what people often think of as innovation, as we have noted innovation includes adapting or modifying products and processes that are new for one's own society, as well as creating something completely from scratch. Over time, imitators become modifiers and modifiers start to make original breakthroughs. The latter stage China is still seeking to move to, and it may be succeeding.

42 Tse, *China's Disruptors*, 55-57, 81; Li Yuan, "Censoring China's Internet for Stability and Profit," *New York Times*, January 2, 2019.

43 Manning and Engelke, *Global Innovation Sweepstakes*, 17-18.

44 President Clinton's March 8, 2001 speech at Johns Hopkins University on the China Trade Bill, "Full Text of Clinton's Speech on China Trade Bill," *New York Times*, March 9, 2001. Nee and Opper, *Capitalism from Below*, 225-60; Kishore Mahbubani, "What China Threat? How the United States and China can avoid War," *Harper's Magazine*, February 2019, p. 40; Dominique Jolly, Bruce McKern, and George Yip, "The Next Innovation Opportunity in China," *Strategy and Business*, July 27, 2015.

45 Vijay Govindarajan, et al., "Which U.S. Companies are doing the Most R&D in China and India?" *Harvard Business Review*, March 26, 2015.

46 Edward Tse, "The Rise of Entrepreneurship in China," *Forbes*, April 5, 2016; Nee and Opper, *Capitalism from Below*, 225-260; Manning and Engelke, *Global Innovation Sweepstakes*, 18; Tse, *China's Disruptors*, 10-12, 56, 78-79; Philip P. Pan, "China Rules: How China Became a Superpower," *New York Times*, November 18, 2018.

47 Fuller, "China's Political Economy," 122.

48 However, workers in private industry typically have very short employment tenures, making it challenging for firms to provide the necessary internal training they need.

49 Manning and Engelke, *Global Innovation Sweepstakes*, 4-5, 20; Koh Gui Qing and Salvador Rodriguez, "In Silicon Valley, Chinese 'accelerators' aim to bring startups home," *Reuters*, May 17, 2018; J.F. Gauthier, Dane Stangler, Marc Penzel, and Arnobio Morelix, *Global Startup Ecosystem Report* (Startup Genome and Global Entrepreneurship Network, 2018), 191; Hui Li and Dexter Roberts, "Making Billions Off China's Worried Parents," *Bloomberg Businessweek*, June 18, 2018; Silvia Massini et al., "Emerging Trends in Global Sourcing of Innovation," 279, and Michael Witt, "Implications from South Korea's Experience," 94, 102, both in Lewin, Kenney, and Murmann, eds., *China's Innovation Challenge*.

50 Rein, *End of Copycat China* , 17, 35-36; Manning and Engelke, *Global Innovation Sweepstakes*, 1-4, 17-18; Regina M. Abrami, William C. Kirby, and F. Warren McFarlan, "Why China Can't Innovate," *Harvard Business Review*, March 2014; Nee and Opper, *Capitalism from Below*, 200-225.

51 Keith Bradsher and Li Yuan, "China's Economy Became No. 2 by Defying No. 1," *New York Times*, November 25, 2018; Mark Zachary Taylor, *The Politics of Innovation: Why Some Countries Are Better than Others at Science and Technology* (Oxford University Press, 2016), 74; *Global Startup Ecosystem Report*, 191-192, 202-203.

52 Martin Ravaillion and Shaohua Chan, "China's (Uneven) Progress Against Poverty," World Bank, 2016; Philip K. Pan, "The Land that Failed to Fail," *New York Times*, November 18, 2018; Nee and Opper, *Capitalism from Below*, 1-3; Manning and Engelke, *Global Innovation Sweepstakes*, 18.

53 Technically South Korea is a presidential representative democratic republic with a multi-party system and Taiwan has changed from a one party military dictatorship to a multiparty democracy with a semi-presidential system. Nonetheless both nations have political systems and traditions that are much less like those of the western democracies in actual operation.

54 Sharma, *Rise and Fall of Nations*, 82-91.

55 Michael Schuman, "What if China Really is Exempt from the Laws of Economics?," *Bloomberg Businessweek*, January 29, 2018.

56 Chan, "Chinese Entrepreneurship," 481; Will Knight, "China's AI Awakening, *MIT Technology Review*, October 10, 2017; Alec Ash, "How China's Tech Revolution Threatens Silicon Valley," *The Atlantic*, May 14, 2018; Ruchir Sharma, "The Coming Tech Battle With China," *New York Times*, June 28, 2018; Cade Metz, "As China Marches Forward on A.I., the White House is Silent," *New York Times*, February 12, 2019; Cade Metz, "The Race is On to Protect Data from the Next Leap in Computers: And China Has the Lead," *New York Times*, December 4, 2018; Edmund S. Phelps, "Will China Out-Innovate the West?," *Project Syndicate*, March 5, 2018; Manning and Engelke, *Global Innovation Sweepstakes*, 20; Sui-Lee Wee, "China Halts Work by Scientist Who Says He Edited Babies' Genes," *New York Times*, November 29, 2018; Kishore Mahbubani, "What China Threat? How the United States and China Can Avoid War," *Harper's* (February 2019), 40.

57 Manning and Engelke, *Global Innovation Sweepstakes*, 18, 20; Alec Ash, "How China's Tech Revolution Threatens Silicon Valley," *The Atlantic*, May 14, 2018.

58 Alec Ash, "How China's Tech Revolution Threatens Silicon Valley," *The Atlantic*, May 14, 2018; Manning and Engelke, *Global Innovation Sweepstakes*, 17-18; *The Global Innovation Index* 2018, p. xxxi.

59 Tse, "Rise of Entrepreneurship in China"; Philip P. Pan, "The Land that Failed to Fail," *New York Times*, November 18, 2018.

Chapter 7

1 Robert A. Manning and Peter Engelke, *The Global Innovation Sweepstakes: A Quest to Win the Future* (Atlantic Council, Scowcroft Center for Strategy and Security, 2018), 15-19.

2 A problem also in other parts of the world, where the significant positive impact of immigrants on the economy is being underestimated by those opposed to immigration. See Ian Goldin and Benjamin Nabarro, "Losing it: The Economics and Politics of Migration," October 24, 2018 at https://voxeu.org/article/losing-it-economics-and-politics-migration.

3 Manning and Engelke, *Global Innovation Sweepstakes*, 8-21.

4 Ruchir Sharma, *The Rise and Fall of Nations: Forces of Change in the Post-Crisis World* (W. W. Norton, 2016), 46-48.

5 Sharma, *Rise and Fall of Nations*, 53.

6 Though Prime Minister Shinzo Abe has tried to change this policy, nonetheless it would require a tenfold increase just to offset the decline in Japan's population caused by falling birth rates. Sharma, *Rise and Fall of Nations*, 48.

7 Manning and Engelke, *Global Innovation Sweepstakes*, 5, 25-28. Japan of course, is still one of the wealthiest nations in the world and highly innovative in certain sectors. It was once deemed to be the next great world economic leader, in the 1980s and 90s, but faltered and has experienced a long period of slow economic growth since then.

8 L. Felipe Monteiro, "Selective Attention and the Initiation of the Global Knowledge-Sourcing Process in Multinational Corporations," *Journal of International Business Studies* 46 (January 2015): 505-27.

9 Manning and Engelke, *Global Innovation Sweepstakes*, 7-11; CBINSIGHTS, "1B + Market Map: The World's 360 Unicorn Companies in One Infographic," June 12, 2019 at https://www.cbinsights.com/research/unicorn-startup-market-map/.

10 Manning and Engelke, *Global Innovation Sweepstakes*, 36-38. In contrast to many other nations, Swedes (like the Chinese) are not particularly fearful of revealing themselves or protecting their privacy from the state. David Flaherty, *Protecting Privacy in Surveillance Societies: The Federal Republic of Germany, Sweden, France, Canada, and the United States* (University of North Carolina Press, 1992).

11 Manning and Engelke, *Global Innovation Sweepstakes*, 38-41.

12 Richard Peach and Charles Steindel, "Low Productivity Growth: The Capital Formation Link," *Liberty Street Economics*, June 26, 2017 at https://libertystreeteconomics.newyorkfed.org/2017/06/low-productivity-growth-the-capital-formation-link.html.

13 Germany ranks high, and Austria, Finland, Denmark even higher in the public spending on training as a percentage of GDP. This high percentage is not confined to the traditional "northern European" group either, as Portugal is one of the top spenders in this category. The United States ranks near the bottom. Business Roundtable, *Innovation Nation: An American Innovation Agenda for 2020* (Business Roundtable, 2019), 7-8.

14 Manning and Engelke, *The Global Innovation Sweepstakes*, 6.

15 Raj Chetty, David Grusky, Maximilian Hell, Nathaniel Hendren, Robert Manduca, and Jimmy Narang, "The Fading American Dream: Trends in Absolute Income Mobility since 1940," May 5, 2018 at https://voxeu.org/article/trends-us-absolute-income-mobility-1940. The lack of mobility is especially high among the poor and the non-white in America. See Juan C. Palomino, Gustavo A. Marrero, Juan Gabriel Rodríguez, "Intergenerational Mobility in the US: One Size Doesn't Fit all," January 3, 2019 at https://voxeu.org/article/intergenerational-mobility-us.

16 Ruchir Agarwal and Patrick Gaulé, "Invisible Geniuses: The Advancement of the Knowledge Frontier," December 23, 2018 at https://voxeu.org/article/invisible-geniuses-advancement-knowledge-frontier.

17 Alex Bell, Raj Chetty, Xavier Jaravel, Nevianna Petkova, and John Van Reenen, "Who Becomes an Inventor in America? The Importance of Exposure to Innovation," November 2018 at http://www.equality-of-opportunity.org/assets/documents/inventors_paper.pdf.

18 Peter Temin, "Finance in Economic Growth: Eating the Family Cow," Institute for New Economic Thinking, Working Paper 86, December 17, 2018 at https://www.ineteconomics.org/uploads/papers/WP_86-Temin-Finance-in-Economic-Growth.pdf; Elizabeth McNichol, "It's Time for States to Invest in Infrastructure," Center on Budget and Policy Priorities, March 19, 2019 at https://www.cbpp.org/research/state-budget-and-tax/its-time-for-states-to-invest-in-infrastructure; Jeffrey M. Stupak, "Economic Impact of Infrastructure Investment," Congressional Research Service, January 24, 2018 at https://fas.org/sgp/crs/misc/R44896.pdf.

19 Life expectancy has declined in the United States for the past five years, whereas it has held steady or risen in most other highly developed nations. See, "CDC Data Show U.S. Life Expectancy Continues to Decline: Suicides, Drug Overdose Deaths Named as Key Contributors," December 10,2018 at https://www.aafp.org/news/health-of-the-public/20181210lifeexpectdrop.html; Lisa Rapaport, "Life Expectancy Declines seen in U.S. and Other High-Income Countries," *Reuters*, August 22, 2018 at https://www.reuters.com/article/us-health-lifeexpectancy/life-expectancy-declines-seen-in-u-s-and-other-high-income-countries-idUSKCN1L723R; Heather Marcoux, "Why American Moms are the most Stressed Out Moms in the Western World," *Motherly*, March 14, 2019 at https://www.mother.ly/news/why-american-moms-are-the-most-stressed-out-moms-in-western-world.

20 Sari Pekkala Kerr and William Kerr, "Immigrant Entrepreneurship in America: Eight Important Facts from the Survey of Business Owners," September 21, 2018 at https://voxeu.org/article/immigrant-entrepreneurship-america.

21 Sharma, *Rise and Fall of Nations.*

22 Based on this sort of "complexity" ranking the United States sits 10th, behind Japan, South Korea, Singapore, Germany, Switzerland, Finland, and Austria: see http://atlas.cid.harvard.edu/rankings/.

23 Lee G. Branstetter, Britta Glennon, and J. Bradford Jensen, "The IT Revolution and the Globalization of R&D," *Innovation Policy and the Economy, Vol. 19* eds. Josh Lerner and Scott Stern (University of Chicago Press, 2019), 1-37.

24 Ewing Marion Kauffman Foundation, *2017 Kauffman Index of Startup Activity* at https://www.kauffman.org/kauffman-index/reporting/startup-activity/~/media/c9831094536646528ab012dcbd1f83be.ashx.

25 Manning and Engelke, *Global Innovation Sweepstakes*, 24.

26 Dan Breznitz and Michael Murphree, *Run of the Red Queen: Government, Innovation, Globalization, and Economic Growth in China* (Yale University Press, 2011), 13-18.

27 Gintautas Dumcius, "Boston moves up in KPMG's ranking of promising world technology hubs," *Boston Business Journal*, February 22, 2019.

28 Zack Weisfeld, "Corporate Accelerators: What's in it for the Big Companies?" *Forbes*, February 23, 2016.